KINGDOM FINANCE REVOLUTION

Kingdom Finance Revolution: Building your Life as an Altar of Blessing

Copyright © 2024 William Abraham

All rights reserved.

No part of this publication may be reproduced in a retrieval system, or transmitted in any form or by any means—electronic, mechanical, photocopying, recording, or otherwise—without the prior written permission of the publisher.

I want to acknowledge supporters of this vision who provided encouragement and input, particularly Amy Ford for her editorial review that helped to guide the process. —WA

This manuscript has undergone viable editorial work and proofreading, yet human limitations may have resulted in minor grammatical or syntax-related errors remaining in the finished book. The understanding of the reader is requested in these cases. While precaution has been taken in the preparation of this book, the publisher and author assume no responsibility for errors or omissions, or for damages resulting from the use of the information contained herein.

Scriptures quoted and marked *NKJV, NIV, AMP, KJV, AMPC, ESV, NLT, CEV, ABT*. Full permissions are available following endnotes.

This book is set in the typeface *Athelas* designed by Veronika Burian and Jose Scaglione.

Paperback ISBN: 979-8-3481-2173-0

A Publication of *Tall Pine Books*
119 E Center Street, Suite B4A | Warsaw, Indiana 46580
www.tallpinebooks.com

| 1 24 24 20 16 02 |

Published in the United States of America

KINGDOM FINANCE REVOLUTION

BUILDING YOUR LIFE AS AN ALTAR OF BLESSING

WILLIAM ABRAHAM

This book serves as a Clarion Call to break free from the shackles of the Baal system and step out from among those who adhere to it. It strongly urges divine alignment with God's end-time plan for the Nations. Through its powerful and uncompromising message, this book confronts the status quo and aims to eradicate the Babylonian spirit that has plagued and ravaged the true Kingdom wealth of Nations.

I believe the transformative message that it delivers will act as a supernatural catalyst for Kingdom Reformation and Restoration. The Author of this book boldly proclaims the Urgency of the hour and the necessity for Believers to Rise up and take their place in God's Kingdom Agenda. It is a Wake-up call for the Church to shake off the complacency and compromise that have held it back and to boldly step into the Destiny that God has ordained for His people.

With powerful insights and prophetic revelation, this timely book is a powerful tool for equipping and empowering the Saints to walk in the fullness of their Calling and to be Agents of Change and transformation in their Communities and Nations. It will certainly challenge Readers to break free from the stranglehold of Baal that has long ensnared many and to Align themselves with the End-Time purposes of God for this Generation and for the Next....

As readers engage with the message of this book, I believe they will be activated and inspired to take their place on the front lines of the Battle for the Kingdom Inheritance and Birthright of the Nations.

The time is now to rise up, break free, and align with God's end-time plan....The stakes have never been higher, but the rewards are Eternal. Will we heed the Call and commit to Joining the Ranks of those who are now Standing in the gap for the True Identity and Destiny of Nations in the Valley of Decision?

—Prophet Veronika West
Ignite Ireland Ministry and Ireland's Destiny Hub

This powerful new book is essential reading for anyone concerned about their personal finances or the wider extension of the Kingdom of God. This biblically researched publication comes from the pen of an author who has endeavoured throughout a long and successful career and ministry to put these fiscal principles into practice. It covers a wide spectrum and concerns itself not only with how to receive but also how to give. Perhaps its greatest value to the reader however is its focus not only on the proffered hand of the believer but especially on their heart. Motive is prioritised over method. It is a pivotal book in the life of the Church today.

—John Glass
Speaker, Writer, Broadcaster and
General Superintendent of *Elim Pentecostal Churches (2000-2016)*

In 12 weeks God fundamentally altered our church and ministry toward a God centered finance model that puts Jesus, and not the world's systems, at the heart of our belief systems regarding money. There were an innumerable amount of A-ha's as we became secure in Jesus in the midst of a shifting sands economy. That alone is priceless.

—Angela Meer
Lead, *FireHouse International*

I appreciate your sharing on Kingdom Finance. It has reminded me to focus on resting in the security of the Lord and on what He says and not on what I see or my own thoughts. Even in the blessings, keeping the focus on what He is saying and praying His words and promises. Thank you for great insight!

—Pamela Teel
FireHouse International

I was struck by your language, "willing", today. The difference between being willing to sow as opposed to getting WORD/ VISION from Father as starting point. So many shifts happening in my perspective on giving William. Thank you for creating a platform for change!

—Kathleen Krohn
FireHouse International

William's book is one of the best I have read for some time! I believe it is going to have a great impact on the church. It is written in the same spirit that the likes of Bill Johnson, Kris Valloton, Andrew Wommack, Charles Capps and others write in, and the same spirit that Creflo Dollar, Jesse Duplantis and Kenneth Hagin teach in. The richness of the book is it is deeply rooted in scripture and vulnerable testimony, further strengthened with structured tools for stepping into freedom e.g. 'The Good Samaritan Test and 'The Shame Test'. The reading of his book for me was on the same experience level as reading Ron Macintosh's The Greatest Secret/The Missing Ingredient'. In the same way that Ron provides vision and the tools to step into renewed thinking, so William does with regards to living a life of Kingdom Giving and Receiving. Highly recommend getting a copy!

—Andrew Rodgers
Principal at *Odgers Berndtson*

Kingdom Finance Revolution brings an edge to finance that is needed and has been lacking. This is more than understanding a balance sheet and proper budgeting. William Abraham accesses language that cross-pollinates deeply spiritual concepts like unseen war and eschatology with financial systems. It's refreshing and practical! It's a now word and a word that will last in its relevance and impact. If you're going to read a finance book this year, make it this one!

—Conifer Review of Books

This book is dedicated to my wife, Donna, and daughter, Spencer-Marie, who have shared in the cost of this journey and been my unwavering support.

Contents

Foreword xiii
Preface xvii

Part One
Shifting Our Perceptions

1. HAVES AND HAVE-NOTS 3
   George's Story 3
   Financial Blessings 6
   The Prodigal Son 7

2. WHAT IT MEANS TO BE RICH 9
   Identity of the Believer in Christ 11

3. SLAVERY 15

4. LACK AND BLESSING 21
   The Outhouse of Lack 21
   The Blessing 24

5. BREAKING FREE 29
   The Good Samaritan Test 29
   Parable of the Good Samaritan 30
   Breaking Free From Slavery 34
   Not Me - I'm Okay 37
   More Than Social Welfare 39
   Isaiah 58 Calling 40

6. A REALITY CHECK 43
   So How Are We Doing, Really? 43
   The Floor and the Ceiling 45

Part Two
Concluding the Past

- 7. RATS IN THE BASEMENT — 53
- 8. PERSONAL INVENTORY — 59
  - Taking Stock - What is our Heritage? — 59
  - Personal Inventory — 62
  - What is the Fruit in Our Lives? — 63
  - Revelation of the Strategy for Victory — 70
  - There is Hope, Even for the Tax Man — 72
- 9. MOVING INTO BLESSING — 75
  - Deliverance and Lordship — 76
- 10. IS THIS AN ATTACK? — 79
  - What about the Attacks? - My Hezekiah Testimony — 82
  - Continuum of Release — 90
  - Scriptural Examples - How was this implemented in the Bible? — 92
- 11. SIN IN THE CAMP — 97
  - Is There Sin in the Camp? — 97
- 12. POSITIONAL TRUTH — 101
  - Experiential Truth vs Positional Truth — 104
- 13. GENERATIONAL SIN — 111
  - Iniquity Comes for a Visit — 111
  - Daniel's Generational Prayer for Today — 120
- 14. LEAVING THE PAST BEHIND — 123
  - God's Will is for Us to Flourish — 123
  - God is Good All the Time — 125
  - Lordship — 127

Part Three
The Way Forward

- 15. SHAME — 133
  - True Anointing Will Not Operate with Shame — 134
  - How Do We Move on from Failure? — 135
  - What is Shame? — 136
  - Freed from Shame — 139

Some Tests for Shame	140
Impact of Shame	141
Shame and Hypocrisy	142
Remedy for Shame	144
16. GIVING	**147**
God is the Great Giver	147
We are Called to be Givers	148
What is Biblical Giving?	150
We Give to God, Not Man	153
Honour in Giving	155
Giving Breaks Bondages	157
Purposeful Giving	159
Practical Points for Giving	165
Giving Traps	168
Traps from the Perspective of the Receiver	178
Giving to Believers	179
Radical Giving - The Special Anointing or Calling to Give	185
17. OFFENCE	**189**
Offences are Wrong	191
Dealing with Offenders	193
The Field of Pain	195
Pride Deceives	197
Crooked Dealing	198
Taking Offence - Pierced but Not Wounded	199
I Have a Plane to Catch	201
Being Offended at God	202
Godly Confrontation	205
The Watchmen	207
The Battle is the Lord's	209
18. DEBT	**211**
What About Debt?	211
What Does the Bible Say About Debt?	213
Am I Oppressed?	215
A New Mindset	218
The Lesson of King Josiah	221
Is Debt Sin?	224

Strategy for Victory over Debt	228
What about Loans and Mortgages?	231

19. VICTORY — 237

What About Victory?	237
Principles of Victory	241
Obedience the key to victory	242
What was the secret of Jesus' miracle-working power?	243
Vision	246
The Word from the Lord	249
Obedience Through Faith	250
Lesson Learned - Faith, Hope and Love	252
Satan's IF	253
Eternal Victory	255
Faith in Action - God's Strange Acts	259
Greater Works and Financial Miracles	266

20. KINGDOM BUSINESS AS USUAL — 271

It is NEVER Just Business	271
About the Author	275
Endnotes	277
Permissions	280

Foreword

I write the forward of William Abraham's book, deeply challenged by the implications of its message. To be honest, I am unsure of how to walk it out myself. All of us in ministry face the challenge of raising finances. The temptation to hype, to manipulate, and to depend on worldly models faces us all. Likewise, those in the marketplace are deeply challenged to stay true to Kingdom values in a world of fierce competition and greed. It is into this challenging system, God wants to raise up a prophetic voice and understanding: "How then shall we live?"

William Abraham, a dear friend and businessman, witnessed the excesses and the compromise of certain Christian businesses that functioned in peaceful coexistence with worldly motivations and practices of our modern economic system. Faced with a great decision, he risked everything and left the system. Like Elijah, he would not bow the knee to Baal. He has been tested severely, but out of that testing has come this book, as a provocation and trumpet sound to come out of Babylon. I believe that there are thousands of Christian businessmen like him who have not bowed the knee to these ever-present temptations.

Elijah lived for three and a half years under the prophetic providence of God, not under self-serving motivations. Throughout my history, I have seen that any business man who seeks to follow God in his practice, will at times be upended by unscrupulous and greedy men and partners. The temptation to compromise because of the loss of potential millions of dollars could be the greatest challenge, for "the love of money is the root of all evil." The man or woman of God in business must be to go through great offence and loss of all, in order that they may know that they love God more than mammon –you cannot serve both.

Recently, I spoke with an amazing businessman who refused to compromise his vision: that a portion of the sales of his project would feed children around the world. The business partners refused, and so the businessman gave up everything rather than compromise the God-given vision. Then, born out of that stand of faith, came a product five times better. Since then, millions of children have been fed around the world. This was the process of death and resurrection.

Seventeen years ago, a woman came to me and said, "You don't know who I am, but the Lord told me to pay your salary this year, because you're going to start something with the youth of America in prayer that is going to change the destiny of this nation." Out of this, TheCall was born, and that widow paid my salary for seventeen years. I know the Lord commanded to fund TheCall. She no longer can pay my salary, and now I am asking the question that William Abraham is asking, "How do I live?" Do I get into a whirlwind of frantic activity raising finances? Do I wait for God to command ravens?

I don't have all the answers. All I know is that I want to remain pure – that if He asks me to give, I'll give all. Even if I don't reap immediately, I wait for the reaping. Do I compete with my brothers and question how I can posture our ministry, so that we can get an edge of financing? Or do I consider my brother's ministry more important than my own? These are big questions. As you read this book, let God search you so that you can truly say: "The prince of this world cometh but he hath nothing in me." These are searching questions in a system of big investment, hedge funds, mega music labels; in a world of massive world needs, world-wide poverty, refugee crises. God help us.

Let God speak to you as you read.

—Lou Engle
Intercessor and International Minister

Preface

This book is about **breaking free into liberty** - getting freedom from the things that have held us back from walking in our full inheritance and blessing, including finances. I believe that there is a group of set-apart men and women who are part of God's plan in this next season. People for whom this book is like a spring of water that leaves them thirsting and calling out for more.

The new Kingdom Financiers know that the key to the Kingdom is that there is a King and that if we want to access Kingdom resources we need to partner with this King in His mission to destroy the works of the enemy (1 John 3:8). They are anointed worshippers who are sold out servants for Jesus and will do what He asks them to do. Like Gideon and other heroes of faith, they will obey God and see His abundant release. They will prophesy, lead movements, speak to countries, and have influence to a degree that has not yet been seen on the earth. They will have clean hands and a pure heart (Ps. 24:4) operating according to God's standards not man's.

John the Baptist moved in the spirit and power of Elijah (John 11:14). This is the spirit of confrontation and consecration which has inspired this book. The book leads us to cleanse the "altar of our lives" so that the fire of God can fall and change a nation. Elijah impacted the economy and destroyed the ungodly system that Ahab and Jezebel operated under. Right now, God wants to change His church to be what He intended it to be, operating in the level of power and financial blessing needed to change the world. There are no small visions, but a truly global calling and mandate.

As new leaders with a Kingdom Finance calling and vision move forward, God will open doors for flow and blessing that are beyond what we can ask or even think. Those who have paid the price to conclude the past and to press in to Him for His direction and calling will operate in unprecedented release and blessing. The qualification is not being rich, connections, or having money - that was the old season. Now the qualification is to be called and anointed for end-times Kingdom Finance. God has a detailed plan for great things that need to be done in these last days and it will not be released to those dining at Jezebel's table.

A number of years ago, I was visiting a major ministry in the US and was given a prophetic word that God had seen my heart, that I believed I was alone, but that God was releasing to me seven "silver arrows of truth". God had been downloading some of these Kingdom Finance principles to me and I had been working through them but it was true that I also felt very much alone, unrecognised and a long long way from any manifestation of financial blessing! I had had my "Joseph's brothers" experience (if you don't immediately know what I mean then read the story) and my share of personal upheavals. The first silver arrow of truth was that I was operating in the spirit and power of Elijah and, like Elijah, despite feeling alone, there were 7,000 others who had not bowed the knee to Baal (the world's system). This was the genesis of The 7000 (www.the7000.com), the book writing process, and my search for the 7000 "Kingdom Finance Elijahs" who are called for God's end-times funding release.

Of course the teachings in the book can apply to everyone who wants more liberty and freedom, but I believe that there is a core team of people God will bring to this book who see themselves as patterning their lives on this Elijah calling. Those whose hearts are yearning to be radical, sold out, releasers of Kingdom blessing! Doing things that can only be done when God brings the fire. People who are seeking a deeper relationship with the King, not just funding. Imagine an army of 7,000 Kingdom Financiers doing the greater works of Jesus and breaking ungodly dominions and powers. Those who are willing to tackle the issues in their lives and generations that have held them back in order to see the release of blessings needed to fund the destinies on the lives of Christians. People who say, "NO MORE" to the plans of the enemy that have kept them in bondage. This is part of what has inspired the book - how to get free and into liberty. Not just givers, but modern day Elijahs!!

A common characteristic of these modern-day Elijah Kingdom Financiers is that they have been called to unusual fasts or God has asked them to do some strange things. They will also almost always have the goal to give radically or to reverse tithe in some manner. Many have also had real struggles financially as they set out on their journey. No surprise here, as the enemy will also try to thwart the callings and destiny of those who are sold out to Him. It seems that in many cases the unclean "old" must be swept away to create a clean platform for God's "new".

As with any work such as this book, take the good and use it to empower you on your journey. There is a release of anointing and breakthrough for those who are willing to radically move forward to rest and abide in Jesus. His plan is to bless and to prosper you, your family, and believers everywhere. Let's walk into this breakthrough!

If you feel you are one of those called to release Kingdom Finance in this generation then this book represents a foundation - the first steps to cleanse the altar of your life so that the fire of Heaven can fall. Are you one of these ones who are planning to partner with Jesus to destroy the works of the enemy? I hope so.

—William Abraham
www.the7000.com

Part One

Shifting Our Perceptions

Chapter 1

Haves and Have-Nots

George's Story

George walks slowly into the building, slouching and looking side to side, clearly unsure of where to go and what to do. His jacket hangs loosely over his tall frame and his trousers are cinched tightly, giving the impression of a teenager wearing his father's clothes. This first impression is quickly dispelled at the notice of his greying hair and haggard features. He appears gaunt, dazed, and profoundly sad - like a prisoner released from a concentration camp. He looks ashamed and in disbelief to find himself in a food bank. As the pastor manning the desk walks over to greet him, George holds out his referral slip as though he is presenting an invitation to a party.

The pastor smiles and is welcoming; it is not the first time he has seen this reaction- the embarrassment of the usually self-sufficient person in a time of need. He notes the referral is from a suicide prevention charity in the next town, and time seems to slow down. This is his divine appointment for the day. He knows that this is a pivotal crossroads moment in George's life. He takes George through the process, gets him a coffee and takes the time to chat with him. As he fills a box with food basics, George asks quietly if he can get it in sturdy bags, and the pastor realises George is on foot. He also *learns he has walked six miles from the next town and has the same distance to walk back. Keeping in mind the divine appointment, the pastor arranges to drive him back. He enters the rooming house and sees the stripped-bare, depressing room and the totally empty shelves. As time progresses, he learns a bit of George's story: the illness of his wife, the breakdown, his lost job, the bills piling up, his wife's passing, financial collapse, and the slow stripping away of the structures and supports of normal life. George felt his only options were suicide or the long walk to the food bank. Thankfully George met a modern-day "Good samaritan" who was looking for a divine appointment and George's journey to restoration and recovery began.*[1]

> **We cannot move in Kingdom Finance and blessing until we know the King and His plan!**

Are you in the position you had hoped for or dreamed of at this stage of your life? Do you feel you are fulfilling your calling in life? Are debts or lack of funds holding you back? Have you lost some of your fire and motivation because it seems so hard to break through to something better? Do you identify more with George or with the pastor who wants to do more to help him?

We live in a broken world and in broken communities with needs that we are called to meet. In many cases there are also critical needs in our own families. Throughout the church, Christians are not operating at the level of finances they should be, and that is what this book is about.

We need to have liberty in our finances so that we can meet our needs and fulfil our Kingdom calling. However, it is impossible to move into true Kingdom Finance and blessing until we know the King and His plan. If we look at things objectively, it appears that we may have made Him Lord of our lives to a point, but there is a

---

1. Based on a recent true story.

blockage when it comes to finance. God wants a new level of Lordship in our lives that includes finances. There is work to be done!

God is calling us in this generation to take a stand and change things for ourselves and for our future generations. We don't have to fully understand all the implications to know that we are not where God wants us to be, as individuals or the corporate Body of Christ - the Church. It does not measure up to God's plan for us.

I am sure that most of the people that God has led to read this book fit mainly into this camp – we know that there is a higher path that we should be walking in, but just don't know how to move forward and access it. We want to change things, we see the needs around us and want to do something, we have a fundamental dissatisfaction with the way things are, and we are praying for release and repositioning. However, even if today you are privileged to be able to say you are "doing OK", there are needs all around us that God calls us to meet. Are we really fulfilling our calling in Kingdom Finance when a host of needs around us go unmet? As a group, we need to be fruitful in the area of finance and indeed **we are called to be.**

We need to move into a new release of blessing so that we can bring positive changes to our lives, families, churches, communities, and nations. We must confront this difficult and often contentious area head-on, not only in our personal lives and families, but also in the church and society. I believe that if you are reading this, your spirit intuitively knows this truth, and you are crying out for more: more of life, more of Him, more intimacy, more fellowship, more peace, more joy, more resources, more blessing, and more victory.

In this book I will share how we can connect with the anointing God has for Kingdom finance and tear off any "veils" that blind us, demolish strongholds where the enemy has operated in our lives, and bring the Kingdom release of provision to our lives in a new way. I know that the fact that God has led you to read this book means you have been separated for breakthrough. Ungodly dominion over your life and your generations will be broken. The name of Jesus brings liberty, and through the study of His Word, our minds will be renewed.

We long to join with Jesus in His calling to destroy the works of the devil in our lives, our families, and in the world:

> "...The reason the Son of God was made manifest (visible) was to undo (destroy, loosen and dissolve) the works the devil (has done)." (AMPC 1 John 3:8)

This is the definition of Kingdom Finance for this generation: To partner with Jesus in His anointing to destroy the works of the devil.

Financial Blessings

Blessing, riches, prosperity, and provision are areas that many in the church have simply neglected or abandoned as being too difficult to understand or too controversial to address. Indeed, nothing gets a more immediate and mainly negative reaction from many Christians than a discussion about money and prosperity. People raise instant walls of judgement and condemnation associated with the disapproval shown towards some televangelists and high-profile jet-setting Christian leaders. Some of us condemn the "prosperity merchants" living the high life and at the same time others condemn those bound in a "poverty spirit". These labels are walls that deflect us from addressing the issues, so we do not really deal with the lack of Biblical prosperity or the lack of Kingdom Finance in evidence in our lives.

In addition to deflecting by condemning the speakers, we have wallpapered over these cracks in our financial foundation with religious mumbo jumbo sayings and folksy one-liners that do not result in a godly assessment of our true

> **KINGDOM FINANCE -** to partner with Jesus in His anointing to destroy the works of the devil.

financial foundations. "Bless you" has been devalued to mean, "Goodbye", with no real connection to giving nor understanding of the blessings to which we are entitled. Can it be that there is no "meat" in the blessing? Does the blessing really leave you hungry, thirsty, or on the side of the road needing a ride? Not according to the patterns set out in the Word where blessing makes rich and adds no sorrow (Proverbs 10:22).

Another witty half-truth designed to justify lack is that God has only promised to meet our needs, not our wants. What image of the Father does this represent - an unloving father that does not care about the desires of his children, nor in cultivating godly wants and desires in His children? Does this line up with the image of the Father shown to us by Jesus in the story of the Prodigal Son? In this parable, Jesus portrayed the true nature of God as a father running and falling on his estranged son's neck, blessing and restoring him.

THE PRODIGAL SON

> *Then He said, "A certain man had two sons. The younger of them [inappropriately] said to his father, 'Father, give me the share of the property that falls to me.' So he divided the estate between them. A few days later, the younger son gathered together everything [that he had] and traveled to a distant country, and there he wasted his fortune in reckless and immoral living. Now when he had spent everything, a severe famine occurred in that country, and he began to do without and be in need. So he went and forced himself on one of the citizens of that country, who sent him into his fields to feed pigs. He would have gladly eaten the [carob] pods that the pigs were eating [but they could not satisfy his hunger], and no one was giving anything to him. But when he [finally] came to his senses, he said, 'How many of my father's hired men have more than enough food, while I am dying here of hunger! I will get up and go to my father, and I will say to him, "Father, I have sinned against Heaven and in your sight. I am no longer worthy to be called your son; [just] treat me like one of your hired men."' So he got up and came to his father. But while he*

*was still a long way off, **his father saw him and was moved with compassion for him, and ran and embraced him and kissed him**. And the son said to him, 'Father, I have sinned against Heaven and in your sight; I am no longer worthy to be called your son.' But the father said to his servants, **'Quickly bring out the best robe for the guest of honor and put it on him; and give him a ring for his hand, and sandals for his feet. And bring the fattened calf and slaughter it, and let us invite everyone and feast and celebrate; for this son of mine was as good as dead and is alive again; he was lost and has been found.'** So they began to celebrate. (Luke 15:11-24 AMP emphasis added, brackets and some notes removed)*

The garment, ring, restored position, tears, and fatted calf were not just "meeting a need", rather these blessings demonstrated the extravagant love and undeserved favour of a loving and generous Father. It was done for love, with no merit on the part of the Prodigal Son. Indeed, the parable is clear that the Prodigal Son sowed his fortune on reckless and immoral living. In this parable, Jesus sets out the truth about the heart of God and His desire for us to be fully restored.

Essentially, these one-liners and arguments are preemptive attacks designed to shut down dialogue and avoid self-examination. At first glance, they seem to have some merit, but the purpose is to deflect from any examination of a person's real situation and the lack of financial blessing. Like the Prodigal Son, we must soberly examine our condition and ask the question: Are we really walking in the Kingdom blessing as God intended?

Chapter 2

What it Means to be Rich

One of the things that God wants to deal with and correct in us is our conception of what it means to be rich. We cannot move forward with a Kingdom Finance vision and into godly prosperity without knowing our *starting point* and our goal and *destination* - we need to know what God has intended for us (our destination or calling) and not be blinded to our current situation (our starting point). If we deal with our true state and honestly look at our condition, no papering over cracks in our foundations, then we can then move forward towards a life of genuine liberty. Can our understanding be awakened and renewed in the area of riches and finance? Can we get a vision of our Kingdom destination and calling? There are so many competing views that some clarity and focus in this area is desperately needed – what does the Word say?

As you read this book there is an anointing that will be released over you to break ungodly perceptions and beliefs and to put in place a godly view of what it means to be prosperous, rich, and to walk in Kingdom financial blessing. It is not wrong to be rich, but our definition of what makes a person rich is wrong.

Let us shut out distractions just for a moment and see what comes to our minds when we speak the words "Rich", "Rich Man", "Rich Woman", or even "Rich Minister". What preconceived notions or pictures came to our mind? Have we immediately begun to redefine "rich" to suit our world view? Do we engage in one-liners and deflections to avoid these topics?

> It is not wrong to be rich, but our definition of what makes a person rich is wrong.

I am confident that our reactions will be varied, but some associations that commonly come to mind are what we see day-to-day in society, social media, and entertainment magazines. We see billionaire politicians, movie stars, and influencers getting out of their limousines and private jets expressing a careless self-centred attitude which shouts that money is not an issue for them.

For others, their definition of a rich man is someone released from the pressure of the weight of bills, on a nice holiday, or moving into a new home. For those of us focusing on the altruistic side or even wanting to be seen as more spiritual, it could be helping the hungry and poor – the red thermostat of a fundraising drive at the very top.

So, what does the Bible instruct people who have money or are rich to do? Not to pursue extra above your needs? To give it all away? Or, not to keep any extra?

> *As for the rich in this present world, instruct them not to be conceited and arrogant, nor to set their hope on the uncertainty of riches, but on God, who richly and ceaselessly provides us with everything for our enjoyment. Instruct them to do good, to be rich in good works, to be generous, willing to share [with others]. In this way storing up for themselves the enduring riches of a good foundation for the future, so that they may take hold of that which is truly life. (1 Timothy 6:17-19 AMP)*

What are our instructions? To keep our key focus on God, to do good, to be rich in good works, to be generous and to be willing to share! Being rich in this world comes with Kingdom obligations and instructions.

As you read this book you will learn that we are called to serve Him, not to be slaves and in any form of bondage. Like the children of Israel being freed from slavery in Egypt, freedom was not the ultimate goal, it came with obligations and instructions.

> *For long ago in Egypt I broke your yoke and burst your bonds **not that you might be free, but that you might serve Me**... (Jer. 2:20 AMPC parenthesis removed and emphasis added)*

Their freedom from slavery and bondage also came with great riches described as the plunder of Egypt (Ex. 12:36). Likewise, when we are freed to serve Him our riches are for service in His Kingdom. Our liberty is not about freedom, self-actualisation, pursuing happiness or any similar concept or goal, as good as these things may be. We are freed to serve and our riches are part of this. Indeed, the children of Israel were harshly judged for taking some of this wealth and using it for their own desires, making a golden calf (Ex. 32).

Identity of the Believer in Christ

All creation is travailing for us to discover who we are in Christ, to see the manifestation of a Spirit-led, praying, Jesus Generation coming into victory - lands get healed, and the miracle-working power of God is released. We are called to rule and reign in relation to finance, and Jesus has paid the price to redeem us from all of the curse.

I had a vivid vision some time back that illustrated this point to me in a startling fashion. Here are the notes I made at that time:

> *Lack - I had a vision of people who were neither white or black, but who were stained like drippings from the top down. This was the stain of the*

curse and lack coming in from the generational lines - impurities of people who did not rely on the Lord for supply and have brought their entire generational lines under the curse and bondage of lack. I then had a picture of these generations asking God to bless their banquets and feasts, but the dishes on the table were contaminated by faeces and urine - I felt a spiritual reaction almost like vomiting - spiritual revulsion. These people were embracing lack, relishing in undeserved pride in their table and were oblivious to its disgusting nature. The key take-away was that their speech was approving of lack, mediocrity, and a "just get by" mentality.

I then had a strong picture that God was raising up a new generation of breakers - people who have paid the price and carry a great anointing to break this yoke off the body of Christ - a mighty work to break lack. I then heard the words, "and you are one of them". I think we are entering into a new release of anointing - the breakthrough that we win in our call to holiness, fasting, and pressing into God will result in a season of great anointing to move people with us.

My challenge to each of us is to see ourselves as the breakers and pay the price - any price - to walk closely with the Lord. We are a "Moses generation" taking the Church from the bondage of lack into the promised land of service and blessing; an "Elijah generation" re-establishing Kingdom operation and destroying the ungodly dominion of Baal.

There are a number of scriptural parallels to this vision. In Malachi we see God's heart revealed when dealing with areas of non-reflective spiritual blindness. It is similar to the spiritual revulsion I felt in my vision. God will not accept the co-mingling of the anointing and His Glory and the things of the world. Throughout the Bible there is a call to recognise sin and spiritual blindness and to repent.

"'A son honors his father, and a servant his master. Then if I am a Father, where is My honor? And if I am a Master, where is the reverent fear and respect due Me?' says the Lord of hosts to you, O priests, who despise My name. But you say, 'How and in what way have we despised Your name?'

*You are presenting **defiled food upon My altar**. But you say, 'How have we defiled You?' By thinking that the table of the Lord is contemptible and may be despised. When you [priests] present the blind [animals] for sacrifice, is it not evil? And when you present the lame and the sick, is it not evil? Offer such a thing [as a blind or lame or sick animal] to your governor [as a gift or as payment for your taxes]. Would he be pleased with you? Or would he receive you graciously?" says the Lord of hosts. "But now will you not entreat God's favor, that He may be gracious to us? With such an offering from your hand [as an imperfect animal for sacrifice], will He show favor to any of you?" says the Lord of hosts. "Oh, that there were even one among you [whose duty it is to minister to Me] who would shut the gates, so that you would not kindle fire on My altar uselessly [with an empty, worthless pretense]! **I am not pleased with you," says the Lord of hosts, "nor will I accept an offering from your hand.** For from the rising of the sun, even to its setting, My name shall be great among the nations. In every place incense is going to be offered to My name, and a grain **offering that is pure**; for My name shall be great among the nations," says the Lord of hosts. "But you [priests] profane it when you say, '**The table of the Lord is defiled**, and as for its fruit, its food is to be despised.' You also say, 'How tiresome this is!' And you disdainfully sniff at it," says the Lord of hosts, "and you bring what was taken by robbery, and the lame or the sick [animals]; this you bring as an offering! Should I receive it with pleasure from your hand?" says the Lord. "But cursed is the swindler who has a male in his flock and vows [to offer] it, but sacrifices to the Lord a blemished or diseased thing! For I am a great King," says the Lord of hosts, "and My name is to be [reverently and greatly] feared among the nations." (Malachi 1:6-14 AMPC emphasis added and some notes removed)*

The people God addressed through Malachi had strayed into worldly financial practices and saw the requirements and desires of the Lord as drudgery and weariness. They had mixed the Holy and the profane and still expected God to bless them. In a manner similar to Isaiah 58, they had the forms but not the Spirit. Just like in my vision, we had a table of filthy food dishes completely awash with this world's system and people completely blind to how far away they were from the pure table of financial blessing the Lord had designed. Indeed, God records that the cry for justice is WEARYING to Him where our actions have this co-mingling.

> *You have wearied the Lord with your words. Yet you say, In what way have we wearied Him? [You do it when by your actions] you say, Everyone who does evil is good in the sight of the Lord and He delights in them. Or [by asking], Where is the God of justice? (Malachi 2:17 AMPC)*

I would ask us to consider "our financial table" – how we live and operate in the area of finances. Could it be that our financial beliefs and actions are not in line with God's plans and purposes? God is the revealer of truth, so let's be quick to come into agreement with His plans and purposes and to repent where we have got it wrong. Let us commit to operate Kingdom principles in our lives and walk in revelation, not as the world walks.

> *So this I say and solemnly testify in the name of the Lord as in His presence, that **you must no longer live as the heathen (the Gentiles) do in their perverseness in the folly, vanity, and emptiness of their souls and the futility of their minds.***
>
> *Their moral understanding is darkened and their reasoning is beclouded. They are alienated (estranged, self-banished) from the life of God with no share in it; this is because of the ignorance (the want of knowledge and perception, the willful blindness) that is deep-seated in them, due to their hardness of heart to the insensitiveness of their moral nature.*
>
> *In their spiritual apathy they have become callous and past feeling and reckless and have abandoned themselves a prey to unbridled sensuality, eager and greedy to indulge in every form of impurity that their depraved desires may suggest and demand. (Ephesians 4:17-19 AMP emphasis added and parenthesis removed)*

Chapter 3

Slavery

Slavery is defined as *1. drudgery, toil; 2. submission to a dominating influence; 3. a. the state of a person who is a chattel of another; b. the practice of slaveholding.*[i]

The church is mired in lack and financial constraint. I have seen prophetic leaders who are losing their homes or who are unable to pay small sums of money to meet critical needs. This situation should not be so in the body of Christ, and this area needs to be fully reclaimed in our lives and in the Church for this age. I know that we can go through seasons of "just in time" provision and enemy attack, but if that is the case, then the operative model in the Church should be that there are a host of Good Samaritans - empowered people who rush to our aid when necessary. We also need a host of Kingdom Finance equippers and empowerers to come around us to fund the vision and the destiny that God has given to us. Working alone and unaided allows the enemy as a roaring lion[1] to pick people off one by one and to thwart what God is calling us to do.

---

1. I Peter 5:8

> **Slavery in the church is financial bondage and one of the hardest to break.**

Many of us have languished in complete ignorance, not recognising the limitations the enemy has managed to erect in our lives to hinder our future and limit our destiny. In effect, the enemy has stepped into the vacuum, exerted his influence in our lives, completely hiding and blinding us to our true state - he has occupied the gate of financial blessing, and we need to reclaim this territory. Many of us have accepted the status quo and in most cases are completely non-reflective about it. That is the fruit of co-operating with the deceiver - to be deceived and blinded to the truth. In this way our current state of being has become so ingrained in us that for many it has become the dominant world view. Thank God that through the Blood of Jesus, truth can be revealed and we can be restored to our God-ordained positions.

We are in a battle against an active enemy whose mission statement is to steal, kill, and destroy (John 10:10). There is no vacuum – either we occupy this area and take dominion, or we have abandoned it to an active enemy whose plan is to enslave and harm us. We must come out of agreement with the enemy's plan for our lives and declare that His Kingdom comes to the area of finances. We also must ensure that our minds are renewed to the Scriptural vision of godly riches. **We declare that HIS KINGDOM will come to this area of our lives NOW.**

> *Our Father who art in Heaven.... Thy Kingdom come Thy will be done on earth as it is in Heaven (Lord's Prayer Matthew 6:13 KJV)*

We are to declare this every day, allowing in our lives only what would be His will in Heaven. The test of what God's will in Heaven actually looks like, is one we will continually apply as we look at Kingdom Finance.

What is the true reality for people in the Church? If the facades are stripped away and our lives are laid bare, the situation of many if not most people in the church is dire and could be characterised by bondage and slavery. We are not living in the Blessing we should be, and the reality for many is not the destiny that God intended.

Sadly, it seems that, with a few exceptions (thank God for some godly pathfinders), people in the Church are in deep bondage and are struggling with crippling levels of debt. Most people seem to be in economic slavery, broke, and waiting for a handout. The current state of affairs in the world illustrates the difficult financial environment impacting Christians. A quick look at the debt statistics for your country will give you a picture of the bleak state of affairs.[ii]

Even if some do have funds, then they do not seem to be happy and are not walking in fruitfulness and blessing. People are in slavery *without* money and in slavery *with* money as they are not walking in the Blessing! What I observed in many cases was arrogance and pride, people using money to separate themselves from the needy and oppressed, not to get closer to them to minister to their needs. As far as I can discern there were few, if any, examples of people with financial means who also truly reflect the life of Christ.

A key characteristic of slavery that people sometimes miss is that it is essentially about money - slavery is economic bondage. For Christians, slavery and bondage means not being able to walk in the destiny God has for you. Remember, slave owners do not want elderly unproductive slaves - it is not the *person* that a slave owner really wants to own, but the person's economic productivity. Indeed, during the era of slavery there were laws that required slave owners to bear the financial burden of older non-productive slaves.[iii] Slavery is about the slave owner usurping the economic productivity and destiny God purposed for the slave and appropriating this for themselves. The first-hand account of the American slave Bill Simms (born in 1839) speaks to this reality:

> *If a man was a big strong man, neighboring plantation owners would ask him to come over and see his gals, hoping that he might want to marry one of them, but if a Negro was a small man he was not cared for as a husband, as they valued their slaves as only for what they could do, just like they would horses. When they were married and if they had children they belonged to the man who owned the woman.*[iv]

It seems we are blind to the financial slavery we are living in - at best some of us may have understood that something is wrong but without an understanding of what was needed to fix the problems. We know that we and many other Christians are continuing to struggle financially and we have an inner feeling of frustration that things should be better than they are. We can see that most Christians are not walking in material blessing and breakthrough, and the few that have material wealth appear to be just as worldly and broken as everyone else.

> **We were designed to soar freely like eagles but instead most of us hop along chained to our perches.**

Of course, we can still have lack in operation in our lives if we have lots of money - a quick read of recent suicide stories will settle any argument on that side.

We have accepted, without much reflection or awareness, the enslaving dominion of the world's financial system and its values. We think things should be better than they are, we want to walk in blessing, but we feel we are locked in, and there is a sense of powerlessness. We were designed to soar freely like eagles, but instead most of us hop along chained to our perches.

Many have been so beaten down in their lives and in generations past that there is simply no awareness of the need to even bring this area of our lives into active dominion and liberty. The pressures of debt and making ends meet occupies most of our focus. Christians plod on in bondage to lack - with the enemy holding on to their economic blessing and frustrating their destiny. People everywhere seem to be suffering: debt pressures are massive, homes are being lost, destinies are thwarted, and there is great pain and suffering. People are in extreme situations and under heavy weights and pressures and are looking for a way out and rescue - like George in our story, many are brought low.

In almost every situation where I speak to a crowd, there are people who are facing life changing financial pressures. Students are buried under debt and looking at paying off student loans into their 50s. Christians that have stepped out to pursue a vision are losing everything - it seems like something is preventing the flow of needed provision. It may be that the cross section of people in the Church is no worse than in the general population, but no one can dispute that there are deep problems in the Body of Christ and that people are in situations which do not line up with God's plan for their lives to be blessed.

Many others seem to be comfortable with their status quo, not realising that their ability to move forward with God's plans for their lives is severely impacted by the level of bondage in their lives. These are the "happy slaves" who do not recognise their bondage as they are doing "OK". They may be getting by, but they could not change their situations easily due to their financial obligations and constraints. Young couples with godly destinies are locked into a month-by-month grinding cycle of payments that have them completely bound. Complacency and being "OK" may not mean they are financially secure as their precarious financial situation can be easily unbalanced. It may not take too much upheaval to "upset the apple cart". Illness or one partner losing their job can result in real hardship in a very short time frame.

We need to recognise that in addition to financially desperate Christians, there are also believers who are barely stable and lack resources to move forward into their callings.

Chapter 4

Lack and Blessing

The Outhouse of Lack

I have a vision of the world system and the current state of affairs as being like the outhouse named LACK. The world system we operate under is connected to defilement and lack, not the blessing. Imagine two buildings: one is an outhouse called Lack and the other is a beautiful building called the Blessing.

Outhouse of Lack <————————————————————> *The Blessing*

You may remember or have heard of the old outhouses set above a hole dug into the ground. I remember these outhouses from my childhood camping days. There were wooden benches with holes in them for the toilet seat and all of the waste goes directly into the hole in the ground. When the hole fills up, the wooden structure would be moved to a new location above a new hole. Of course, they were usually away from buildings, and they were not pleasant places to spend any length of time!

Figuratively, those with some money and education have clambered out of the muck and are trying to keep as far away from those unfortunate enough to be still at the bottom - they are at a better level, but they are all still in the outhouse. We can work to improve our conditions, to do better under the world system of lack, but this is not The Blessing that God intended for us. People can be blind to the fact that they are still in the outhouse. So, too, we can be blind to the world of Kingdom Finance and Blessing. Spiritually, the outhouse is a symbol of lack and the curse that we operate under, whether we have some money or no money.

> **The goal of people in the Outhouse is to get ahead and use their money to work hard to climb the ladder to separate them from those less fortunate – to rise above the masses.**

The goal of people in the world system's Outhouse is to **get ahead** and use their money to work hard to climb the ladder to separate them from those less fortunate - to rise above the masses. The ultimate illustration of this would be a gated home or private island with no interaction with the community, with guards, minders, and a chauffeured limo to a private airfield to keep the people isolated from the needs of others. None of these things are wrong in and of themselves, but **lack is in full operation if the goal is isolation.** You can isolate and separate yourself to the point where you have convinced yourself there is no lack in your life. However, this is a delusion because you are still in the Outhouse, and the operating power in your life is still lack and the curse, not the blessing that makes one rich and adds no sorrow. You may not be in the muck, but you still carry the odour of lack with you no matter what designer perfume you use! Like the vision of the table of defilement, even the offerings are tainted. Kingdom Finance does not separate us from those in need but drives us closer to meet their needs and to pull them into prosperity and the blessing. It is the anointing to rescue and deliver others.

The enemy has been controlling things for too long, and he does not mind money moving around in his kingdom even in the hands of Christians. As long as everyone is in satan's outhouse called Lack, he does not mind you helping a few people. This type of social welfare "good act" does not break the enslaving power over their lives and does not set them free. Our goal is not just to do good but to deliver people from bondage in the Outhouse of Lack and take them to the new building of Kingdom Blessing. We are not looking to just improve their lot in the Outhouse! Like the Prodigal Son, we want to take them out of the pig pen and put them fully restored in the Father's Home of Blessing.

Social justice movements and charities which help people are good, but the goal of Kingdom Finance is to destroy the works of satan, including the entire structure of lack. The goal is to destroy the empowering connection of sin and lack in operation in our lives and to connect us to the river of blessing through Jesus: The Blessing that makes rich and adds no sorrow. This is where the social justice movement utterly misses the mark as it focuses only on improving people's relative position in the outhouse without breaking the dominion of lack and moving them into the new operating paradigm of Kingdom Finance Blessing. Merely taking from those at the top to give to those in the bottom does not make it Kingdom. We need to break the dominion of lack and move people across to the new building of Blessing. The goal of Kingdom Finance therefore is not to rise to the top of worldly structures but to eclipse them completely by building something new and undefiled. No whitewashed outhouses in the Kingdom!

> Our goal is to deliver people from bondage in the Outhouse of Lack and take them to the new building of Kingdom Blessing. We are not looking to just improve their lot in the Outhouse!

The Blessing

Contrast the lifestyle of the Outhouse with the plan of God for us to live in Blessing. God's best for us is not to do a bit better under the curse - He has redeemed us from the curse.

> *All men of faith share the blessing of Abraham who "believed God". Everyone, however, who is involved in trying to keep the Law's demands falls under a curse, for it is written:* **'Cursed is everyone who does not continue in all things which are written in the book of the Law, to do them.'** *It is made still plainer that no one is justified in God's sight by obeying the Law, for: 'The just shall live by faith.' And the Law is not a matter of faith at all but of doing, as, for example, in the Scripture: 'The man who does them shall live by them.' Now* **Christ has redeemed us from the curse** *of the Law's condemnation, by himself becoming a curse for us when he was crucified. For the Scripture is plain: 'Cursed is everyone who hangs on a tree. (PHILLIPS Galatians 3:9-13 emphasis added)*

We are set free. He does not lift us to a higher status under lack but still leave us in the outhouse of defilement. He takes us to a new building of Blessing! No odour or influence of the curse, but the fragrant anointing of Heaven.

> **We are not blessed to be better slaves but to be free men and women.**

To be clear, there is a sense in which we can be "blessed" under the curse - or in the Outhouse of Lack - but this acknowledges the enslaving dominion of the enemy in operation in our lives. Here is how it works: If you are a slave being beaten five times a day, it is *a blessing* to be sold to an owner that only beats you once a day or treats you nicely - BUT this is not THE BLESSING of Abraham that we are to walk in. We are not blessed to be better slaves but to be free men and women. We have been redeemed or purchased out of the curse and slavery through the blood of Jesus.[1]

Jeremiah 29 deals with being blessed **under the curse,** and I have seen this Scripture used to illustrate how we are intended to prosper and multiply in an evil world system. However, in Jeremiah's day the Jews had rebelled and entered into judgement and captivity in Babylon for their sins.[2] Paraphrasing the above, what God is saying is that "you might as well prosper under the curse as you are not going to be freed until the judgement time is completed". It was the mercy of God that they were given a blessing to prosper *even in* their captivity. We can still see the heart of God's mercy to bless even in this season, **but this was not His will - it was not what He wanted for them and not what He wants for us.** The Lord's prayer for His will to be done on earth as in Heaven would not apply to them in captivity. More importantly, we are not under judgement in the New Covenant, as Jesus has taken our punishment. We are free.

God did not improve the conditions of the Children of Israel in slavery, He took them out of slavery to a land flowing with milk and honey. This is a picture of what he does in our lives. He does not cause us to be improved; He gives us a new citizenship, a new identity, a new family, and new financial sources. We are not in the Outhouse of Lack anymore but are seated with Him in Heavenly places (Ephesians 2). He wants us to restore Eden on earth so that we can walk with Him in the cool of the day (Genesis 3:8) with the blessing operating that makes one rich and adds no sorrow to it.

The blessing of the Lord brings wealth, without painful toil for it. (Proverbs 10:22 NIV)

or

---

1. I Peter 1:19; I Corinthians 7:23
2. Jeremiah 29:1, 4-14

The blessing of Adonai is what makes people rich, and he doesn't mix sorrow with it. (Complete Jewish Bible)

In making us rich, He wants us to join with him in His mission of freeing others - that is His **purpose** for our riches. If we are following Him, we don't want to get up and walk away from those who are stuck in the mire; we want to get close to them to rescue them as we are in a good place and have the tools to pull them out. Remember, we have joined with Jesus in His Kingdom Finance mission to destroy the works of the enemy.

> **In making us rich, He wants us to join with Him in His mission of freeing others – that is His purpose for our riches.**

Using our Outhouse image, we are now in a beautiful place of blessing, but we go back to the outhouse called Lack and pull people out. While this is true in terms of salvation, it should also be true in terms of money. Our financial blessing is one of the PRIMARY tools that can pull someone free from the Outhouse of Lack - remember that money answers all things.

A feast is made for laughter, and wine maketh merry: ***but money answereth all things****. (Ecclesiastes 10:19 KJV)*

What is the use (profit), my brethren, for anyone to profess to have faith if he has no [good] works [to show for it]? Can [such] faith save [his soul]? If a brother or sister is poorly clad and lacks food for each day, And one of you says to him, Good-bye! Keep [yourself] warm and well fed, ***without giving him the necessities for the body****, what good does that do? So also faith, if it does not have works (deeds and actions of obedience to back it up), by itself is* ***destitute of power*** *(inoperative, dead). (James 2:14-17 AMPC emphasis added)*

*...I delivered the poor who cried, the fatherless and him who had none to help him. I was eyes to the blind, and feet was I to the lame. I was a father to the poor and needy; the cause of him I did not know I searched out. And **I broke the jaws or the big teeth of the unrighteous and plucked the prey out of his teeth.** (Job 29:12, 15-17 AMPC emphasis added)*

These Scriptures speak of the role of a godly rich person, being capable of reaching out practically and responding to needs. People are trapped in poverty and lack, and we in the church should have the answer and should be able to meet the need! Money is part of the solution, and we have the good news that they can be freed and released and walk in blessing.

*The steps of a [good] man are directed and established by the Lord when He delights in his way [and He busies Himself with his every step]. Though he falls, he shall not be utterly cast down, for **the Lord grasps his hand in support and upholds him.** I have been young and now am old, yet have **I not seen the [uncompromisingly] righteous forsaken or their seed begging bread.** (Psalm 37:23-25 AMPC emphasis added)*

Psalm 37 says that the Lord grasps the hand of one who stumbles. This verse is in the context of being established in His way and not being forsaken financially or begging bread. Begging bread is a strong indication of lack and shortfall in operation in our lives. As the old song says, we are to be His hand extended reaching out to the oppressed. We are not to be reaching out with witty sayings or a meaningless "bless you", but with practical help, money, and the anointing to break the power operating in people's lives and to connect them with the blessing.

Chapter 5

Breaking Free

The Good Samaritan Test

For many if not most Christians today, even being the "Good Samaritan" and meeting critical needs would be impossible due to our lack of free resources. **Can we, without credit or borrowing, be the Good Samaritan?**

> *25 And a certain lawyer [an expert in Mosaic Law] stood up to test Him, saying, "Teacher,* **what must I do to inherit eternal life?"** *26 Jesus said to him, "What is written in the Law? How do you read it?" 27 And he replied, "You shall love the Lord your God with all your heart, and with all your soul, and with all your strength, and with all your mind; and your neighbor as yourself."*
>
> *28 Jesus said to him, "You have answered correctly; do this habitually and you will live." 29 But he, wishing to justify and vindicate himself, asked Jesus, "And who is my neighbor?"*

Parable of the Good Samaritan

> *30 Jesus replied, "A man was going down from Jerusalem to Jericho, and he encountered robbers, who stripped him of his clothes [and belongings], beat him, and went their way [unconcerned], leaving him half dead. 31 Now by coincidence a priest was going down that road, and when he saw him, he passed by on the other side. 32 Likewise a Levite also came down to the place and saw him, and passed by on the other side [of the road]. 33 But a Samaritan (foreigner), who was traveling, came upon him; and when he saw him, he was **deeply moved with compassion [for him]**, 34 and went to him and bandaged up his wounds, pouring oil and wine on them [to sooth and disinfect the injuries]; and he put him on his own pack-animal, and brought him to an inn and took care of him. 35 On the next day he took out two denarii (two days' wages) and gave them to the innkeeper, and said, 'Take care of him; and whatever more you spend, I will repay you when I return.' 36 Which of these three do you think proved himself a neighbor to the man who encountered the robbers?" 37 He answered, "The one who showed compassion and mercy to him." Then Jesus said to him, "**Go and constantly do the same.**" (Luke 10:25-37 AMP emphasis added)*

The Good Samaritan Test is a good, "Jesus approved", starting point in looking critically at our finances since we were commanded by Jesus to "**constantly** do the same" as the Good Samaritan. If our finances limit our ability to be a Good Samaritan, then we need to address our situation seriously, as it is evidence that we are in bondage and lack. We may be just covering our own expenses, but if we fail this test, we need to seek God in prayer and fasting to fix the problem.

So, what do we need to be modern day Good Samaritans - to pass the Good Samaritan Test? Here are what I think are a list of basic requirements:

- To be mobile - The Good Samaritan was on the road travelling and engaged - he was not stuck at home due to a

shortage of funds. We need to be out and active and able to be on a journey.
- To be able to communicate - The Good Samaritan was able to book a room, engage with a doctor, and take care of what was needed. In our modern age, this would require a different set of tools such as a phone we can use, wifi, and the ability to book a hotel etc.
- To have transportation - The Good Samaritan was on the road travelling and had the extra capacity on his pack animals (read *car* for us) to take the injured man with him. We are not much help to the needy without these basics in place.
- To have "oil and wine" - The Good Samaritan was able to provide food and supplies. We need to have with us those things which are needed for such a situation. Practical service needs practical goods such as emergency response and first aid.
- To have funds available - The Good Samaritan had funds in hand to support the injured man, pay for his care, and hotel. He had these resources with him.
- To have more than enough - The Good Samaritan did not just give a contribution - he left the tab open to provide a full response. We need to have additional resources to pick up any extras - to leave an open tab.

Let us not cheat here and say we can call an ambulance to push the cost onto someone else or use our credit card to rack up debt. We use this parable to see what is the basic level of prosperity that should be in operation personally for each Christian! Remember the Good Samaritan was also travelling away from home, so he was already spending money for his journey.

I tried to do a rough calculation of the cost, but the rates vary depending upon the jurisdiction; you can do a rough calculation for your area. Food, medical supplies, private doctor's attendance,

> **We are not meeting the standard Jesus set for us if we cannot meet His call to be Good Samaritans as we go on our journey in life.**

gasoline, transportation, hotel charges, and extras would certainly add up to a fairly large five figure bill. Just imagine your last week-long foreign holiday bill, then double it and add on severe life threatening medical costs, clothing, and food. I think we can agree that it would not be cheap. I am calling this minimum level of financial prosperity the FLOOR for us as Christians - a level of financial prosperity and freedom we should all be able to agree on.

We can argue about planes and high living - the CEILING - but we should all be able to agree on this FLOOR. When people deflect by trying to argue about Christians with nice cars or a plane, I make the point that I will spend time discussing the ceiling once we have all agreed and are operating at the FLOOR level. The CEILING is not the major problem among Christians right now; it is lack and the need for us all to move up to be operating at this floor level! If you are facing a tough time financially, you already know you are in need and are crying out for help.

Setting our biblical FLOOR means that everyone in the Body of Christ needs to be moving at this basic level of financial freedom without going to the lenders to borrow! I set a challenge to us all: even if our personal needs are met, we are not fully operational in Kingdom Finance until we get to our Good Samaritan FLOOR level. We need the Good Samaritan standard or test to break many people out of the malaise of comfort. We are not meeting the standard Jesus set for us if we cannot meet His call to be Good Samaritans continually as we go on our journey in life. We need to live at a level of Kingdom Finance blessing that we can operate as Jesus described so that we do not fail the test.

However, this is just the basic test for us as Christians because it does not address any calling to a greater work in the Kingdom. To truly make an impact and influence culture will require a lot more funds than our Good Samaritan FLOOR test. We need to be financially free and empowered to fulfil the plan that God has for us in life. Think of the requirements to alleviate poverty, bring clean water, free the slaves, eliminate corruption, and change financial systems. That is why I described this test as the floor - it is the starting point that God can build on.

Perhaps the "Test of the Good Samaritan" should really be called the "Test of the Naked Victim". We may have always seen ourselves as givers, but Jesus set the test by identifying his listeners with the victim. If you find yourself like George in our story, or if you are facing an impossible situation, what kind of person do you want to pass by at your time of need? When you find yourself attacked and almost taken out by the enemy, what kind of neighbour do you want to walk by? I want an empowered Good Samaritan with money, not another victim with no ability to help. If I am crying out to God for a desperate need, I don't want someone to religiously mumble "Bless you" or a faithless "I'm praying for you"- I want the Good Samaritan. Part of walking in victory as Christians should be our ability to support each other practically when we are going through a time of attack.

> **We need to be financially free and empowered to fulfil the plan that God has for us in life.**

Just as someone in our path who is in need is a test for us, **sometimes we can be the person in need.** That is also the message Jesus described. When we are in need - proverbially beaten, robbed and left naked in a ditch - we are a test to those around us who must respond, either by failing the test and walking past or by stepping up and meeting the needs. Remember, we are all in a battle, and if we are under attack, we need those around us to help. Who comes to beat and rob us? The enemy, of course, as the thief comes to steal, kill, and destroy (John 10:10). When we are in trouble we need neighbours who do not pass by us.

If you find yourself under attack and in need, it is amazing how quickly those around you can melt away and distance themselves from your need. How quickly the prosperous facade of many Christians is revealed as they do not have resources to help. The well-dressed, Mercedes driving Christian may be living on credit and actually may have no money to help. In 2023, the US Federal Reserve reported that 63% of Americans would be unable to pay $400 in cash (or cash equivalent such as a credit card paid off that month) for emergency expenses.[i] According to another source, almost 80% of us are reported to be living paycheck to paycheck.[ii]

How many of us would fail the Good Samaritan Test? The test is to help, not to be willing to help but unable! **I do not say this to condemn us if we are not in the place we should be, but it should be a challenge to recognise that we have the taint of bondage on our lives, families, and churches, and God wants to break it off.**

> **The test is to help, not to be willing to help but unable!**

Jesus approves of the Good Samaritan and wants us to be like him, and He will empower us to walk at this minimum level of freedom. The first step is to recognise that things are not as they should be and that we need to move forward to financial freedom and blessing. We must see our need so that we can address it and deal with it.

Breaking Free From Slavery

Worldly positive thinking is useful and addresses the paradigm shifts that can happen when people begin to look at these constraints, but we are talking about something much more fundamental. We are breaking out of the outhouse of ungodly dominion - the slavery and lack the enemy has held us in, so that we can move into the Kingdom that God has ordained for us to operate in. First, He brings us to our floor level of prosperity so that we can pass the Good Samaritan Test, and then to the level of financial freedom needed to fund our destiny callings.

Moses' experiences are an illustration of how difficult it is to break free from slavery. It required the anointing to declare the word of the Lord for the people and to repeatedly enforce it in the physical world. Moses was not raised in the lack and oppression of his people since he was raised in the palace. When he saw the Israelites' true circumstances he immediately perceived they were oppressed and in lack. Later he declared the word of the Lord that God would take them from slavery and into their inheritance:

> *Therefore, say to the children of Israel, 'I am the Lord, and **I will bring you out** from under the burdens of the Egyptians, and I will free you from their bondage. I will redeem and rescue you with an outstretched (vigorous, powerful) arm and with great acts of judgment [against Egypt]. 7 Then I will take you for My people, and I will be your God; and you shall know that I am the Lord your God, who redeemed you and brought you out from under the burdens of the Egyptians. 8 I will bring you to the land which I [d]swore to give to Abraham, Isaac, and Jacob (Israel); and I will give it to you as a possession. I am the Lord [you have the promise of My changeless omnipotence and faithfulness].'" 9 **Moses told this to the Israelites, but they did not listen to him because of their [e]impatience and despondency, and because of their forced labor.** (Exodus 6:6-9 AMP emphasis added)*

The Orthodox Jewish Bible translates "forced labour" as "cruel bondage" or slavery. It is the reaction of Moses' kinfolk to the promise that is illuminating - they could not "hear" the truth of what he was saying. They did not listen to him and the vision of freedom and blessing that he was speaking about was not something they could see or comprehend. Slavery had shut down the Israelites' ability to see themselves operating in their destiny!

This "blindness" is part of the curse that says:

> *... you will be groping at noon [in broad daylight], just as the blind grope in the darkness, and nothing you do will prosper; but you will only be oppressed and exploited and robbed continually, with no one to save you. (Deuteronomy 28:29 AMP)*

> **Slavery had shut down their ability to see themselves operating in their destiny!**

Blindness to the truth of our situation is a sign of the curse in operation in our lives. How similar to the deflection and hardness of hearing that we encounter from some people when we present to them the blessing and level of prosperity that God has for us today! Christians today have become used to the constraints, compromises, and pressures they live under. Many of us in the church have accepted debt and a standard of limitation that blinds us to the curse in operation in our lives. People have become blind to their own situation and lack of blessing and worse, blind to the word of Kingdom Finance and blessing. We may not even realise the state we are in as, like the Israelites, we plod on in our cruel bondage to debt and lack. When someone comes with a message of hope we can respond by deflection and rejection just like the pattern we see with Moses and the Israelites.

We too have been given a challenge in the area of finance. At a minimum, that challenge is to pass the Good Samaritan Test, but it is much more than this, as we are called to change things and to bring His Kingdom to this world. We need to become alive to the issues facing the church and the world and move into financial freedom like we have never walked in as believers before. Ungodly systems need to be shifted and nations need to be changed, and that requires His people to operate freely in the area of Kingdom Finance.

Another obvious truth about slavery is that the enemy does not want us to be free. Standing on and claiming the word of God for freedom can be a real battle! Pharaoh held the Children of Israel as slaves for economic reasons - "their forced labour". Moses came with the word of the Lord for freedom and declared it, but Pharaoh refused to let them go over and over. They only achieved freedom and were able to move towards their destiny after **repeated demands** in accordance with the word of the Lord and the intervening manifestation of the **power of the Lord** extracting a great cost from the enslaving power of Egypt. Only the anointing broke the yoke.

We speak of "Egypt" today as an example or type of these old limiting modes of thinking and acting. In Egypt, the Children of Israel were enslaved and under bondage. They were constrained by an oppressive system that did not allow them to fulfil their destiny. However, it was familiar, and people were held in bondage through force and belief. After the period of transition in the wilderness, God had a new paradigm for them. They were to rule and reign in the Promised Land. We will refer back to the paradigm of Egypt and slavery in our discussion of Kingdom Finance because God wants us to be free - free from lack and constraint, operating as rulers not slaves.

In a similar manner the liberation of Christians and the Church into their financial destiny is heavily contested, and it is no surprise that the apparent answer to our declarations of blessing may result in no immediate change. Economic bondage (our "Egypt") is difficult to break and, as such, once we are free, we need to avoid coming again into any form of bondage. We are not to remain in Egypt nor be bound by the rules of Egypt as we move forward.

Not Me - I'm Okay

Finally, what about the Christians that seem to be doing well financially? At the other end of the wealth continuum are those who are more well off but are not always modelling a life of service and worship to Jesus. They are entrenched in a worldly system of money and wealth with little direct revelation of what the Kingdom might be about. The key question is whether they are in the Outhouse of Lack or in the House of Blessing. Are they just doing better than others, but with the real power in their lives being dominated by lack? Are they operating in the Kingdom or just doing well with their finances?

The purpose of being free is to be free to worship God:

> *"Let my people go, so that they may <u>worship</u> me." (Exodus 9:1 NIV emphasis added)*

and

> *"For long ago in Egypt I broke your yoke and burst your bonds <u>not that you might be free, but that you might serve me</u>..." (Jeremiah 2:20 AMPC emphasis added and brackets removed)*

From a worldly perspective, all the focus is on being free, but from a Kingdom perspective the goal is NOT about being free - the goal is about **being free to worship.** There is a calling and a purpose to our walking in prosperity and that is what moving into Kingdom Finance is really about.

Some of the wealthy also seem to be locked into an ungodly system and are on a treadmill. I think of this as "Christian brothel-keeping" - where Christians are fully entrenched in a world system and businesses that may be completely contrary to God's call for them and even His values, but smug and contented that they are doing well financially and better off than others. How many Bibles are sitting on desks in businesses that people consider "Christian" but where the source and flow of power is not from God? My goal is not to condemn or judge, as we are all on our journey, but to call us to really look at what God wants to do in our lives, in the church and in the world. We also need to examine what we are doing to see if it is part of the Outhouse or part of the Kingdom.

> *"Come [quickly] now, you rich [who lack true faith and hoard and misuse your resources], weep and howl over the miseries [the woes, the judgments] that are coming upon you. 2 Your wealth has rotted and is*

> ruined and your [fine] clothes have become moth-eaten. 3 Your gold and silver are corroded, and their corrosion will be a witness against you and will consume your flesh like fire. You have **stored up your treasure** in the last days [when it will do you no good]... On the earth you have lived luxuriously and **abandoned yourselves** to soft living and led a life of wanton pleasure [self-indulgence, self-gratification]..." (James 5:1-3; 5 AMPC emphasis added)

Financial freedom is not given to us to do better in the Outhouse or to separate us from those in need. Freedom in Kingdom Finance is so that we can worship and serve God. Our treasure is not stored up for our freedom to abandon ourselves, rather it is to enable and empower us to partner with Jesus to destroy the works of satan. The funds we take out of Egypt are for service, not to build a Golden Calf! The sad reality is that in many cases Christians are in the Outhouse of Lack: in bondage with money and in bondage without money. We need to know His plan for us so that we can align our lives to do His will. His will is to be a giver and to minister to those in need.[1]

> But those who want to get rich fall into temptation and a snare and many foolish and harmful desires which plunge men into ruin and destruction....
> (1 Timothy 6:9 NIV)

If we truly see that we are free to serve Him and His Kingdom plan then our resources are not free to be spent on foolish and harmful desires.

More Than Social Welfare

Isaiah 58 shows us that the critical requirement for our corporate breakthrough requires practical service. We are freed so that we can worship and serve. If we are looking to break through to the freedom of peace and prosperity in our lives and churches, it comes along with

---
1. Luke 6:31

the action steps of freeing the oppressed, feeding the hungry, helping the homeless, and clothing the naked. Not mere social justice activity, but being Jesus' hands to those in need. Does this bring to mind Jesus' parable of the Good Samaritan? When Jesus was describing the Good Samaritan, He was describing a man walking in Isaiah 58 calling.

Isaiah 58 Calling

*Yet they seek, inquire for, and require Me daily and delight [externally] to know My ways, as [if they were in reality] a nation that did righteousness and forsook not the ordinance of their God. They ask of Me righteous judgments, they delight to draw near to God [in visible ways]. Why have we fasted, they say, and You do not see it? Why have we afflicted ourselves, and You take no knowledge [of it]? Behold [O Israel], on the day of your fast [when you should be grieving for your sins], you find profit in your business, and [instead of stopping all work, as the law implies you and your workmen should do] you extort from your hired servants a full amount of labor. [The facts are that] you fast only for strife and debate and to smite with the fist of wickedness. Fasting as you do today will not cause your voice to be heard on high. Is such a fast as yours what I have chosen, a day for a man to humble himself with sorrow in his soul? [Is true fasting merely mechanical?] Is it only to bow down his head like a bulrush and to spread sackcloth and ashes under him [to indicate a condition of heart that he does not have]? Will you call this a fast and an acceptable day to the Lord? [Rather] is not this the fast that I have chosen: **to loose the bonds of wickedness, to undo the bands of the yoke, to let the oppressed go free, and that you break every [enslaving] yoke? Is it not to divide your bread with the hungry and bring the homeless poor into your house—when you see the naked, that you cover him, and that you hide not yourself from [the needs of] your own flesh and blood? Then shall your light break forth like the morning, and your healing** (your restoration and the power of a new life) **shall spring forth speedily;** your righteousness (your rightness, your justice, and your right relationship* with God) shall go before you [conducting you to peace and prosperity], and the glory of the Lord shall be your rear guard. Then you shall call, and the Lord will answer; you shall cry, and He will say, Here I am. If you take away from your midst yokes of oppression [wherever you find them], the finger pointed in scorn [toward the oppressed or the godly], and every form of false, harsh, unjust, and wicked speaking, **And if you pour out that with which you sustain your own life for the hungry and satisfy the need of the afflicted, then shall your light rise in darkness, and your obscurity and gloom become like the noonday. And the Lord shall guide you continually and satisfy you in drought and in dry places and make strong your bones. And you shall be like a watered garden and like a spring of water whose waters fail not. And your ancient ruins shall be rebuilt; you shall raise up the foundations of [buildings that have laid waste for] many generations; and you shall be called Repairer of the Breach, Restorer of Streets to Dwell In.** (Isaiah 58:2-12 AMPC emphasis added and some punctuation removed)

Breaking every enslaving yoke - that is what God says is a true fast which results in breakthrough for our needs. It is not enough to improve someone's lot - we must break the enslaving yoke and have them move from the power of lack operating in their lives and families, and then have them move into the operation of the blessing in Kingdom Finance. The key to corporate breakthrough and restoring our foundations is practical Isaiah 58 service.

Chapter 6

A Reality Check

So How Are We Doing, Really?

So, how are we doing? What is our current status? Are we able to meet people's needs, and have we been restored like the description above? Are we operating in the blessing of Kingdom Finance? This is what it means to be blessed - to have the ancient ruins of our lives rebuilt (Isaiah 61). It seems from my observations that many, if not most of the churches are in debt and burdened with monthly payments and cares that inhibit their ability to give and act as they would like. I remember one high pressure building fund "Missions" drive which was really better described as a church mortgage reduction drive, and the "hard-sell" for the congregation was the amount of money that could go to missions and other good causes if only the monthly payment was reduced.

The model for release from financial bondage is not pressure and regret - the Isaiah 58 model would have called for repentance and fasting coupled with radical giving. However, I don't remember any repentance for the years of lost missions giving due to taking on the debt in the first place and not seeking God for His solution to funding the church. In the Church we may have had a measure of release and revelation for salvation and a little bit for healing, but when it comes to financial blessing there is little fruit evident.

Not only are many people buried in debt but so are many churches. Again, I do not mean to condemn, but to illustrate that there is room for improvement in our walk. It is time to change this reality to come in line with God's plan for blessing. If you are in a place where you are struggling financially or have funds, but there are other major issues requiring restoration, then you know you need things to be better. If you were in the "Doing OK" category, then I trust that your eyes have been opened and that you now believe that things could and should be better.

It is time for money to be released and flowing in the Church so that needs can be met for individuals, families, churches, cities, and countries.

Another way to think of this is that money is to our destiny as oxygen is to our physical body. Just imagine for a moment having to complete a complex task requiring significant mental and physical exertion. A motivated, enthusiastic person could do the task in a few minutes. In a room without oxygen, desire and passion are irrelevant as the physical impact of reduced oxygen impairs our ability to undertake even the most basic tasks - we stop being effective, start staggering around, and eventually fall over. Of course, the end result is brain impairment and death.

> Another way to think of this is that money is to our destiny calling as oxygen is to our physical body.

Not having money to do what we need to do is like being starved of oxygen - it can be disastrous to our mission. One of the best strategies for the enemy is to have a cash-strapped, crippled and ineffective body of Christ where believers are cut off from being able to access the supply of provision that God intended for them to have. Lack exerts a fundamental limitation on our capacity to achieve our destiny, and if we operate in agreement with lack, we have shut down or at best crippled our effectiveness and potential.

There is another justification for Christian lack which rises up in my experiences with believers and churches - the "just in time" financial miracles of God. I love these miracle stories and God certainly works through miracles, but what we are discussing here is the base state that we should be living and abiding in. The question we should ask is, "In what state do we need to be so that we can be His hand extended rescuing others?" Not, "What God can do to rescue us?" God provided for the flight of Joseph, Mary, and Jesus to safety in Egypt by bringing rich men with gifts of gold, frankincense, and myrrh - imagine a chest of gold when most people had never seen even one gold coin (Matthew 2:11). Roman soldiers could not readily use gold coins as people did not have enough change in silver![i] Blessings indeed.

God's plan is for us to abide in Him in such a manner that we can walk in the blessings and do the works of Isaiah 58, Job 29, and be the Good Samaritans of our time. This is our identity as believers. If we are connected to the King and operating in the blessing then our provision will come, not through striving and the world's system, but through the blessing. This is Kingdom Finance in operation.

THE FLOOR AND THE CEILING

We have established that there is a "Floor", a minimum level of blessing that we should be walking in. A manner of living that allows us to operate in the Blessing so that we can be His hand extended to rescue others. We have also established that the majority of us fall well short of this standard and need help. Even if we were in the category of feeling "OK" this is usually with reference to our immediate needs and not the mission Jesus has for us - it does not take account of our destiny calling, and we may not press into our destiny as it will upset the financial status quo.

People misquote Moses and say that he told Pharaoh God had said to "Let my people go", when what he really said was to: *"...Let my people go, that they may serve Me"* (Exodus 8:1). The purpose of freedom and liberty is not vain self indulgence but to serve Him. How do we serve Him? One of the primary ways is by meeting the needs of others following the model of the Good Samaritan and Isaiah 58.

This is the foundation stone upon which we re-establish the vision of what it means to be a godly Rich man or woman - PURPOSE. The purpose of our liberty from the slavery of lack is to serve Him, and service is all about destroying the works of the enemy in people's lives.

So if this is the floor what is the ceiling? I think if most of the Body of Christ were living at the FLOOR level of liberty, acting according to the purpose of service as Good Samaritans, then there would be little contention about the ceiling. If we abide in Him and walk in the blessing, then we will be doing His will. It may be easier to identify those not doing his will with much but it is the same failure. Larger amounts of money should mean we have a service requirement that requires this along with a greater capability to do the work Jesus asks us to do!

There are some amazing examples in the Bible of our forerunners, and Psalm 112 is one of my favourites:

> *Praise the Lord! (Hallelujah!)*
> *Blessed [fortunate, prosperous, and favored by God] is the man who*
> *fears the Lord [with awe-inspired reverence and worships Him*
> *with obedience],*
> *Who delights greatly in His commandments.*
> *His descendants will be mighty on earth;*
> *The generation of the upright will be blessed.*
> **Wealth and riches are in his house,**
> *And his righteousness endures forever.*
> *Light arises in the darkness for the upright;*

He is gracious and compassionate and righteous (upright—in right standing with God).
It is well with the man who is gracious and lends;
He conducts his affairs with justice.
He will never be shaken;
The righteous will be remembered forever.
He will not fear bad news;
His heart is steadfast, trusting [confidently relying on and believing] in the Lord.
His heart is upheld, he will not fear
While he looks [with satisfaction] on his adversaries.
*He has **given freely** to the poor;*
His righteousness endures forever;
His horn will be exalted in honor.
The wicked will see it and be angered,
He will gnash his teeth and melt away [in despair and death];
The desire of the wicked will perish and come to nothing. (AMP Psalm 112 emphasis added)

This passage describes the lifestyle of a godly rich man - **blessed, established, confident, and giving.** This pattern can be seen throughout the Bible.

- *There is **precious treasure** and oil in the house of the wise [who prepare for the future]..., (Proverbs 21:20 AMP emphasis added)*

- *Great and **priceless treasure** is in the house of the righteous one... (Proverbs 15:6 AMP emphasis added and parenthesis removed)*

- *A good man leaves an **inheritance** to his children's children, And the wealth of the sinner is stored up for [the hands of] the righteous. (Proverbs 13:22 AMP emphasis added)*

- *The blessing of Adonai is what makes people rich, and he doesn't mix sorrow with it. (Proverbs 10:22 CJB)*

- *Now, behold, in my trouble I have prepared for the house of the Lord an hundred thousand talents of gold, and a thousand thousand talents of silver; and of brass and iron without weight; for it is in abundance: timber also and stone have I prepared; and thou mayest add thereto. Moreover there are workmen with thee in abundance, hewers and workers of stone and timber, and all manner of cunning men for every manner of work. Of the gold, the silver, and the brass, and the iron, there is no number. (I Chron. 22:14-1 KJV)*

- *Now at Caesarea Maritima there was a man named Cornelius ... He made many charitable donations to the Jewish people, and prayed to God always. About the ninth hour (3:00 p.m.) of the day he clearly saw in a vision an angel of God who had come to him and said, "Cornelius!" Cornelius was frightened and stared intently at him and said, "What is it, lord (sir)?" And the angel said to him,* **"Your prayers and gifts of charity have ascended as a memorial offering before God.** *(Acts 10:1-4 AMP emphasis added and notations removed)*

- *Now Abram was extremely rich in livestock and in silver and in gold. (Genesis 13:2 AMP)*

- *Then Isaac planted seed in that land as a farmer and reaped in the same year a hundred times as much as he had planted, and the Lord blessed and favored him. And the man Isaac became great and gained more and more until he became very wealthy and extremely distinguished; (Genesis 26:12-13 AMP parenthesis removed)*

Clearly, the Lord wants to bless us in prosperity so that we might be a blessing. It is time to shift our perspective. If you are ready to move into your place as a godly, rich man or woman, here is a prayer and confession to read aloud:

Jesus, I acknowledge you as Lord of my life. I repent for myself and on behalf of my generations for not walking the way you designed in the area of finances and material blessing. I repent for not looking to you as my source, the author and finisher of my faith, in the area of finance. Father, on behalf of myself and my generational lines, please forgive us for not trusting our care to you. We have relied on the world's system, we have not gone to you and sought you, but we have accessed debt and allowed the enemy to seed our generations with lack. We have not left inheritances to our children and grandchildren, thereby causing them to start out life in lack and bondage. We have excused certain debts which we need because of this lack of inheritances, forgetting that "Your Kingdom come on earth as it is in Heaven" would mean that not having these debts would be the fullest expression of blessing! We repent for allowing debt into our lives and for not walking fully in the blessing you had for us that makes us rich and adds no sorrow to it.

Jesus, forgive us and cleanse us by your blood and as we study this area. We ask that you would lead us into all truth and that any blinding and limitation would be broken off so that we can see your truth, bring all sin under the blood for cleansing, and have our minds renewed.

Jesus we decree your Kingdom come into our lives in the area of finances. We believe that you reveal the secret things (Mark 4:22) and that you will reveal anything in our lives and generations that is not your plan and perfect will for us.

Father, we come out of agreement with sin and any force that has been active in our lives that is not godly. In particular we repent on behalf of ourselves and our generations for not walking in godly humility, but in the "I am" of pride and unbelief – not casting our cares upon you but working and striving to provide for our own needs and coming up with our own solutions instead of believing that you will provide. We have cooperated with and adopted the world's way of thinking about money and have not given according to your pattern - at times we have not looked after family (Is 58), the poor, and the ministers who have fed into our lives.

We have pooled money when we did have it and not entered into the flow (James 5). (Now, wait for a moment and listen and then repent for any specific matters that God brings to mind.)

By acting contrary to your Word, we have not "hearkened to your word" and have activated the power of the curses in Deuteronomy 28. We repent for this and ask that you forgive us for not casting all of our cares upon you, particularly (name your cares specifically). We acknowledge that these are not the truth for our situation, merely facts that you can change. We realign ourselves with the Word and what it says about us and our situation. We know that you cleanse us from sin and, like the Prodigal Son, you will restore us.

Father, we repent and ask that you would forgive us because of the sacrifice of your Son Jesus, and that you would cleanse us and our family lines from every stain. We choose the Blessing (read Deuteronomy 28).

Thank you for your restoration activity now working on behalf of myself and my generations. I decree and declare that lack is broken in my life and in my family's generational line – it stops with me, and I thank you Holy Spirit for doing a great work of restoration to move me into the place of blessing God has for me.

Part Two

Concluding the Past

Chapter 7

Rats in the Basement

On two separate occasions we discovered a rat in the basement and a bat in a bedroom. I learned a valuable lesson from this in that every other priority became secondary to getting these encroachments dealt with. Once identified, there was nothing more important to deal with to move on with our our lives. The first step in understanding and operating in Kingdom Finance blessing is to receive a revelation of the issues in our lives that could affect us or hold us back and then dealing with them. These issues are like rats in the basement as they can be well hidden; however, once they are revealed and identified, getting rid of them becomes the most important agenda item in your day!

Whether you call them rats or thistles as Jesus did, the clear admonition from Scripture is to get rid of them. Today can be the day that we deal with the issues that have held us back! Picture your life as a clean, prosperous garden full of great fruit where the first hint of a

> Once you find rats in the basement or bats in the bedroom, getting rid of them becomes Priority Number 1!

weed of lack is ruthlessly eliminated. Or picture a clean house where the first sign of a rat results in a visit from the exterminator. That is what I mean by concluding the past, and with the help of Jesus, we have the power to deal with the "rats" and move on to do the good works He wants us to do and to live the good life he has made ready for us.

> *For we are God's own handiwork His workmanship, recreated in Christ Jesus, born anew that we may do those **good works** which God predestined (planned beforehand) for us taking paths which He prepared ahead of time, that we should walk in them **living the good life** which He prearranged and made ready for us to live. (Ephesians 2:10 AMPC parenthesis removed and emphasis added)*

God is calling on this generation to take a stand and change things for ourselves and for our future generations, to deal with and move away from anything that holds us back from the full manifestation of God's will for our lives.

We don't have to fully understand all the implications to know that we, as individuals and as the church, are not where God wants us to be. I believe that if you are reading this book, your spirit intuitively knows this and is crying out for more: more of life, more of Him, more intimacy, more fellowship, more peace, more joy, more resources, more blessing, and more victory - to walk in the blessing.

We will look at some practical and biblical actions to conclude the past, cutting off these influences and dealing with repentance, generational issues, and financial repentance. We will look at steps to realign ourselves with God's will and purposes and to move on in victory. Critically, this includes the area of finance where the roots of contamination are eliminated and the weeds of covetousness and lust are eradicated. We will join with Jesus in the destruction of the works the devil has done in our lives and families. We cannot fully move forward in Kingdom Finance as godly rich people without dealing with and concluding the negative influences of the past over our lives.

We may have caught the vision and want to rush ahead to get into the work of the Kingdom as we see it. We want to take territory immediately - and in many cases, this masks the mixed motivation to get rich quick and do some good once we have money. Why not? After all, we are saved and covered by the blood of Jesus, right? However, there is a true fork in the road for us to choose. One road leads to a model of mixed effort combining self, works, and mere "Christian effort" based social justice. The other road leads to intimacy with Jesus, allowing Him to put in place His godly order as we commit to do His will in our lives. The path God desires for you is intimacy, anointing, power, and deep communion with Him. This second road of intimacy with Jesus is the only way that we can abide in Him, and only on that foundation can we really connect with His vision for Kingdom Finance.

A calling for Kingdom Finance sounds great, and many people want to sign up immediately. The prophetic calling for handling wealth can seem appealing, but this calling is not to be confused with our worldly examples. Moving into Kingdom Finance does not usually start with a "golden ticket", lottery win, or a sudden inheritance. Rather,

> I believe that if you are reading this that your spirit intuitively knows this and is crying out for more: more of life, more of Him, more intimacy, more fellowship, more peace, more joy, more resources, more blessing, and more victory - to walk in the blessing.

it is a process of intimacy with Jesus, concluding the past, shaking off anything that hinders us, and seeking the will of the Lord.

The process can put people off, as we generally want it all now. I recall a young man from a Christian home who had been living a worldly and ungodly lifestyle. He came to some prophetic meetings and had a real touch from the Lord, and he received an amazing prophecy of what God wanted for his life in the arts and media, which was close to his heart. There was a rush of enthusiasm which was dashed a very short time later due to pre-existing money issues. These issues had been caused by his lifestyle choices, but somehow he became offended that God had not dealt with them, that there was no "golden ticket" or quick escape from the issues in his life. He soon fell away. He put the weight of belief on his circumstances and not on the Word of God for his life.

In relation to God's will we know that:

- It is God's will for us to flourish - personally and economically (Jeremiah 29:11, Deuteronomy 28)

- God is good all the time - like the Prodigal Son's father, He wants us blessed, and we are to repent for bitterness and attributing to God the works of the enemy

- God's desire is for us to walk as Good Samaritans in the land, having the financial and emotional capital to reach out to those in need with real help

- His desire is for us to be connected to those He cares about, breaking the jaw of the oppressor to release the captives (Job 29)

- We need to reclaim our identity as kings and priests and rediscover what it means to be a godly believer (Psalm 112 and Proverbs 31)

- God has a purpose in this time to destroy the works of the enemy (1 John 3:8), and we each have a calling to operate in Kingdom Finance and need to cooperate with Jesus to fund that purpose (Luke 5:11-32 and John 15)

These principles may seem obvious, but if that were true, wouldn't each of our lives be full of blessing? Wouldn't the norm in our lives be victory and success with abundant godly fruit? After all, the Word says that everything we touch will prosper.[1] If the norm in our lives were godly success and prosperity, wouldn't the church be full of fruitful, thriving, giving, godly people? Is it?

This is the place where we lay to rest one of the key fallacies of religion. Yes, the work of Jesus on the cross transforms us from one kingdom to another, and our spirits are born anew.[2] The power of sin is also broken in our lives and we need no longer serve sin.[3] We also inherit the blessing of Abraham and the promises.[4] However, the Christian life in operation is the daily working out of this salvation through His power.[5] This process of appropriating the blessing brings the reality of our new position in Him to our lives, families, and finances. That is why many Christians still struggle with issues in their lives - the chains of sin may be gone, but like an animal tied to a mill wheel, we still can tend to focus on and tread the same old paths. These old patterns of the past which still hold some influence in our lives need to be identified and broken as we pray daily for His Kingdom to come and His will to be done fully in our lives. His will is for us to bear godly fruit:

> *You will fully recognize them by their fruits. Do people pick grapes from thorns, or figs from thistles? (Matthew 7:15-19 AMPC)*

> *But thanks be to God, Who in Christ always leads us in triumph as trophies of Christ's victory and through us spreads and makes evident the fragrance of the knowledge of God everywhere, For we are the* **sweet** *fragrance of Christ which exhales unto God, discernible alike among those who are being saved and among those who are perishing: (II Corinthians 2:14-15 AMPC parenthesis removed and emphasis added)*

---

1. Deuteronomy 28:8; 30:9
2. Colossians 1:13
3. Romans 6:6
4. Galatians 3:14
5. Philippians 2:12-13

If we are honest with ourselves, is the fruit we see in our lives and in the church giving off "sweet fragrance" unto God? I believe there is room for improvement. Would you like to deal with issues that are holding you back in life and keeping you from prospering and living in the way that God intended? Or, phrased differently, if living the life of blessing God intended means we have to deal with some issues, would you be willing? I think for all of us, the answer will be a resounding yes!

Chapter 8

Personal Inventory

Taking Stock - What is our Heritage?

It was clear to me that, despite many blessings, my life and my experience of the church did not measure up to the biblical standard. Frankly, I was not seeing this Blessing in operation in my life or in the church, particularly in the area of finances. Something was broken and needed to be fixed.

Each of us have our family, cultural, economic, national, and social background. The things that give us identity and our "fit" in the world we live in. In this context, the nation and family in which we are born are very important, as is our family background.

> *And he showed me a pure **river of water of life, clear as crystal, proceeding from the throne of God and of the Lamb** (Rev. 22:1 NKJ emphasis added).*

Picture your life as a body of water like a lake with conduits and rivers flowing into and out of it. Then imagine that some of these old conduits are polluted and black and full of waste and defilement. In all of our lives there are things that flow into or impact our lives that are not godly and need to be dealt with. We need to allow into our lives only the pure flow from the Kingdom.

It is time to deal with the rivers of poverty, sickness, defilement, anger, abuse, lust, and anything else that does not flow from the Spirit of God.

In many families, issues have gone on for a long time, and it is time to draw the bloodline - a line that says that the sin issues, health issues, and curses that have plagued us and our families will stop with us because of the blood of Jesus. God has not just saved us and made our spirits to be one with Him, He has given us the power to bring victory to every area of our lives.

> ...the "apple" of our lives has been grafted into the vine (John 15) so the "tree" it falls from is Jesus.

Poverty, lack, anger, rebellion, abuse, sickness - every conduit or stream entering into our lives that is not connected to Him can be stopped NOW. Not only can these ungodly rivers be stopped, but we can open the new conduits of blessings: abundance, love, peace, healing, prosperity, and all the blessings of the covenant. We are the generation of people called to turn the tide of poverty and lack and restore what God intended for us and for our children. We can then increase the flow of blessing coming from the reservoir of our lives to those in need.

Never again should the curses of heritage or family be used in relation to us, such as:

- "The apple doesn't fall far from the tree"
- "Bad blood" or "Blood will tell"
- "It's just my Irish (or any other nationality) temper"

These are not the rivers into our lives we want to grant access. Our citizenship is now in Heaven, and we are joint-heirs with Jesus - we have a new family with new character. As Christians, our lives are being transformed and we are made free - the "apple" of our lives has been grafted into the vine (John 15) so the "tree" it falls from is Jesus.

> But **we are citizens of the state (commonwealth, homeland) which is in Heaven** ... *(Philippians 3:20 AMPC emphasis added)*
>
> The Spirit Himself [thus] testifies together with our own spirit, [assuring us] that we are **children of God**. And if we are [His] children, then **we are [His] heirs also: heirs of God and fellow heirs with Christ [sharing His inheritance with Him]**... *(Romans 8:16-17 AMPC emphasis added)*
>
> But all of us who are Christians have no veils on our faces, but reflect like mirrors the glory of the Lord. **We are transfigured** by the Spirit of the Lord in ever-increasing splendour into his own image. *(II Corinthians 3:18 Phillips, emphasis added)*

As Christians we must accept as an irrevocable truth that what God wants for us will be fully in alignment with the Lord's Prayer - it is God's purpose that His will would be done in my life and family as it is in Heaven.[1] He wants us to have the full blessing of our new Heavenly heritage and citizenship. ANYTHING influencing or operating in our lives, families, and businesses that is not in accordance with His will for us in Heaven must be dealt with now - we need to conclude the past that has held us back and move forward in blessing. God wants us to walk in tune with Heaven and in a Heavenly anointing and blessing, reflecting His glory, and in order to do that we need to completely eradicate from our lives anything that is keeping us from full victory.

---

1. Matthew 6:9-13

Personal Inventory

The first step in this process is to take a candid look at your own life and family. You will know that you are not where you should be by the fruit in your life and your family line, or indeed by the unsatisfied hunger in your heart. This hunger is all that is required to move forward to seek Him first in our lives.

> God is calling on us in this generation to take a stand now and change things for ourselves and for our future generations.

In order to be released into Kingdom Finance we must humble ourselves to understand that there may be areas where we are blind to what God wants in our lives. Remember that part of the curse in operation is blindness to the truth of our situation.

And you shall grope at noonday as the blind grope in darkness... (Deut. 28:29 AMPC)

We can be in the Outhouse of Lack living under the curse and think the status quo is normal. Worse yet, we could be like the Pharisees standing aloof in our pride, one step above the muck in the outhouse, thankful that we are so much better than the unfortunates below us and, figuratively, trampling on their heads. Jesus described this as being like a whitewashed tomb or a cup that is clean on the outside and dirty on the inside.[2] The lake of our life can be stagnant and polluted with little or no outflow and polluted inflows. We do not even meet the test of the Good Samaritan, and yet we can be blind to our true state.

We can be like the generational slaves in Egypt who could perhaps only grasp the vision of a better working environment, friendlier overseers, and owners, but initially could not see the full vision God

---

2. Matthew 23:26 -27

had for them - they were blinded under a curse of hard labour. Compared to the blessing God had for them, they were groping around not seeing, evidencing the curse of Deuteronomy 28:29 in practical application. The freedom and self determination that God intended for them was too far removed from their reality to be comprehended. It was too big a leap and only a few, if any, relied on God to the extent that their belief in His word outweighed what they knew and saw.

Likewise, our first step must be to recognise that there may be areas where the light of revelation needs to shine, so we see how the deceiver has lied to us and to our families and used our agreement with these lies to bring us into a state of bondage. This is particularly true in the area of financial dealings, as this area has generally been kept separate from the Kingdom using mantras such as "That's just business". We need to bring all of our dealings under the Lordship of Jesus. As you read further, enquire of the Lord if any issues we discuss could be relevant to your life and your family.

Father, as I read about concluding the past, I really want to shed from my life everything that could hold me back. Give me wisdom and the Spirit of Revelation so that I can see any issues that may affect me and deal with these issues once and for all. Father, I know there is more of You - more blessing, more relationship, more love, more destiny, and more fulfilment. I come out of alignment NOW with anything that is not of You and pray that as I work through this chapter, I will have concluded the past and entered into a new stage of destiny and blessing for me and for my family.

WHAT IS THE FRUIT IN OUR LIVES?

At a conference recently, I asked if one or more of the following questions seemed relevant to the audience. As you read through the list, allow the Holy Spirit to reveal to you anything that may be relevant in your life or any patterns in your family history:

1. Are you in debt?
2. Does it seem like things you work on flounder?
3. Are other people enjoying the deals you put together or running businesses you started?
4. Do you do a lot of work and work hard but seem to come up short?
5. Are you not really enjoying your family as you should, or have your children fallen away?
6. Are you not with your partner, or has your relationship failed?
7. Does it seem like others who are not following God are doing fine, but you are suffering?

Interestingly, almost 100% of the crowd lifted a hand, as they were facing or had faced these issues in their lives and businesses. As we will see, each of those questions were taken directly from the curses described in Deuteronomy 28. The crowd I spoke to had the curse in operation and manifestation in their lives and didn't fully realise it. I think it is the same broadly throughout the church. It was certainly not a picture of His will for us on earth as it is in Heaven! The bondage of Egypt is rampant in the church today particularly in the area of finances.

God wants us to prosper and to walk in the blessing, but there are spiritual laws of blessing and cursing put in place that we can activate and reap the consequences. Think of these curses as being similar to the physical laws of gravity that God also put in place. We can violate this law as we have free will, but if we do violate the law, the negative consequences will surely follow. Using Old Testament language, if you step off a building (thereby engaging with the law of gravity) God will "strike you down". This is the permissive use that confuses many when we deal with the curse in operation. Our actions can put us in the "cursing territory", just like our gravity example, and in many cases it is only the mercy of God that He continually calls us back, providing a way of escape and repentance.

We know that, as with gravity, Kingdom Finance principles operate because God has put these laws in place. If I act "on faith", but in reality I am actually operating in pride and presumption (violating a Kingdom Finance principle), then likewise I will have bad fruit and may "fall" financially. I will have been "struck down" by a principle of Kingdom Finance. It is critical to understand what these Kingdom Finance principles are and operate in accordance with God's plan for release!

We must allow the Holy Spirit to open and renew our minds to see what He would have us see at this time so that we are not operating in constraint. We must remove the principles of Egypt from our thinking and operate His way. The limitations of the past must be overcome so that we can fulfil our destiny callings in this pivotal time.

God wants us to operate on the blessing side, not the cursing side, of life! Perhaps you have read the blessings of Deuteronomy 28:1-14 before, but their opposites are the curses found from verse 15 onwards. Sometimes we need to consider these curses to see what fruit is manifesting in our lives and in our families. As we go through this list (and there are more indicators than these), prayerfully consider if one or more of these things seems to be relevant in your life or in your family. Read Deuteronomy 28 to see what is manifesting in your life and in your generations, and allow God to identify a list that affects you.

1. Are you in debt?

He shall lend to you, but you shall not lend to him; he shall be the head, and you shall be the tail. (Deuteronomy 28:44 AMPC)

God's will is for you to be blessed with abundance so that you can lend to many nations but not borrow and to be the head and not the tail (Deuteronomy 28:12-13). There is no debt in Heaven, so debt is not His perfect will for us - remember, Thy will be done on earth as it is in Heaven! This means all debt, including mortgages and debts for investing - these debts are not part of our Heavenly inheritance. It is not perhaps a sin in the same context as overt sins such as theft, but it can be an example of living at a level that is less than the level of blessing God truly intended for us. We must begin to deal with debt so that we can be in a position to lend to those in need.

2. Does it seem like others who are not pressing in to God are doing fine, but you are suffering?

The transient (stranger) among you shall mount up higher and higher above you, and you shall come down lower and lower. (Deuteronomy 28:43 AMPC)[3]

God is a covenant God, and what He is saying here is that people in the world who are not covenant people (transient strangers) are mounting up above us, and we are falling low. We have a better covenant, and the covenant commands blessing on our lives. It is a spiritual law, and yet we seem to have the opposite being manifested. How often we hear Christians in a family noting and complaining that those that are not following Christ seem to be getting ahead. They are "mounting higher and higher". It is clear that this is the curse in operation in some manner. This is a fruit in our lives that indicates that something needs to be adjusted as we are to be the head and not the tail.

3. Are other people enjoying the deals you put together or running businesses you started?

"...you will build a house, but you will not live in it; you will plant a

---

3. Psalm 73

vineyard, but you will not use its fruit." (Deuteronomy 28:30 AMPC)

So often people have invested time and money in businesses, and then lost them due to a lack of cash flow, hostile take-over, or outright shady dealings. In many cases this has happened over and over - there seems to be an ungodly cycle at work here. Many people I know have lost homes or farms, and not that long ago this principle was driven home to me quite clearly. I remember standing on the balcony of a beautiful wine farm in Italy that represented a substantial investment of a close friend and Christian brother. Not long after this time it was sold for a nominal sum due to debts and lack of cash flow, and he lost most of his investment! There were a number of reasons for this, but I remember the strong revelation that this was wrong; it was the curse, and the result was not what God had intended. It was literally planting a vineyard but not gathering the grapes. We need to have a strategy to eradicate these outcomes in our lives and families.

4. Does it seem like everything you work on flounders?

"The Lord shall send you curses, confusion and rebuke in every enterprise to which you set your hand, until you are destroyed..." (Deuteronomy 28:20 AMPC)

If enterprises to which you are setting your hand to are not prospering as God intended, then is there an aspect of the curse in operation in your life? Do you do a lot of work and seem to come up short? This is probably the most common theme I hear from Christians struggling with disappointment and discouragement who say that they have tried everything. We know that it is the thief whose goal is to steal, kill, and destroy and that God's will is for us to have life and that more abundantly:

The thief comes only in order to steal and kill and destroy. I came that they may have and enjoy life, and have it in abundance (to the full, till it overflows). (John 10:10 AMPC)

Notice the permissive tense above. It is always God's will and plan to bless you. He can only ever give good gifts, but somehow we may have moved out of the blessing zone and into the cursing zone. We are to walk in the blessing where everything we put our hand to prospers.

5. Are you not really enjoying your family as you should or have your children fallen away?

*You shall beget sons and daughters **but shall not enjoy them**, for they shall go into captivity. (Deuteronomy 28:41 AMPC emphasis added)*

Have we lost our children in some manner, or are we so consumed with business issues and struggles that we are not enjoying them? Have they gone off into some form of ungodly addiction or bondage? Indeed, it seems in the church of the 21st Century our children are launched into life with a yoke of debt and student loans instead of a mantle of blessing. If so, this is the curse in full operation. Any father or mother who is struggling with debt knows what it is like to lose them to this type of captivity. This captivity ties our hands from blessing and empowering our children. The sweet voice that asks: "Will there be a holiday?" or "Daddy, why are we walking?" As poignant as this may be, let us also think of those facing hunger, drug addiction, war, and bondage. It is time to break this power at work in our lives, families, and communities; joining with Jesus to destroy the works of the devil in our families.

6. Are you not with your partner, or has your relationship failed?

You shall betroth a wife, but another man shall lie with her.... (Deuteronomy 28:30)

Perhaps the clearest evidence of the operation of the curse is the high rate of marriage breakdown. God's will is a flourishing husband and wife relationship - prospering. I must add here that this is not meant to condemn people who have had to leave difficult and abusive relationships. It is never God's will to stay in a situation where even greater harm is done, such as when the spouse or children are being abused. However, even if we have failed through our own fault, there is a great future God is building for us if we call on Him and walk in repentance. We should all be able to agree that divorce and remarriage is not the blessing that God intended as His first prize.

What if you have been reading the above list and have checked one or more of these points? I believe that the majority of Christians today will have some of these curses in evidence in their lives. We can also use this list as a daily checklist as we pray for God's Kingdom to come and His will to be done. This is the

> **We need to have revelation if any of our righteousness has the odour of the outhouse on it not the aroma of heaven!**

battleground area of life where the enemy is working to bring about destructive consequences. To be very clear: if these curses are in action in our lives, we know for a fact that it is not what God wants, and we must move forward to break out of any structures that tie us down and keep us away from the BEST that God has for us. This list gives us reference points to prayerfully look at our lives and to determine what impacts us - the Blessing or the curse.

Revelation of the Strategy for Victory

I am sure that going through the list above will have brought to light areas of the curse that are active in our lives and families. Once we have a revelation of our current situation, we can use a proven and godly strategy to deal with these issues. Our mission is to destroy the works of the devil in our lives and in the world, so treat this as a call to greater action.

Even if you are moving from victory to victory, it is still a good exercise to examine our blessings and wealth and see if it flows from the blessing and Lordship of Jesus, not self-sufficiency and our own works. We need to continually examine our lives to see if any element of our "victory" simply relates to us climbing above those less fortunate. Are we still in the Outhouse of Lack just doing well by reference to others?

Which source are we plugged in to? Having money does not mean that we are fully in the correct alignment with God - we can be in lack with money and without money. This analysis was done by Jesus in relation to a rich young ruler who was trusting in his money and position. He was one of only a select group of people that Jesus asked to follow Him like His twelve disciples. He was also the only one recorded who walked away from this offer - I like to think he was the preferred replacement for Judas. He may have kept the commandments, but Jesus identified that there was still a key area of **lack** in his life as his security and trust was in his money. Jesus said that he should sell all and follow Him. In error, many have used this to justify a poverty vow in the church, but let's look at the story more closely.

> *And as He was setting out on His journey, a man ran up and knelt before Him and asked Him, Teacher, ...what must I do to inherit eternal life [that is, to partake of eternal salvation in the Messiah's kingdom]?... And Jesus, looking upon him, loved him, and He said to him, You **lack** one thing; go and sell all you have and give [the money] to the poor, and you will have*

treasure in Heaven; and come [and] accompany Me walking the same road that I walk]. At that saying the man's countenance fell and was gloomy, and he went away grieved and sorrowing, for he was holding great possessions. And Jesus looked around and said to His disciples, **With what difficulty will those who possess wealth and keep on holding it enter the kingdom of God!** *And the disciples were amazed and bewildered and perplexed at His words. But Jesus said to them again, Children, how hard it is for those who trust (place their confidence, their sense of safety) in riches to enter the kingdom of God!...Jesus said, Truly I tell you,* **there is no one who has given up and left house or brothers or sisters or mother or father or children or lands for My sake and for the Gospel's Who will not receive a hundred times as much now in this time—houses and brothers and sisters and mothers and children and lands,** *with persecutions—and in the age to come, eternal life. (Mark 10:17, 21-30 AMPC emphasis added and notes removed)*

Jesus identified a key area of lack in the young man's life even though he was rich. He may have been at the very top of the Outhouse not looking like he needed help in the natural world, but Jesus still loved him and wanted him to be delivered and walk in the Kingdom. He walked away from a life with Jesus because he held onto and trusted in his money as his source. Jesus had just taught about giving and receiving and God's power to provide. He had also taught about the power of the Kingdom in finance. Even the Scriptures, which the young ruler would have known well, stated that if you give to the poor you lend to the Lord (Proverbs 19:17). Jesus then confirmed this by stating that if you have given up property, lands, or position for Him you would receive a hundred times as much of the same things, now in this time. He made certain we would not be confused into a poverty or anti-possession mindset. We will receive back IN THIS TIME and IN KIND. Jesus had a hundred-fold material blessing in mind for the young ruler, plus he would have been a disciple, and he would have had eternal life - what an amazing plan!

We don't know what happened to the young ruler who walked away in lack and sorrow, but we do know that approximately 50 years later, the Roman Emperor Titus sacked and destroyed Jerusalem, and it is likely that the rich young ruler would have been alive to see the wealth he relied on totally destroyed. Jesus had laid out a much better plan for him.

> There is even hope for the tax man!

Like the rich young ruler, we need to ask Jesus to give us the revelation if any of our righteousness or wealth has the odour of the Outhouse of Lack on it, not the aroma of Heaven, and be willing to follow him!

There is Hope, Even for the Tax Man

> *He also told this parable to some people who trusted in themselves and were confident that they were righteous [that they were upright and in right standing with God] and scorned and made nothing of all the rest of men: Two men went up into the temple enclosure to pray, the one a Pharisee and the other a tax collector. The Pharisee took his stand ostentatiously and began to pray thus before and with himself: God, I thank You that I am not like the rest of men—extortioners (robbers), swindlers [unrighteous in heart and life], adulterers—or even like this tax collector here. I fast twice a week; I give tithes of all that I gain. But the tax collector, merely standing at a distance, would not even lift up his eyes to Heaven, but **kept striking his breast**, saying, O God, **be** favorable (be gracious, be **merciful) to me**, the especially wicked sinner that I am!*
>
> *I tell you, this man went down to his home justified (forgiven and made upright and in right standing with God), rather than the other man; for everyone who exalts himself will be humbled, but he who humbles himself will be exalted. (Luke 18:9-14 AMPC emphasis added, punctuation and parenthesis removed)*

Unlike the rich young ruler's circumstances, the fact that things are not right in our lives usually makes it easier for us to grasp our need for God to intervene. The tax collector who cried out to God knew he needed help! When everything has fallen into pieces in our lives, it is easier to see our need for Jesus. We may also be convicted of personal sin and need to deal with it like the tax collector above.

> **He didn't want you to be where you are, but He wants YOU whereever you are.**

If you are reading this and have failed businesses, lost homes, broken relationships, or any other manifestation of lack in your life, then be greatly encouraged that God has a plan to take you from where you are now into the full blessing He has for you. If you have a calling for Kingdom Finance, I would expect some of these challenges, as God chooses the weak in this world to confound the wise.[4] I know some will read this from prison or sitting shell-shocked after bankruptcy or the loss of a home. We must be clear - it was not God's will for those things to happen to you, and He did not put you there - His will is always to bless you, and His yoke is easy and His burden is light. Capture this truth: ***He didn't want you to be where you are, but He wants YOU wherever you are.*** Jesus portrayed the heart of God as that of the father of the Prodigal Son who had lost everything **through his own fault**. Jesus gave us the 100% at fault example so that we would understand the goodness of the Father, and so that we would not disqualify ourselves due to our own failings. The Prodigal Son ended up poor, naked, and covered in defiling pig manure which was abhorrent to the Jews. BUT THE FATHER LOVED HIM and ran to him. Not only did he love him, but the personal and financial miracle was that he restored the Prodigal Son into fellowship, sonship, position, and wealth. Please be assured that wherever you are and whatever situation you are in, God wants you and will show His mighty power to manifest His blessing over you.

---

4. 1 Corinthians 1:27

If you are in the top of the Outhouse of Lack with riches like the rich young ruler, or if you are in the bottom of the Outhouse of Lack like the Prodigal Son, then, in both cases, Jesus wants you to be pulled from there into the Kingdom.

Father, I know that I have sinned and I am sorry. I am in a mess, and even if not a total mess, I am not where I know I should be. I know that Jesus died for my sins so that I could have an abundant life. Please forgive me and cleanse me from the consequences of my sin. I thank you that, like the father of the Prodigal Son, you receive me and have a plan to undo the destruction in my life and to restore me to a life with you.

Chapter 9

Moving into Blessing

If we have identified areas in our lives and generations which are not fully manifesting the Blessing, then we need to look seriously at what could be hindering us. What is holding us back or allowing the enemy to work in our lives? How are any of these curses in operation? What negative "rivers" or "conduits" are flowing into our lives?

Here are several key areas where our breakthrough can be hindered. All of them can be relevant and are not mutually exclusive, so we will consider each one in detail.

> **1. Is this hindrance an attack?** - Is what is happening to us all the work of the enemy or, are we blind or unaware of what is really going on?
>
> **2. Is there sin in the camp?** - Is there personal sin or ungodly connections in our lives that have opened a door allowing the enemy to bring his attacks? There are the big sins which everyone can recognise, but Jesus expanded this list greatly in order to show us that we cannot save ourselves. We need Jesus

to forgive our sins and to cleanse us from all unrighteousness. If we continue in sin, we are out of the flow of blessing since the curse is in operation in the world and in our lives when we sin. Like gravity will apply to "strike you down" if you step off the roof of a building, so the curse will operate in your life if you continue in sin, Christian or not.

3. Are we Joseph in prison? - Are we doing what is right and in right standing just waiting for God's promise to be made manifest?

4. Are there generational issues? Blessings are for a thousand generations, but the curse impacts for three or four generations and longer if it has never been acknowledged and repented for in the generations. Daniel was in captivity because of the actions of his family and people. Is there anything in operation in our lives that needs to be closed off using Daniel's example?

Deliverance and Lordship

Once we have dealt with the issues that may have allowed the enemy to attack, we need to shut down any ongoing attack and establish the Lordship of Jesus over 100% of our lives so that we can walk in victory. There are a number of pictures that people have used to describe this: "open doors", "landing-strips", "soul ties", or some kind of access point that allows the enemy to operate in our lives. We need to shut these all down and cut off any area of our lives where it seems the enemy is in control or attacking.

Yes we are made free in Christ but we are admonished to stand fast and not to be entangled again with the yoke of bondage.

> *Stand fast therefore in the liberty by which Christ has made us free, and do not be entangled again with a yoke of bondage. (Ephesians 5:1 NKJV)*

and

And you shall know the truth, and the truth shall make you free. (John 8:32 NKJV)

We need to know the truth about the impact of lack in our lives and how we should be living so that we can move forward in freedom and liberty.

Dear Jesus, as I look at each of these key areas please open my eyes to see and know the truth and be set free. Please reveal and set me free from any entanglement or yoke of bondage that may be in operation in my life.

Chapter 10

Is This an Attack?

Are the issues we are dealing with attacks of the enemy calling us to battle in spiritual warfare, or are they manifestations of the curse in operation against us requiring us to repent?

> "...your fight has not been with flesh and blood, but with Principalities and The Rulers and The Powers of this dark world and with wicked spirits which are under Heaven." (Ephesians 6:12 ABT)

We know that every calling, word of destiny, and prophetic word over our lives will be challenged. We must always keep in mind that God is seeking to bless us, but the enemy is trying to steal, kill, and destroy. Jesus spoke of the word as a seed sown which is immediately attacked:

> "Listen then to what the parable of the sower means:19 When anyone hears the message about the kingdom and does not understand it, the **evil one comes** and snatches away what was sown in their heart. This is the seed sown along the path. 20 The seed falling on rocky ground refers to someone who hears the word and at once receives it with joy. 21 But since they have no root, they last only a short time. When **trouble or**

***persecution** comes because of the word, they quickly fall away. 22 The seed falling among the thorns refers to someone who hears the word, but the **worries of this life and the deceitfulness of wealth** choke the word, making it unfruitful. 23 But the seed falling on good soil refers to someone who hears the word and understands it. This is the one who produces a crop, yielding a hundred, sixty or thirty times what was sown." (Matthew 13:18-23 NIV emphasis added)*

> **This is our season to walk as overcomers - only at this time on earth can we contend for the word of God that has been spoken over our lives.**

If we seek God in our lives, and particularly in the area of Kingdom Finance, then we can expect the enemy to resist in every way he can. There are spiritual forces at work against us if we partner with Jesus. This is particularly true if we are taking a stand in Kingdom Finance since the enemy's first target seems to be the source and flow of money needed for a Kingdom venture. Every word of promise or prophetic word over your life has to be enforced in faith, battling it to fruition. Jesus showed us the way by calling us to decree daily that His will in Heaven be done on earth in our lives. This is the battle for victory against the enemy.

The first attack is to try to steal the word from our lives, crush our destiny and purpose, and hinder our blessing. This is our season to walk as overcomers and walk forward in faith into our callings- only at this time on earth can we contend for the word of God that has been spoken over our lives. It is here that we have a choice to believe the word and walk in victory.

> *For whatever is born of God is victorious over the world; and this is the victory that conquers the world, even our faith. Who is it that is victorious over [that conquers] the world but he who believes that Jesus is the Son of God [who adheres to, trusts in, and relies on that fact]? (I John 5:4-5 AMP)*

When you set out to do Kingdom Finance, you are in effect making a decree on earth and in the Heavens that bondages will be broken and territory taken, as you have partnered with Jesus to destroy the works of the devil. You are not just performing good works from a worldly social justice perspective, you are declaring war on the enemy and saying you are taking back this ground for the Kingdom. You decree that what you establish is done in the name of Jesus and will be of God and have its life source from God. In this you are saying you will break the jaws of the oppressors and set the captives free:

> "...I delivered the poor who cried, the fatherless and him who had none to help him. The blessing of him who was about to perish came upon me, and I caused the widow's heart to sing for joy. I put on [a]righteousness, and it clothed me or clothed itself with me; my justice was like a robe and a turban or a diadem or a crown! I was eyes to the blind, and feet was I to the lame. I was a father to the poor and needy; the cause of him I did not know I searched out. **And I broke the jaws** or the big teeth **of the unrighteous and plucked the prey out of his teeth.**" (Job 29:12-17 AMPC emphasis added)

Many Christians have stepped out to do what they feel God has called them to do, not realising they have joined a life and death battle, which may be one of the reasons that things didn't work out well initially. Setback after setback occurs, and the attack of the enemy may not be recognised. The old aphorism is true: "you don't know what you don't know", but like the rats in the basement, once revelation knowledge is in place we can join in the battle! I know that many Christians have suffered through the failure and loss of businesses as well as difficult personal financial issues. Don't be discouraged! You have joined a battle and your anointing and calling is in contention. We need to understand the rules of warfare so that we can walk in the victory promised for us. Kingdom Finance is war - economic war. After all, setting the captive free can only be done by engaging in a battle against bondage.

> **Kingdom Finance is war - economic war.**

If you feel a call to operate in Kingdom Finance in some manner, then move quickly to seek the Lord for His direction and enter into the process to conclude your past and establish a secure foundation to move forward. In the meantime please pray this prayer of protection and hiding:

"Father, I thank you that I have a calling to do something for your Kingdom in the area of Kingdom Finance [be specific if you can]. Please give me a heart of flesh to understand your word and your will in my life and to draw close to you. Give me ears to hear and break off from me any hindrances or scales so that I can see clearly. Father, I seek your face, and in your word (II Chron. 7:14) it says that if I humble myself and seek your face and turn from my wicked ways then I would hear from Heaven and you would forgive and heal my land. As I go through this process please hide me in your high tower of Psalm 91 and protect me from the attack of the enemy. Where there may be grounds for any attack against me, my family, or my business please extend mercy and show me what steps to take so that I can move forward in authority and power in my calling. I declare that no weapon formed against me, my family, or my business will prosper in the name of Jesus".

What about the Attacks? - My Hezekiah Testimony

Assuming we conclude the past and do the steps below, what about the attacks? Will these attacks stop?

I remember praying about these questions a while back during the last phase of a long and difficult litigation process. The revelation was that this attack from the enemy was not a curse, but was actually covered under the blessing framework of Deuteronomy 28! The Blessing did not state that there would be no enemy attacks. The blessing we walk in is not immunity from attack, but guaranteed victory face-to-face.

> *"The Lord shall cause your enemies who rise up against you to be defeated before your face; they shall come out against you one way and flee before you seven ways." (Deuteronomy 28:7 AMPC)*

I will share a personal story and, although it involved aspects of the other categories, there was clearly a spiritual battle. It illustrates a strategy for dealing with enemy attack, particularly where there is economic threat and litigation.

I have been a Christian since the age of four, from a Christian family, and have had a calling on my life since an early age. However, I have not always pressed into the Lord the way I should. I lived in Asia for a time, and even though I went to church, I made a renewed dedication and truly decided to follow after the Lord and His calling for my life in Kingdom Finance. I was literally starting on a journey toward a deeper level of intimacy with Jesus.

Shortly after this re-commitment, I was on a plane from India travelling with a person senior to me in the company. Over a series of drinks he began ranting about Christians and how they were not trustworthy. Either he did not realise I was a Christian, or he was aggressively challenging my faith! As I was sitting there on the plane, I felt strongly that silence would mean I was agreeing with what he was saying. It was like Jesus was saying to me, "If you remain silent you are denying me before men!" I was very challenged by this conviction, so I spoke out that I was a Christian and agreed that some Christians were not great examples but that Jesus was what it was all about. Immediately, it was as if a switch was turned. This man's attitude towards me changed completely and he became quite hostile and unfriendly.

This antagonism continued after the trip ended and, not too long after this event, I decided to leave the company. This resulted in an increasingly difficult and confrontational situation. I received a letter from this person refusing to pay substantial amounts owed and making some serious threats. I immediately sought the Lord in prayer and was taken to the story of King Hezekiah's letter. Like me, he also had received a letter. His letter was from King Sennacherib of Assyria which essentially said that Hezekiah would be destroyed and that the God of Israel would not save them (Isaiah 36 and 37). In modern language, the letter I received said the same thing as Hezekiah's letter: that Hezekiah would not be blessed, would not be able to continue living and enjoying life and what God had for him.

My circumstances had similarities. This letter was from a major company against me who, as an individual, was a much weaker party. The meaning behind the legalese was that nothing I could say or do would matter: "We're big, we're bad, and we will blow your house down." In effect, they said that the word of the Lord regarding blessing would not apply to me. They contradicted Deuteronomy 28 and stated I would not be blessed coming in and going out, and that I would not be the head, rather I would be the tail.

Hezekiah rent his clothes and sought the Lord when he first heard of the threat, but when he got the letter, he went before the Lord, spread the letter before Him, and prayed to the Lord.

> *And Hezekiah received the letter from the hand of the messengers and read it. And Hezekiah went up to the house of the Lord and spread it before the Lord. And Hezekiah prayed to the Lord: (Isaiah 37:14-15 AMPC)*

For me, this is one of the great battle prayers in the Bible, so I was moved to do the same thing. I put the company's letter in my Bible at Isaiah 37 and prayed my own version of Hezekiah's prayer, making decrees in line with the word - the letter is still in my Bible today.

As you read through the story of Hezekiah it is quite sobering. After seeking the Lord, he receives the word of the Lord about the situation.

First, God releases miraculous provision on the land as a manifestation of His blessing:

And [now Hezekiah, says the Lord] this shall be a sign [of these things] to you; you shall eat this year what grows of itself, and in the second year that which springs from the same and in the third year sow and reap, and plant vineyards and eat the fruit of them. (Isaiah 37:30 AMPC)

Next, God determined the fate of the attack by destroying the plans of Sennacherib:

*By the way that he came, by the same way he shall return, and he shall not come into the city, says the Lord. For I will defend this city to save it, for My own sake and for the sake of My servant David. And the **Angel of the Lord went forth**, and slew 185,000 in the camp of the Assyrians; and when [the living] arose early in the morning, behold all these were dead bodies. (Isaiah 37:34-36 AMPC emphasis added)*

Note that God acted on Hezekiah's behalf "for the sake of My servant David". This is God reminding him of the blessing and that He had a covenant with David (II Samuel 7:8-16).

Likewise, I have a covenant with God and could be confident in His power for me. The same is true for every believer. We have a new covenant in the blood of Jesus (Luke 22.20; Galatians 4; 24-26; Hebrews 9:15) - a better covenant.

> **WE ARE A COVENANT PEOPLE. God will move on our behalf.**

*And for this reason He is the Mediator of the **new covenant**, by means of death, for the redemption of the transgressions under the first covenant, that those who are called may receive the promise of the eternal inheritance. (Hebrews 9:15 NKJV emphasis added)*

We are also inheritors of the Blessing and we are entitled to everything that Hezekiah claimed under the promise of the Blessing!

> *Christ purchased our freedom [redeeming us] from the curse (doom) of the Law [and its condemnations] by [Himself] becoming a curse for us, for it is written [in the Scriptures], Cursed is everyone who hangs on a tree (is crucified); To the end that through [their receiving] Christ Jesus,* **the blessing [promised] to Abraham might come upon the Gentiles, so that we through faith might [all] receive [the realization of] the promise of the [Holy] Spirit...** *For in Christ Jesus you are all sons of God through faith. For as many [of you] as were baptized into Christ [into a spiritual union and communion with Christ, the Anointed One, the Messiah] have put on (clothed yourselves with) Christ. There is [no distinction] neither Jew nor Greek, there is neither slave nor free, there is not male and female; for you are all one in Christ Jesus. And if you belong to Christ [are in Him Who is Abraham's Seed], then you are Abraham's offspring and [spiritual] heirs according to promise....And because you [really] are [His} sons, God has sent the [Holy] Spirit of His Son into our hearts, crying, Abba (Father)! Father! Therefore, you are no longer a slave (bond servant) but a son; and if a son, then [it follows that you are]* **an heir by the aid of God, through Christ.** *(Galatians 3:13-14; 26 -29; 4:6,7 AMPC emphasis added)*

With this revelation from the Lord fresh in my spirit, I had a strategy to deal with this seemingly impossible situation. I repented for anything that I may have done wrong, particularly in relation to my life at this company. I cleared everything and got things right with God. I dealt with any sin in the camp, however minor. I then forgave and released everyone involved from that company.

As I prayed this prayer, I had a very strong image or picture of the Angel of the Lord descending into the top of the office tower with sword extended, and I was reminded of the part of Hezekiah's story where the Angel of the Lords slays 185,000 of the enemy in one night (Isaiah 37:36). I immediately prayed words to the effect that, of course, they should be spared from this aspect of the Scripture!

I had great confidence in the Spirit, I was right with God and my sins were forgiven. However, the situation seemed hopeless and deteriorated resulting in a litigation process that went on for years and seemed to gain momentum.

I tried to settle the litigation in every way possible but was met by intransigence and anger. Hundreds of thousands of dollars went to legal fees and it seemed that the strategy of trying to win by lawfare and bankrupting the weaker party (me) seemed to be working. During this time I was still standing on the Word against this attack. I was modelling the strategy I saw in Scripture. Essentially, a modern day Hezekiah and my prayer was written down and in my Bible along with their letter.

I remember seeking prayer from other Christians during this time. When I mentioned litigation, most people's faith seemed to drain away, and at best I got faithless "your will be done" prayers. I was in a battle for my financial life, in distress, and it seemed there was no one willing and able to stand with me. As many Christians do not even acknowledge we are in a spiritual battle, the worldly view that where there is smoke there must be fire seems to prevail in these circumstances. I don't think most Christians understand that we are in an existential battle, but I came to fully understand it during this time!

We want to live close to Jesus with the anointing resting on us, but that does not change the fact that we have an enemy, and that the enemy will attack those setting out in their calling, particularly if it involves Kingdom Finance.

At this time I was seeking the Lord, but I had not learned many of the lessons included in this book, and I am sure this is a factor in the length of this ordeal. It is my belief that, by implementing the steps set out in this book and gaining revelation on how to implement God's plan for your life, those of you reading this book can move through to victory more quickly or be in a place where unnecessary battles can be avoided.

Of course we want to be wise and in tune with the Spirit and avoid all the entanglements we can, but if we step out in our destiny to attack the kingdom of darkness and take territory, we cannot be surprised if there is an attack. Remember that Joseph ended up in prison with damaging charges against him, and David was a wanted fugitive! Even Jesus as a baby had to flee to Egypt to avoid being murdered. There will be attacks, but if we are truly walking in the Spirit, there will be preparation and escape.

One day I was deeply troubled by the suit against me and seeking the Lord about what to do. I couldn't give in, or I would be bankrupt, and, although I was earning a good salary, I could not continue to fight much longer.

I went through my prayer in Isaiah again including confessing that Hezekiah heard from the Lord (Isaiah 37:21). That night, I was awoken with a picture in my mind of a Christian magazine that had come in the mail the day before and was still unopened, wrapped in plastic. I had a picture of a page with a specific layout: heading, columns, picture, etc. It was vivid, and I remember fighting in my mind as I lay in bed. I ended up by saying to myself that if it was just my own thoughts, the worst that would happen was that I read a Christian magazine in the middle of the night! I got up, found the magazine, opened it, and found the exact page I was seeking - it looked exactly like the picture God had shown me. It was an article about how we need to surrender issues to the Lord and not tie His hands by our words. He knows best what to do in each situation.

While I was reading this article, I was instantly reminded of my prayers when I first got the letter from the company and I had had a picture of the Angel of the Lord descending into the building, and how my response had been to say words like, "don't let that happen, Lord", and I felt I needed to repent for this. I went through all of the Hezekiah prayer again, only this time I repented for hindering the Lord at all and trying to sort out the situation my way. I trusted Him to sort this out. I forgave everyone again and released them all to His mercy and righteous judgement.

It was incredibly sobering when I learned that, at around the same time I was woken to read the magazine and pray this prayer, this same antagonist pressing the litigation was in a different time zone holding a meeting in the company boardroom when he began to shake and then fell to the floor dead.

King Sennacherib learned not to attack God's covenant people, and we too are covenant people.

I thought this would be the end of the matter, and there was a welcome lull in proceedings and costs; however, this litigation continued on for several years and finally came to trial.

During the trial, God was with me in strong anointing, and I was reminded that we wrestle not against flesh and blood but principalities and powers. There were huge binders of documents, and each night I was led to the exact pages to mark and the issues that would come up the next day. Each day was painful and difficult but resulted in victory after victory as lies and half-truths were exposed. One example I remember well, was marking an obscure email exchange from another office sending me documents to look at and requesting my help. For some reason, I marked these obscure sections, and the next day it was alleged that my possession of these documents was somehow proof of wrongdoing. After all, they said, why would I have them? You can imagine the scene when I was able to direct them to my obscure yellow sticky marker in a particular volume of documents and expose the truth of the situation and the lie of the allegation. Each lie and false assumption was exposed.

I asked the Lord during this time why this process went on for so long, and I received the revelation that I was witnessing the blessing in action.

> *The Lord shall cause your enemies who rise up against you to be defeated before your face; they shall come out against you one way and flee before you seven ways. (Deuteronomy 28:7 AMPC)*

My enemy came at me one way, and He was ensuring that I saw them flee from me seven ways. The blessing operated so that I could see the victory and vindication which was done in a complete 100% victory.

Although God was merciful, I am sure this situation could have been avoided or the difficulty lessened. For example, I could have been led to leave the company earlier or to not join it in the first place. What we are talking about in this part of the book is how to get into the right position for our destiny to be fulfilled and to extract ourselves from situations and relationships that are not God's perfect will.

> *What we are talking about in this part of the book is how to get into the right place for our destiny to be fulfilled and to extract ourselves from situations and relationships that are not God's perfect will.*

What is the lesson for us from this? First, we must be in the place God wants us to be, with our lives in order and our past concluded. If we are in this place and hearing from the Lord many of these situations can be avoided before they arise and get out of hand.

Continuum of Release

Essentially, there is a continuum in life with regard to Kingdom Finance:

Unsaved/Backslidden/Mess—>Moving in Kingdom Finance—>Kingdom Financier

Let's assume that you have set out in Kingdom Finance and have concluded your past and moved forward, but now are suffering an attack. Remember, it is part of the blessing that attacks will come along with the expected victory. Of course, we want to minimise the number and frequency of any attack by being in the situation where God wants us to be. Also, when these attacks do come, we also want to minimise the impact by receiving early revelation and strategies from the Lord.

I am setting out a very simple scriptural strategy based on II Chronicles 7:14.

> *If My people, who are called by My name, shall humble themselves, pray, seek, crave, and require of necessity My face and turn from their wicked ways, then will I hear from Heaven, forgive their sin, and heal their land. (II Chron. 7:14 AMPC)*

If, like my story, you find yourself in a mess and are in a battle, then use the Hezekiah strategy. The strategy for us is based upon this Scriptural formula:

> **1. Be a Person Called by His Name:** Accept Jesus as Lord over your life, including your finances, either for the first time or by re-dedication. As we see above, this brings you fully into the operative power of the COVENANT and the BLESSING.

> **2. Pray for Protection:** If you are stepping out for the Lord in Kingdom Finance first pray the prayer of hiding and protection set out above.

> **3. Humble Yourself:** Hezekiah did this by prayer and fasting. He set aside his grand plans and schemes and recognised the solution was not his but God's.

> **4. Seek the Lord's Face:** Seek the Lord as your urgent necessity. Stop what you are doing and seek His face and gain the level of intimacy with Him that can minimise the attack of the enemy.

5. Turn From Any Wicked Ways: Repent and clean up and have God reveal what is wicked in us. Be ready for revelation because God's view of what qualifies as "wicked" may be very different from ours.

6. He Will Cleanse Us from Our Sins: According to 1 John 1:9, if we confess our sins, He is faithful and just and will forgive them and cleanse us from all unrighteousness, which is everything not in conformity to His will in purpose, thought, and action. Think of it, we are not just forgiven, but the consequences are cleansed in our lives.

7. Listen: Listen and we will hear a Word from the Lord - declare and recite the covenant petition. Write it down and anchor your faith in this and stand firm. He will start to undertake for us and direct us.

8. Continue to Ask Him: Ask Him if there is any spiritual blindness in you and if there is anything you need to do. Keep short accounts by dealing with issues quickly.

9. Wait on Him - The Work is His: After that, it is His job to do the rest. He will heal our land - this is our ultimate goal - God putting things back the way He intended. There will be restoration like we have seen for the Prodigal Son.

Scriptural Examples - How was this implemented in the Bible?

Hezekiah. As we discussed above, when he heard of the threat, Hezekiah rent his clothes and sought the Lord and recounted the covenant with the Lord. He then heard the Word of the Lord and strategy (Isaiah 37). Result: King Sennacherib of Assyria lost 185,000 men in one night and Hezekiah reaped a miraculous harvest and financial blessing.

Jehoshaphat. He heard about the multitude coming against him and determined his vital need to seek the Lord, and so proclaimed a fast in all Judah. He recounted the covenant and the illustrious acts of the Lord. He heard the Word of the Lord through the prophet and the strategy from the Lord was given, which he implemented. The strategy was to lead with praise and worship. This story is well worth reading in detail and sets out what I call the "war cry" that we are to use when facing any issue - **GIVE THANKS TO THE LORD, FOR HIS MERCY AND LOVING-KINDNESS ENDURE FOREVER!** You will see this example over and over again in Scripture.

> *And when they began to sing and to praise, the Lord set ambushments ... And when Judah came to the watchtower of the wilderness, they looked at the multitude, and behold, they were dead bodies fallen to the earth, and none had escaped! When Jehoshaphat and his people came to take the spoil, they found among them much cattle, goods, garments, and precious things which they took for themselves, more than they could carry away, so much they were three days in gathering the spoil. (II Chron. 20:22-25 AMPC)*

Joshua. The story of Joshua and the Children of Israel crossing into the Promised Land is another great source of inspiration and example. There are a few key points here that support the approach we take when facing issues or attacks. The Promised Land is a type of what God intends for us today. Remember that Eden was God's original plan, and He wanted us to walk with Him in the cool of the day ruling in the authority that He had delegated to us.

Joshua had a personal word and calling from the Lord to take his people forward. The Children of Israel then moved forward in obedience to their calling and crossed the Jordan. They had left the old behind, Egypt, which was a place of bondage, and had moved into the destiny and calling that God had for them. They then renewed their covenant with the Lord and were circumcised, which is a sign of covenant. At this time God said that the reproach of Egypt had been rolled away. This was a new life, a new start, and they had "concluded the past".

We have two realities here or two maps, but only one truth. The true map is the one that included the reality of the Kingdom and what God had said. Joshua was facing the reality that so scared the spies before. They were in a land populated by strong giants of men and these men controlled the resources. On top of that, when they crossed the Jordan the manna from Heaven stopped. Joshua relied on the true map, the reality that included what God had said, namely, that they would be blessed and would win every battle and everywhere their feet trod would be theirs (Joshua 3:2).

> *And the manna ceased on the day after they ate of the produce of the land; and the Israelites had manna no more, but they ate of the fruit of the land of Canaan that year. When Joshua was by Jericho, he looked up, and behold, a Man stood near him with His drawn sword in His hand. And Joshua went to Him and said to Him,* ***Are you for us or for our adversaries? And He said, No [neither], but as Prince of the Lord's host have I now come. And Joshua fell on his face to the earth and worshiped, and said to Him, What says my Lord to His servant?*** *And the Prince of the Lord's host said to Joshua, [a]Loose your shoes from off your feet, for the place where you stand is holy. And Joshua did so. Now Jericho [a fenced town with high walls] was tightly closed because of the Israelites; no one went out or came in. And the Lord said to Joshua, See, I have given Jericho, its king and mighty men of valor, into your hands. You shall march around the enclosure, all the men of war going around the city once. This you shall do for six days. And seven priests shall bear before the ark seven trumpets of rams' horns; and on the seventh day you shall march around the enclosure seven times, and the priests shall blow the trumpets. When they make a long blast with the ram's horn and you hear the sound of the trumpet, all the people shall shout with a great shout; and the wall of the enclosure shall fall down in its place and the people shall go up [over it], every man straight before him…And the city and all that is in it shall be devoted to the Lord [for destruction]; only Rahab the harlot and*

> *all who are with her in her house shall live, because she hid the messengers whom we sent. But you, keep yourselves from the accursed and devoted things, lest when you have devoted it [to destruction], you take of the accursed thing, and so make the camp of Israel accursed and trouble it. But all the silver and gold and vessels of bronze and iron are consecrated to the Lord; they shall come into the treasury of the Lord. (Joshua 5:13-15; 6:1-5; 17-19 AMPC emphasis added)*

We too have the word of God declaring blessing over our lives. We have to stand in faith for this word as "good spies" believing what God has said. We also have personal words or direction for our lives, our callings, and perhaps even prophetic confirmations of what we know God is doing in our lives. Like the Children of Israel, we have to stand on the word of God for our lives and move forward in faith.

Chapter 11

Sin in the Camp

Is There Sin in the Camp?

In a broader sense, all of these negative things in our lives are "attacks" as they are not the fruit of God's plan for our lives and certainly don't represent our daily prayer that our lives should be on earth as it is in Heaven. God is good all the time and His will for us is perfectly expressed in the plan for mankind to rule in the Garden of Eden. Even after mankind, through Adam, had failed and the curse was in operation on the earth, God's plan was to take the Children of Israel out of slavery and into a land flowing with milk and honey. In that sense, if what we see in our life isn't Eden, then it is the enemy.

God is good all the time; it is the thief that comes to steal, kill and destroy. Many Christians are fervently praying against the enemy, and in one sense this is correct and good to do, but it is important to identify where the root of the issue is located. If we have somehow opened the door allowing the enemy freedom to work in our lives, our ability to deal with the issue is

> **If it isn't Eden, then it is the enemy.**

compromised. We must be honest enough to ask God to reveal to us what the issue could be and the biggest of these open doors is personal sin in our lives. Are there any grounds for the enemy to operate? Are we really facing an attack and time of testing, or has sin left an open door for the enemy to work? Is this a pure attack, or is it coming against us as a result of our own sinful actions?

Sometimes this opening is referred to as an "open door", a "landing strip", a "hook", or an "ungodly soul tie". Whatever we call it, we need to make sure we have cleared it out. We cannot be too proud to humble ourselves and ask the Lord to reveal any issues in our lives. Know that God resists the proud, requiring us to humble ourselves and to seek his forgiveness.

> *Whoever exalts himself [with haughtiness and empty pride] shall be humbled (brought low), and whoever humbles himself...shall be raised to honor. (Matthew 23:12 AMPC)*

> *You [are like] unfaithful wives [having illicit love affairs with the world and breaking your marriage vow to God]! Do you not know that being the world's friend is being God's enemy? So whoever chooses to be a friend of the world takes his stand as an enemy of God. Or do you suppose that the Scripture is speaking to no purpose that says, The Spirit Whom He has caused to dwell in us yearns over us and He yearns for the Spirit [to be welcome] with a jealous love? But He gives us more and more grace ([a]power of the Holy Spirit, to meet this evil tendency and all others fully). That is why He says,* **God sets Himself against the proud and haughty, but gives grace [continually] to the lowly (those who are humble enough to receive it).** *So be subject to God. Resist the devil [stand firm against him], and he will flee from you. Come close to God and He will come close to you. [Recognize that you are] sinners, get your soiled hands clean; [realize that you have been disloyal] wavering individuals with divided interests, and purify your hearts [of your spiritual adultery]. [As you draw near to God] be deeply penitent and grieve, even weep [over your disloyalty]. Let your laughter be turned to grief and your mirth to dejection and heartfelt shame [for your sins]. Humble*

yourselves [feeling very insignificant] in the presence of the Lord, and He will exalt you [He will lift you up and make your lives significant]. (James 4:4-10 AMPC emphasis added)

This passage clearly states that our victory and ability to walk in Kingdom Finance can be hindered directly by sin issues and sin requires humility and repentance. After the great victory at Jericho, they were defeated at the very next town of Ai with the loss of 36 lives.[1] An Israelite named Achan had taken some of the things that were devoted to destruction, and this was the reason for the defeat.

> *That is why the Israelites could not stand before their enemies, but fled before them; they are accursed and ... I will cease to be with you unless you destroy the accursed [devoted] things among you. (Joshua 7:12 AMPC)*

In this case, there was no point complaining about the enemy or praying against enemy attack as this failure was due to sin in the camp. Joshua had to seek God and have understanding about why they did not have victory. Once sin was revealed, they had to clean things up and conclude the past so they could move on in victory.

In the same way, when we are facing a setback or series of setbacks, we need to be willing to examine our own lives to see if there is anything in us that is causing or allowing this attack. This runs counter to the current viewpoint prevalent amongst Christians that tends to put the blame 100% on the attacker. Everything is collapsed to a black and white, good versus evil outlook. However, is there anything in operation that is allowing this action to proceed? Even at a national level, an attack may be evil but within the operation of Deuteronomy 28:49-50. The response at a national level is set out in 2 Chron. 7:14 where the nation was to seek His face, humble themselves and "turn from their wicked ways". Repentance and looking for the open doors with humility allows the power of God to

---

1. Joshua 7 and 8

turn the situation around. It is the same mechanism in operation for us. We must be willing to humble ourselves, see what may be wrong, seek God's face and turn from our wicked ways – any open doors must be dealt with and shut.

Chapter 12

Positional Truth

Are we doing the right things, in the right place just waiting for God's timing to elevate us? We have dealt with our sin issues and are standing on the promises of God for our life. These promises include those in the Bible such as the promised Blessing, but also the words God has given us in relation to our personal destiny. Joseph had the written word in the Bible that everything he touched would prosper from the Blessing. Joseph also had a specific dream from God in relation to his destiny (Genesis 37:5-8). We too have the Bible, the Word of God, the Blessing, and an even better covenant through Jesus. We also have specific words, callings, and dreams about our destiny that we may be waiting to see come to fruition. We walk in close communion with God, believing in and standing on His promises for our destiny putting on God's whole armour![1] Remember, even in prison waiting for his destiny, Joseph prospered as: *"...the Lord was with Joseph...and gave him favor..." (Genesis 39:21 AMPC).*

---

1. "Put on God's whole armor [the armor of a heavy-armed soldier which God supplies], that you may be able successfully to stand up against [all] the strategies and deceits of the devil." (Ephesians 6:11 AMPC)

The Blessing was at work on Joseph's behalf, even though to the outside observer it may not have looked like it. In the same way, we need to keep praying and believing, standing on the promises of God for our destiny and future. The period between the promise and its full manifestation can be a difficult phase in our walk with the Lord, but the faith hall of fame in Hebrews 11 gives us some excellent examples of waiting in faith-filled expectation. Abraham had to wait in faith for 25 years for his son of promise (Hebrews 11:8-19). Even though he struggled and fell along the way, trying to bring forth the promise through a maidservant, this failure is not even included in the record of his faith journey in Hebrews 11.

Noah had to follow the word of God for his life while waiting for the promised rain to come. How foolish this was to those around him who said he was deluded or under the curse, when in reality he stood in faith waiting for the specific Word of God for him to be made fully manifest.

> *[Prompted]* ***by faith*** *Noah, being forewarned by God concerning events of which as yet there was no visible sign, took heed and diligently and reverently constructed and prepared an ark for the deliverance of his own family. By this [his faith which relied on God] he passed judgment and sentence on the world's unbelief and became an heir and possessor of righteousness... (Hebrews 11:7 AMPC emphasis added)*

David was anointed King at a young age but was not crowned King for a very long time. It was approximately 15 years before he became King of Judah and another 7 years after that before he became King of all Israel.

> **This is the training for reigning season that we go through as Christians.**

Perhaps there has been a word about our destiny and we are standing in faith believing for it to manifest. The process we saw in Hebrews 11 can be the same process in our lives as we wait in faith for the full manifestation. This is the "training for reigning" season that we go through as Christians.

We do live in an "instant" society and people expect results in a quick time cycle. People want to see the fruits of breakthrough and can sit in judgement when they do not see quick results. It is during these seasons of waiting on the Lord that people can fall away from standing with us as they enter into judgement towards us. Like Moses, as we wait for the fulfilment of what God is doing, people not in the flow of the anointing can lose faith.

> *When the people saw that Moses was so long in coming down from the mountain, they gathered around Aaron and said, "Come, make us gods[a] who will go before us. **As for this fellow Moses** who brought us up out of Egypt, **we don't know what has happened to him**." (Exodus 32:1 AMPC emphasis added)*

This can be painful as people can respond to our faith-filled waiting with judgement, disappointment, or even outright attack. Indeed, in Moses' case they took their gold and threw it into a false Golden Calf instead of waiting for what God was delivering through Moses.

Of course, we must always check to deal with any delusion and sin on our part, but then be fierce to stand on the Word of the Lord for our lives. We must bless those who fall away, forgive them, and continue pressing forward and ask God to reveal our true destiny partners.

Like Abraham, Moses, David, and every other figure in the Bible (except Jesus), we must also forgive ourselves for our failures on our journey. Many feel a call on their lives to step out and do something in the Kingdom. They even receive prophetic words and other confirmations about their callings. However, when they step out, they wonder why they are attacked and have setbacks or personal failures. It is right to heed the call and move forward, but many of us metaphorically "rush from the tent naked to attack the enemy with a toothbrush". We may be on fire with zeal for the Kingdom Finance vision, but with no prayer covering (intercessors), no fellow soldiers (our "tribe"), no weapons (the weapons of our warfare are not of this world), no preparation (prayer and fasting), and many times with significant foundational issues in our lives that need to be dealt with ("open doors"). We then wonder why there have been setbacks!

Am I recommending we don't move forward? Of course not! There is an old saying about destiny, "that you can only steer a ship that is moving", and this is true of moving forward in our calling and destiny. Another adage is that "any journey must start from where you are, not where you wish you were". We must begin to move - like Abram moving from the tent at the Word of the Lord. Even if Abram had started going in the wrong direction, it would have only taken a couple of corrective turns to get him going in the right direction. Like Abram, we need to take our calling, vision, and Kingdom Finance goals and hold them up to the Lord in full submission to Him and allow Him to show us how to move. If we wait to be qualified and have it all together to move forward, we will never take the first step, and we will be stuck in the status quo, never achieving the destiny we have been called to.

Experiential Truth vs Positional Truth

There are two sets of facts at work or two maps of our reality. One set of facts relies on experiential truths, the things we see with our own eyes and uses these truths to create a map or worldview. The other set of facts include positional truths, the things we see by faith and this creates a map or worldview that includes spirit world realities. Like the evil spies and good spies of the children of Israel, the difference was that the good spies included the Word of God and His promises in their map (Numbers 13 and 14). We have heard a great deal of discussion on this topic in the church and there is a lot of confusion. It is critical to take a moment to clear up some of this confusion so that we can determine how we should move forward. What facts are we to have faith in, and which are "fake news"?

Experiential Truth - Experiential or situational truth focuses on our factual circumstances such as our country, socio-economic status, race, education, finances, credit rating, and other facts about our lived experience. Experiential truth generates self-help books and many practical courses on budgeting and dealing with issues but if we are in the outhouse it reproduces all of the constraints that may be "true" in our situation. Focusing on our situation or experience leads to expressions such as "you have to be realistic" or "you are too Heavenly minded". It creates a map to navigate reality that is earth-centred, creates boundaries of our own strength, and gives little credence to Kingdom level realities, prayer, or the ability of God to intervene. At its best, it generates helpful steps to better the lot of the less fortunate, but at its worst, it is limited to what can reasonably be done in our own strength. This leads to comments such as: "after all you cannot change the world".

In many cases our experiential truth is in fact a set of contentious and difficult circumstances. These circumstances seem to stand against what we believe is true about our life and destiny. These situational realities may seem true, but these truths contend with a greater truth, the positional truth of who we are in Christ. Positional truth may say you are blessed, yet the situational truth says you are facing losing your home.

Positional Truth - Positional truth looks at what God has said about the situation or about our lives regardless of whether that is even possible in our lives by natural measures. It creates a map of our reality that includes and gives priority to what God has said about us and our destiny calling. David was anointed King - that was his positional truth according to the Word of God, yet at one point he was hiding with a price on his head and people who helped him were being killed. The Kingdom map of positional truth focuses on what the Word of God says about us: who God says we are without any regard for the culture, family, and countries that have shaped us. If you think of the slaves in Egypt, they may not have been well-educated, may not have believed release was possible, and may have even forgotten their heritage. They were in true multi-generational poverty, with no hope, yet God had a covenant with them and a declaration over them, "*...Thus says the Lord, Israel is My son, even My firstborn. And I say to you, Let my son go, that he may serve Me...*". *(Exodus 4:22-23 AMPC)*. God had a positional truth, destiny declaration over the Children of Israel when their situational truth was that they were slaves and their future involved only brick making.

When was the outcome certain for Jesus, David, Abraham, Moses and others? Their position was settled when the Word of the Lord was given. This is the God who made the Heavens and the earth, and nothing can interfere with his declarations. Abraham's destiny and reality as a father was certain when God said it, not when Isaac was born. When Isaac was born, it was the fulfilment of the Word or the manifesting of the positional truth.

This is most clearly seen in the discussion of Abraham's faith in Hebrews 11 where he is showcased as an overcomer. How did that come about - by hard work and perseverance? No! The Word says that Abraham believed the Lord, and it was credited to him as righteousness (Gen 15:6; Ro 4:3). What did he believe, the map containing the facts about his life or the map that contained the word of God that he would be a father, and that through him the earth would be blessed?

> *For the Law results in [divine] wrath, but where there is no law there is no transgression [of it either].Therefore, [inheriting] the promise is the outcome of faith and depends [entirely] on faith, in order that it might be given as an act of grace (unmerited favor), to make it stable and valid and guaranteed to all his descendants—not only to the devotees and adherents*

of the Law, **but also to those who share the faith of Abraham,** *who is [thus] the father of us all. As it is written, I have made you the father of many nations. [He was appointed our father] in the sight of God in Whom he believed, Who gives life to the dead and speaks of the nonexistent things that [He has foretold and promised] as if they [already] existed. [For Abraham, human reason for] hope being gone, hoped in faith that he should become the father of many nations, as he had been promised, So [numberless] shall your descendants be. He did not weaken in faith when he* **considered** *the [utter] impotence of his own body, which was as good as dead because he was about a hundred years old, or [when he* **considered***] the barrenness of Sarah's [deadened] womb. No unbelief or distrust made him waver (doubtingly question) concerning the promise of God, but he grew strong and was empowered by faith as he gave praise and glory to God, Fully satisfied and assured that* **God was able and mighty to keep His word and to do what He had promised.** *That is why his faith was credited to him as righteousness (right standing with God). But [the words], It was credited to him, were written not for his sake alone, But [they were written] for our sakes too... (Romans 4 15-24 AMPC emphasis added)*

I have highlighted the word "consider", which in context means to give full weight to or to weigh, as in the old fashioned weighing scales. Essentially, what this is saying is that faith is taking the Word of God for your life (remember the Word of God for our lives is primarily in the Bible - the Blessing, but is also the specific Words you have for your destiny provided they do not contradict the Scripture) and putting it on one side of the scale: your Positional Truth. You then put on the other side of the scale the facts that are relevant to your situation: your Situational Truth. In Abraham's case, the Situational Truth included the physical impossibility of Abraham and Sarah having children due to their age. You are not ignoring these facts or denying them, rather you are fully considering them and giving these facts their full weight.

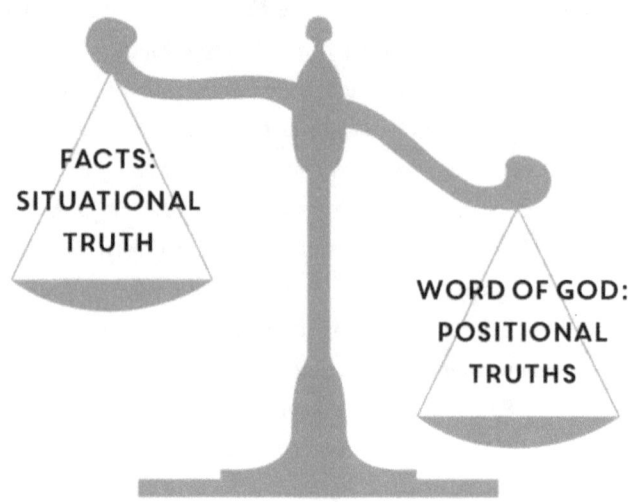

When we look at the scales then, like our father Abraham, we should see God's Word as being much more weighty and important. That is what faith is - waiting for the physical or situational reality - for God to keep His word and do what He promised. This waiting is what is described as the trial of our faith that works patience (James 1:3).

What does that mean in our circumstances today? Remember the story of Joseph in prison. We, like Joseph, know we have the blessing and the WORD of God for our lives. We also know that we have a calling and destiny, yet our circumstances and situational truth may be totally at odds with that word for our life - this is what I meant by contentious and difficult circumstances. Sound familiar? Like Abraham, Joseph, Hezekiah, and others, we have to take what we are facing, the facts of our situation, and put this on the scale. These facts can be heavy and ugly: the letters of creditors, the reality of our current bank balance, our ability to pay for things we need, and judgemental things people may say. Maybe you are in prison like Joseph and the blessing seems like it is a million miles away. Indeed, at times in my life it felt like the weight of these concerns was overpowering and the vision of the future destiny God had spoken about had dimmed.

We will deal with some of these situations in detail, but if we are going to move on in Kingdom Finance, we need 100% of our lives on the positional truth Word of God side of the scale. We must fully face the situational truths and look at our problems clearly - like Abraham, we must "consider" and weigh them. We must also fully look at the Word of the Lord for our lives. We settle in our hearts that the Word of the Lord for our lives is to bless us and make us prosper. We put the Word of the Lord about us on the scale, we make this the operative map of our reality and from this point we declare and know what is the real truth for us. This is faith- standing on His Word as the evidence of things hoped for and the substance of things we do not see yet (Hebrews 11:1). Waiting in expectation, declaring the Word of God over our lives is prophetic contending for the manifestation of God's promises.

Without faith it is impossible to please God (Hebrews 11:6), and it is also how we are saved and brought into relationship with Jesus:

> *For by grace are ye saved through faith; and that not of yourselves: it is the gift of God: Not of works, lest any man should boast. (Ephesians 2:8-9 KJV)*

It is the same process to stand on the word of God for what He has for our lives.

> *So then faith cometh by hearing, and hearing by the word of God. (Romans 10:17 KJV)*

So FAITH comes by hearing the WORD, and without faith it is IMPOSSIBLE to please God.

> *For [if we are] in Christ Jesus, neither circumcision nor uncircumcision*

*counts for anything, but only **faith** activated and energized and expressed and **working through love**. (Galatians 5:6 AMPC emphasis added)*

Every situation in our lives must bow to the Word of God and to His Word for us. Coupled with our actions in concluding the past and moving forward in faith, we will now be an unstoppable force. If God be for us, who can be against us (Romans 8:31)?

Chapter 13

Generational Sin

Iniquity Comes for a Visit

Is it possible that there are negative impacts and influences in our lives which are generational in nature? Can we be negatively impacted by the sins of our family and ancestors? How do we conclude the past if that past occurred before we were alive?

We know that we are in a battle against evil spiritual forces that want to steal, kill, and destroy us. Like Elisha's servant, we may not see it, but there is a spiritual battle all around us. God is working to protect us and bring us into the Kingdom, and the enemy is working to destroy us - it is an ongoing battle.

> *Then Elisha prayed, Lord, I pray You, open his eyes that he may see. And the Lord opened the young man's eyes, and he saw, and behold, the mountain was full of horses and chariots of fire round about Elisha. (2 Kings 6:17 AMPC)*

We have seen that when we sin, we open the door for the curse to operate in our lives, bringing about negative fruit. We have been redeemed from the curse through Jesus and need no longer serve sin; however, when we do sin we allow the enemy to bring the curse into operation in our lives. We can all see this principle in operation when a leader falls into sin such as a moral failure as people are hurt and families break up. The crying spouse and children and the hurt, confused church-goers are clear examples of successful enemy action and the curse in operation. We know from the Lord's Prayer that it is God's will for His Kingdom to be on earth as it is in Heaven - each day. No one could seriously argue that devastated families and broken churches are part of the Kingdom plan!

One of the impacts of personal sin is that it can open a door for the enemy to attack our children and, of course, we are also children ourselves. Exodus 34:7 and Numbers 14:18 state that the iniquity, or sins, of the fathers are visited on the *"children and the children's children, to the third and fourth generation"*. Think about the implications of sins from four generations back impacting your life! As all have sinned and come up short (Romans 3:23), this means there are many potential open conduits or open doors for the enemy to bring ungodly influence into our lives. If there is any chance this could be a factor impacting our lives, we need to look carefully and make sure we have shut off all generational curses that may be impacting our lives.

What does it mean to "visit iniquity" in your life? Iniquity is sin, and we know that sin triggers the curses arising from sin set out in Deuteronomy 28. We can all think of anecdotal stories that could support this such as when addiction or sexual sin seem to run in a family line. What about so-called bad luck, poverty, or the inability to get ahead? The curses we looked at include situations where it seems like others are winning and getting ahead, but we are not.

When I began praying into this, I had an amazing journey of discovery looking at my own genealogy. There was godly inheritance in my family with several generations of preachers, but there was also a troubling thread of devastation, which is evidence of the curse in operation. My experience may provide a useful illustration.

Some time ago, I had one of the most difficult days I can remember. I had a business meeting with some harsh words said which heralded the end of a business I had put in place with the vision of funding the Kingdom. It also meant a very significant personal financial loss. Upon arriving home in a low state, I had to deal with the loss of a baby that we had been praying and hoping for.

With all this going on, I decided not to go to the special meetings at a nearby church. However, my wife, though grieving and ill, insisted that I go as an act of defiance against the enemy. I remember being in the service and writing in my journal that I needed to hear from God. I was concerned I had gotten off track and I wrote that I need to hear from God about my vision and destiny. I was asking whether I had got it all wrong and had moved off to worshipping a god of "wood and stone" that doesn't speak or doesn't hear. I decided I would stop what I was doing to pursue Kingdom Finance if I did not hear something from God directly.

As it happened, it was a special meeting in London with the prophet Jill Austin speaking, and I really don't remember much of the service. I had never met her before, but she called me out as the "man in the blue shirt" and gave me a very detailed word about what I had been going through and what God was going to do moving forward including a *"new release of finances"*.

There was a lot more that she had to say, but she brought a word from the Lord to me which was directly on point, dealing with my calling, words spoken against me, and the assignment of a spirit of death that had tried to destroy me and my family line. She did not know we had lost our baby that day. This experience also led me on a journey to look at my family line in a bit more detail. Here is a summary of some things I found:

- My father, who was a minister and the Director of Youth for Christ, was killed on an outing while mountain climbing with troubled teens the week before I started school. As you can imagine, this was a very devastating time and a huge loss.

- My father was raised by a stepfather in difficult circumstances. His father, my grandfather, was a minister in the move of the spirit in the early 1900s, but died tragically just after my father's second birthday. He never knew him.

- My great-grandfather, who became a lay minister, originally came to Canada from the UK with his sister at the age of eight as orphans under the notorious indentured settlement programme as Annie MacPhearson Home Children.[i] He was indentured until the age of twenty-one. This modern day slavery led to unprecedented levels of sexual and physical abuse.

- My great-great-grandfather lived in London, England and became ill and died, leaving a pregnant wife and young family who ended up in a London workhouse in Mayfair. Two months after his death, his wife gave birth in the workhouse. The baby boy died one month after birth, and his wife died just after the death of the baby, leaving the two surviving children as orphans alone in the workhouse.

Can you see that the truth I discovered about my family matches the revelation I received through Jill Austin's prophetic word about an **"assignment of a spirit of death that has tried to take you and your family line out"?** I think anyone looking at this genealogy would see repetitive generational tragedies playing out.

Before I share the end of this story, I wanted to give some pointers on how to look at this type of information and make some deductions.

We know that it is God's will for us to be blessed, and there are promises of long life in the Bible. We know the Blessing makes rich and adds no sorrow (Prov. 10:22). We also know that it is God's will for things to be done on earth as it is in Heaven. We are also to leave inheritances for our children and grandchildren (Prov. 13:22). This is true for me, and it was equally true for each person in my lineage.

So, when you see premature death, orphaned children left in terrible conditions, and devastation, you see the curse in operation. I am not being unkind to my ancestors to say that it was not God's blessing for a mother and father to die in the same year, leaving the children in a workhouse to be exploited. It is also not wrong to note that none of the relatives obeyed the command of Scripture to look after the widows and orphans - they were not looked after by my ancestor's family, their church, or the government of the day. We can recognise that the curse was in operation in my family and see a pattern of the enemy killing the fathers in my generational line.

The story of how I dealt with this in my life is an example of how we can deal with any ungodly or unblessed pattern you may see impacting your own life and generations. First, we must follow the scriptural pattern. Although there are a number of places that deal with generational issues in the Bible, the best example is that of Daniel. Daniel was by all accounts a godly and devout person who lived according to the Scripture. However, he recognised that he was an exile as a result of a curse brought upon his people due to their sin. Not his sin personally since he was not born at the time they were sent into exile. Look carefully at how he prayed:

> *"And I set my face to the Lord God to seek Him by prayer and supplications, with fasting and sackcloth and ashes; And I prayed to the Lord my God and made confession and said, O Lord, the great and dreadful God, Who keeps covenant, mercy, and loving-kindness with those who love Him and keep His commandments,* **We have sinned** *and dealt perversely and done wickedly and have rebelled, turning aside from Your commandments and ordinances.* **Neither have we listened** *to and heeded*

Your servants the prophets, who spoke in Your name to our kings, our princes and our fathers, and to all the people of the land. O Lord, righteousness belongs to You, but to us confusion and shame of face, as at this day—to the men of Judah, to the inhabitants of Jerusalem, and to all Israel, to those who are near and those who are far off, through all the countries to which You have driven them because of the [treacherous] trespass which they have committed against You. **O Lord, to us belong confusion and shame of face—to our kings, to our princes, and to our fathers—because we have sinned against You.** *To the Lord our God belong mercy and loving-kindness and forgiveness,* **for we have rebelled** *against Him; And we have not obeyed the voice of the Lord our God by walking in His laws which He set before us through His servants the prophets. Yes,* **all Israel has transgressed** *Your law, even turning aside that they might not obey Your voice.* **Therefore the curse has been poured out on us** *and the oath that is written in the Law of Moses the servant of God, because we have sinned against Him. And He has carried out intact His [threatening] words which He threatened against us and against our judges [the kings, princes, and rulers generally] who ruled us, and He has brought upon us a great evil; for under the whole Heavens there has not been done before [anything so dreadful] as [He has caused to be] done against Jerusalem. Just as it is written in the Law of Moses as to all this evil [that would surely come upon transgressors], so it has come upon us.* **Yet we** *have not earnestly begged for forgiveness and entreated the favor of the Lord our God, that we might turn from our iniquities and have understanding and become wise in Your truth. Therefore the Lord has kept ready the calamity (evil) and has brought it upon us, for the Lord our God is [uncompromisingly] righteous and rigidly just in all His works which He does [keeping His word]; and we have not obeyed His voice. And now, O Lord our God, Who brought Your people forth out of the land of Egypt with a mighty hand and secured Yourself renown and a name as at this day,* **we have sinned, we have done wickedly!** *O Lord, according to all Your rightness and justice, I beseech You, let Your anger and Your wrath be turned away from Your city Jerusalem, Your holy mountain. Because of our sins and the iniquities of our fathers, Jerusalem and Your people have become a reproach and a byword to all who are around about us. Now* *therefore, O our God, listen to and heed the prayer of Your servant [a] [Daniel] and his supplications, and for Your own sake cause Your face to shine upon Your sanctuary which is desolate. O my God, incline Your ear and hear; open Your eyes and look at our desolations and the city which is called by Your name; for we do not present our supplications before You for our own righteousness and justice, but for Your great mercy and loving-kindness.* **O Lord, hear! O Lord, forgive!** *O Lord, give heed and act! Do not delay, for Your own sake, O my God, because Your city and Your people are called by Your name. While I was speaking and praying, confessing my sin and the sin of my people Israel, and presenting my supplication before the Lord my God for the holy hill of my God—Yes, while I was speaking in prayer, the man Gabriel, whom I had seen in the former vision, being caused to fly swiftly, came near to me and touched me about the time of the evening sacrifice. (Daniel 9:3-21 AMP emphasis added and some notations removed)*

Do you see the pattern in Daniel's prayer? WE have sinned and WE have done wickedly - the prayer is a personal prayer as Daniel was included, but it is a corporate prayer for his family and his tribe and nation. He also did not blame God since the curse in manifestation was not God's act against him, rather he recognised this was the natural result of the curse in operation. Like the law of gravity, the law of cursing impacts us when we sin.

So here is the biblical pattern that I used in dealing with what I saw in my generation: generational lack, poverty, and premature death. In my case, I took a copy of the death certificate of my great-great-grandfather and wrote out the Daniel prayers. I repented on behalf of myself and my family line for all the sins I could identify such as:

- the sin of not looking after the widows and orphans;

- not walking in the blessing provided for in Scripture, resulting in the curse in operation;

- not leaving inheritances for children and grandchildren; and

- not understanding that the curse and enemy was in operation and blaming God for dealing badly with us.

I also recognised that through sin and the operation of the enemy, there was sickness, disease, and death operating in my family line, and that this was not the blessing that God had intended. I named the enemy acts for what they were and repented for blaming God.

Interestingly, just as I was led to forgive the family for not looking after the orphans, I was also led to forgive the government for not dealing with the orphans correctly and to forgive the Anglican Church that ran the workhouse for how they dealt with these treasured children. In dealing with such a prayer, God will lead you for specifics to pray. In any event, I prayed at length my Daniel-style prayers and wrote them onto the death certificate. We tied the death certificate to a stake and drove the stake into the ground as a prophetic act. We did this in a graveyard in the heart of London while making powerful declarations of God's power and blessing over our lives.

In Daniel's case, he got a quick result, as God sent an angel to him immediately. In my case, there was also a powerful result. A few days after my prayers, I was invited to attend the Canadian High Commission in London on Berkeley Square for a charity board meeting and dinner with the High Commissioner. I was in a grand room in a seat of honour, and I was having a quiet personal reflection saying to myself: "Isn't it amazing that I am here seated in such an honoured location only 200 yards away from the site of the workhouse where my great-great-grandmother died and from where my great-grandfather was sent to Canada." I was thanking the Lord for this quietly when some latecomers from the press arrived, apologising as they had been delayed at Parliament covering the repentance of the UK Prime Minister to the Canadian Home

Children.[1] As the discussion continued, they could not believe that I was a descendant of one of the earliest of the Home Children, and they took me to another part of the building to meet with one of the oldest living Home Children who had travelled to London for the event.

In God's miracle timetable I had repented on behalf of my family for these generational issues and forgiven ancestors, the government, and the Church for not looking after my family. Two weeks later I was in an honoured location, 200 yards away from the workhouse site when the UK Prime Minister repented formally in Parliament to me! What a blessing that only God could coordinate!

We are actually in a much better position than Daniel as we have a better covenant through Jesus. Jesus has borne all our sins and the curse so we have a positional entitlement to freedom and the blessing. This includes these generational curses - Jesus is the answer to these as well. We also know that if we pray for forgiveness, he will forgive us of these sins and cleanse us from unrighteousness (I John 1:9). **The visiting iniquity will be fully cleansed.**

Here is a reminder of the steps:

- Look at issues in your life and in your generations that seem to be persistent or problematic. Perhaps there are sins you have struggled with or ongoing areas of attack such as poverty, barrenness, addiction, sexual sin, broken families, failed businesses and the like. I would include generational and inherited conditions that may come down the family line. This may require some research into your genealogy. Is there something there that is not blessing?

---

1. https://www.cbc.ca/news/world/british-pm-apologizes-to-home-children-1.916446 and https://chameleonfire1.wordpress.com/2017/02/23/house-of-commons-passes-apology-motion-for-british-home-children/

- Go through the steps dealing with blindness to our situation and personal sin and then look at the generations and pray a version of Daniel's prayer.

Daniel's Generational Prayer for Today

Dear Lord, I recognise that you are righteous and you do not bring evil upon us. I recognise that your will is for me and my family to be blessed and to have on earth the Kingdom just as in Heaven. Through the blood of Jesus we have forgiveness of sin and cleansing from all unrighteousness and iniquity. I recognise that in my life and in the lives of my ancestors, we have not walked as closely to you as you intended, and we have not walked in the blessing as we should have. Inheritances were not left for children and grandchildren, and if they were they were not what you would have liked.

On behalf of myself and my generations, we repent for not walking in the blessing in the way you intended. [Note any other sins that you see evident such as not looking after the orphans, hate, strife, sexual sin, and the like.]

I also recognise that operating in my generational line is [name what you see such as poverty, sickness, premature death etc], and this is not part of Heaven and not part of the Kingdom you intended. Therefore, on behalf of myself and my family line, we come out of agreement with these curses and repent for any sins that gave rise to the operation of these curses or to the manifestation of ungodly fruit. I repent on behalf of myself and my generations for having these curses in operation in our lives and ask you to shut the door and cut off the conduit and access points which allow the enemy to operate.

The Bible says that the iniquity will be healed and cleansed, and we ask you to cleanse our iniquity, and in particular that the iniquity visiting us due to generational sin would be cut off and dealt with at the cross. Jesus has borne this curse, and through this prayer we bring all generational curses to Him.

Finally, in prayer, listen to the guiding voice of the Holy Spirit which will lead you specifically in prayer and in revelation.

Chapter 14

Leaving the Past Behind

God's Will is for Us to Flourish

It is God's will for us to be in close communion with Him and to flourish. Let's capture a vision of what it means for us to truly flourish in Kingdom Finance. As a foundational principle, we must come into agreement with the Word that says that He has a great and wonderful plan for each of us, and that this plan includes us thriving financially. We are to be the head and not the tail and to live as kings and priests in this life. No longer are sin, sickness, and disease to rule in our lives and in the lives of our family members. We are no longer to be food for the beasts of the field and the birds of the air to feast on at their will (Deuteronomy 28:26).

Deep in each human being is the knowledge that we have each been created to have a godly purpose and destiny. We are designed to be in connection with God's heart and His purposes in our lives. We know that we have a destiny, that we are to be world-changers, and that there are good works for us to walk in (Ephesians 2:10). This knowledge can be dulled by distractions, sin, or even attacks against us. However, our heart is designed to be in connection with God's heart. Regardless of where life has taken us, at this moment and no matter what our circumstances may be, each one of us has a future and hope - God has a great plan for us!

> *For I know the thoughts that I think toward you, says the Lord, thoughts of peace and not of evil, **to give you a future and a hope**. (Jeremiah 29:11 AMP emphasis added)*

There is something that is not satisfied in the heart of man if there is no realisation of the destiny that God has prepared for us. The core of this is anchored on the love of Jesus, a personal relationship with Him and worship.

> **We are created and wired to seek the presence of the Lord and only in His presence can we be satisfied and fully realise our destiny.**

Without this connection to the heart of God our efforts fall short. In John 4, Jesus spoke to a woman drawing water from the well and illustrated the thirst inside every human being. He offered her "water" to quench the inner thirst and need in her life.

> *Jesus answered and said to her, "Whoever drinks of this water will thirst again, but whoever drinks of the water that I shall give him will never thirst. But the water that I shall give him will become in him a fountain of water springing up into everlasting life." (John 4:13-14 NKJV)*

We are created and wired to seek the presence of the Lord, and only in His presence can we be satisfied and fully realise our destiny.

> *You have said, Seek My face [inquire for and require My presence as your vital need]. My heart says to You, Your face (Your presence), Lord, will I seek, inquire for, and require [of necessity and on the authority of Your Word]. (Psalm 27:8 AMPC)*

If there is any doubt left in your mind about Jesus' will for you to have a future and a destiny, then Jesus' prayer was that you would be made perfect. Think about that - *made perfect*! This is truly His will for us and, if we can just believe it, we can address any issues in our lives that have led us to a place where things are not perfect. Here is Jesus' prayer for us; meditate on it and let it sink into your spirit:

> *"I do not pray that You should take them out of the world, but that You should keep them from the evil one. They are not of the world, just as I am not of the world. Sanctify them by Your truth. Your word is truth. As You sent Me into the world, I also have sent them into the world. And for their sakes I sanctify Myself, that they also may be sanctified by the truth.*
>
> *"I do not pray for these alone, but also for those who will believe in Me through their word; that they all may be one, as You, Father, are in Me, and I in You; that they also may be one in Us, that the world may believe that You sent Me. And the glory which You gave Me I have given them, that they may be one just as We are one: I in them, and You in Me; that they may be **made perfect in one**, and that the world may know that You have sent Me, and have loved them as You have loved Me.*
>
> "Father, I desire that they also whom You gave Me may be with Me where I am, that they may behold My glory which You have given Me; for You loved Me before the foundation of the world. O righteous Father! The world has not known You, but I have known You; and these have known that You sent Me. And I have declared to them Your name, and will declare it, that the love with which You loved Me may be in them, and I in them." (John 17:15-26 New King James Version (emphasis added))

God is Good All the Time

We must anchor in our hearts and minds the truth of the nature of God. God is good all the time. This was brought home to me recently by a dream that God gave me on this point. I was dreaming about a friend who had gone through a very difficult time and had fallen away from a close relationship with God. In the dream I was shown and fully comprehended what he believed about God. He believed that somehow God had not answered his prayers or had brought these difficulties on him.

> **One of the biggest sin issues of this generation is blaming God for the work of the enemy.**

I felt his bitter judgement that God had let him down; that he could have spared him this horrible situation. My perspective then shifted out from the individual to the broader view in the Church, and the word of the Lord came to me that one of the biggest sin issues of this generation is attributing to God the actions of another. In this case, attributing to God the work of the enemy in this man's life and also blaming God for the fruit of his own sinful actions. In the dream, I fully understood how wrong this was and how this bitterness towards God hinders our lives as Christians.

> *I assure you and most solemnly say to you, all sins will be forgiven the sons of men, and all the abusive and blasphemous things they say; but whoever blasphemes against the Holy Spirit and His power [by attributing the miracles done by Me to Satan] never has forgiveness, but is guilty of an everlasting sin [a sin which is unforgivable in this present age as well as in the age to come]. (Mark 3:28-29 AMP)*

Let me say it again and really receive it in your hearts: "God is good all the time". Whatever situation you are in now, no matter how difficult it may be, God is good and has a good plan for you if you align yourself with the blessing that flows for you.

That is why the operation of the enemy is to steal, kill, and destroy the destiny purpose that God has laid out for you. The bright eyed enthusiasm of most nursery school children is such a contrast to the results in many people's lives. Alcoholism, despair, cynicism, offence, and suspicion dog many people's footsteps. How often have we heard from our peers or even said: "Is this all there is?" or "I thought I would have been in a different place". What has happened is that the cares and trials of this world or the attacks of the enemy have broken people down and suppressed their dreams. The defeated looking adult or the nasty social climber bear little resemblance to the child dreaming to be the superhero rescuing those in need.

One thing is guaranteed: we have a calling and a destiny that has captured our imagination and energy. It may be suppressed right now, but if you are reading this, you have a desire to see things done in the Kingdom, to find a new way of operating in finances, and to break the patterns that have held you and your generations down.

You have a God inspired destiny that fires your desire to DO – Do something for God in an area of influence that God has called you to. What is your destiny and calling? Is it to release funds for the gospel, build orphanages, or help the downtrodden with real justice? To provide financial support for ministries God leads you to partner with? Do you want to fund students or education and relieve physical suffering and starvation? Is it to fund and see the end to human sex trafficking and the release of those trapped in horrible situations of abuse? God loves that hunger, as He can work with it. Even if we set off in completely the wrong direction it only takes a few course corrections by God to turn us in the right direction. Take comfort that moving forward is a critical first step.

> **You have a God inspired destiny that fires your desire to DO - Do something for God.**

Wherever you may find yourself today, God can re-animate your destiny calling or awake you to it more fully. Get ready to be the Kingdom superhero or leader you dreamed of being.

Lordship

Once we have dealt with the issues that may have been allowing the enemy to attack, we need to establish the Lordship of Jesus over 100% of our lives so that we can walk in victory. What do we mean by

Lordship, and how do we get into this deeper relationship with Jesus? The only way to see the release of the glory of the Kingdom in and through our lives (and to be released in Kingdom Finance) is through intimacy with Jesus.

In Christian business discussions this intimacy and Lordship seems to be lacking. These discussions seem much more like normal business but with a Christian nomenclature bolted on. Much more like the Pharisees acting in their religious authority, rather than Jesus operating in the miraculous anointing. God wants to be Lord over our finances and our financial vision. To walk in Kingdom Finance we must walk in relationship with the King.

The old paradigms will not work in Kingdom Finance moving forward. How often have we heard the phrase "well that's just business" expressed in the context of Christians applying worldly financial principles to a situation? Has the warmth of worship changed to a chill when money is discussed, as if somehow money is disconnected from worship and the anointing? Has someone rushed emotionally into financial ruin claiming that they were operating and living "on faith", meaning that faith is an excuse for failure?

God has set in place principles upon which Kingdom Finance works and we must learn to walk in these. Thankfully, we have a merciful God who is faithful and just to forgive us our failings and cleanse us (1 John 1:9). I believe that God is releasing a new wave of Kingdom Finance understanding so that we can accomplish what he has called us to do. Here is a lordship prayer:

"Dear Lord Jesus, I know I need you and I accept you as my Saviour, my Deliverer and my Lord.
Please Lord Jesus come now and be Lord over all of my life, the whole of it, every part of it and every part of me.
Lord this is what I truly want and need.
Be Lord of my body, my physical health, how and what I eat, how and when I get exercise, how and when I rest, and what I look like.

Be Lord of my mind, my mental health, what I think, what I believe, what I imagine and my attitude towards everything.
Be Lord of my emotions, how I feel and how I express those feelings.
Be Lord of my will, my desires and all of my decisions.
Be Lord of my needs and of what I think I need.
Be Lord of my sexuality and how I express it.
Be Lord of my family and all of my relationships.
Be Lord of my human spirit, my spiritual awareness and how I worship.
Be Lord of my work, for you and in my job and in and around my family home.
Be Lord of my time and how I use it.
Be Lord of my home and all my possessions.
Be Lord of my finances, how I receive and how I give.
Be Lord of my plans, my future and my ambition.
Be Lord of the time and the nature of the death of my body here on this earth.
Lord Jesus I thank you that your blood was shed for me that I can live and be free from sin and that I may live for ever with you.
Amen."[i]

Part Three

The Way Forward

Chapter 15

Shame

In order to walk in the measure of overcoming victory God intends, we need to abide with Him and have His anointing rest on us as a whole, authentic, and healed person. Shame can result in a fragmented or constructed personality which impedes true release and anointing. Only in the anointing can we fully join with Jesus in destroying the works of the enemy relative to Kingdom Finance.

Shame holds us back as it leads us to paper over or suppress issues in our lives rather than bringing them all to Jesus for His cleansing and empowering. The areas of our life where shame has influence are areas where we are not ABIDING in Jesus. These are areas we have not fully surrendered to Him and, as a result, we are standing in our own strength and righteousness. There is no shame in Jesus, so if we feel it or see its impact in our lives we need to get rid of it!

Shame drives religious legalism and draws us nearer to the darkness. It empowers defilement and addiction in our lives and drives us away from the anointing. It causes us to build a fabricated personality - a facade of how we want to be seen which is not authentic - our "Christian side" and our "worldly side".

True Anointing Will Not Operate with Shame

Most of the pride and bluster around money and image flows from the shame-empowered, fabricated personality. We see people chasing the dream and the love of money and power, with perhaps some lip-service to good works, but lacking in true Holy Spirit anointing and power. Instead of being known by the King, they seek branding and name recognition. They seek self-elevation instead of God-elevation. Then they wonder why the glory of God and the anointing does not fall on their inauthentic lives. If we do not see the anointing flowing through our lives, then consider if shame may be a factor.

God has a vision and plan for each of us to be the godly righteous rich man or woman: someone we may have lost the capacity to see. God has called us to live in Him living a Kingdom lifestyle of freedom - ABIDING IN HIM - moving with His plan in power and anointing.

Think about the life of Moses. In later life, when God called him, he was honest about who and what he was, and God used him in great supernatural power. God's strength was made known through his weakness.

> *Fear not, for you shall not be **ashamed**; neither be confounded and depressed, for you shall not be put to **shame**. For you shall forget the **shame** of your youth, and you shall not [seriously] remember the reproach of your widowhood any more. (Isaiah 54:4 AMPC emphasis added)*

> *It is my own eager expectation and hope, that [looking toward the future] I will not disgrace myself **nor be ashamed** in anything, but that with courage and the utmost freedom of speech, even now as always, Christ will be magnified and exalted in my body, whether by life or by death. (Philippians 1:20 AMP emphasis added)*

How Do We Move on from Failure?

What if you have moved forward but everything has gone wrong and it is all a mess? Is it too late for you? I remember crying out to God after the apparent complete failure of the Kingdom business I believed I was establishing for Him. I had left my secure leadership position in a major London firm to set out and do something I felt called to do. The result seemed to be nothing but strife, division, personal attacks, and a complete mess. Indeed, some of the mess of my own making - like ashes in my hands. How had I gotten it all wrong? Had I gone down the wrong path, trusted the wrong people, or done the wrong things? I felt I had stepped out to do something for Him and had been blindsided. I also knew that I had let Him down in so many ways. I felt broken, misused, and had more than a dollop of self-pity and shame.

In the world's eyes perhaps this response was justified as this was a severe financial blow that would take years to work through. However, as I was in this place of brokenness, fasting, and crying out to the Lord, my reading for the day was about Peter's sermon that launched the New Testament Church. The word of the Lord dropped into my spirit: *"You have had your time of self-pity, get up and proclaim your vision and destiny again."* When I counted the days from the time I got this word to the date of the legal separation of that failed venture, it was exactly the same time from Peter's denial - his great failure; to his sermon - his great success. It was no coincidence that I was led to read about Peter's sermon on that very day– it is how God speaks to us.

Remember, Peter denied Jesus having known Him IN PERSON.[1] He got it wrong, failed, and denied Jesus. However, God restored him to leadership and 53 days later he stood in front of everyone proclaiming Jesus as Lord. What was God saying to me? He was saying that I too was to move on from that place of failure and broken dreams and to

---

1. Mark 14:66-72

press back into the destiny that God had for me. I had my 53 days of shame, and it was time to forget those things which are behind and press on for the prize of His high calling (Philippians 3:13-14). I could not allow shame and what was said by anyone hinder me from the calling God placed on my life.

You too may have had a failure: a broken marriage, failed business, or bankruptcy. There may be people who are holding you in that place and cursing your destiny. Everything may appear to be a muddled mess but Jesus has called us to get up, move forward and run the race, living out the works He has prepared for us to walk in (Ephesians 2:10).

Indeed, I would be surprised if anyone had not experienced setbacks if they have a calling in the area of Kingdom Finance. Why? Because the enemy always attacks us in the area of our calling. Also, God loves to show His true nature and chooses the weak things to confound the wise. David was the least among his brothers and was not even included in the initial line up of the sons of Jesse! Moses came into the world as the son of a slave at a time children of the slaves were being killed. The enemy tried to take out the baby Jesus by killing all children born in the area. Gideon was threshing in the winepress to hide from the enemy. Our weakness, when coupled with God's calling and His strength, is our qualification.

What is Shame?

However good and right this sounds, for many in the Church, we continue to walk in disability, burdened with shame and carrying the odour of the pigpen and outhouse with us instead of carrying the atmosphere of Heaven! We allow the judgement of ourselves and others to hold us back. As we step forward we hear the voice of the accuser in our mind telling us we are not really worthy. The, "Who do you think you are?" accusation of shame. We act like we are broken china that has been glued together which only looks good, but is really broken and incapable of holding our destiny.

Guilt is consciousness of having done something wrong which drives us to make things right. Shame is defining ourselves as being somehow wrong and holding us in that place. It is a still photo or snapshot that holds us to the place of shame, when in reality our lives are to be a moving picture. We are not to remain emotionally fixed at a point where shame can impact our lives but to move to freedom.

Shame is defined as:

> "A painful feeling of humiliation or distress caused by the consciousness of wrong or foolish behaviour... A loss of respect or esteem; dishonour..." [i]

Shame does not lead us into an empowered and anointed lifestyle. Yes, there may be good times, but we are not free and in victory, and many are covering secret sins and addictions. We still walk forward in our lives with reference to the past and not with reference to our future destiny in Him.

To the extent that shame is empowered in our lives, we are unable to fully abide and rest with Jesus. We have a form of godliness, but the power is denied (II Tim. 3:5). There is no place for us to be held back by shame as individuals or as the body of Christ. Just as defilement is the glue that holds lack in operation in our lives, so shame is the repellant that keeps us from operating fully in the anointing.

> *...For what partnership have right living and right standing with God with iniquity and lawlessness? Or how can light have fellowship with darkness?* (2 Corinthians 6:14 AMPC)

Shame can lead us to a place where we are not authentic and transparent with Him or with others. We see ourselves as cracked vessels hiding our flaws and failures. Our internal image is not aligned with our restored and redeemed position in Christ. Worse yet, the religious spirit may blind us to our true state, and we can become prideful of our great fabricated image.[2] Somewhere in our lives, we are hiding: hiding the truth of who we are, believing that if people really knew us, they would reject us. Like the Prodigal Son who initially did not see himself as a son but at best a servant. We can believe this at the core of our being, it becomes who we see ourselves and in doing so we believe a lie and empower the enemy to work in our lives.

Shame will always try to hold us in a place of failure or point out the imperfection in what we do. Have you failed 10%, 50%, or even 90%? God has a great plan to restore you. He set the standard at 100%! The amazing thing about Jesus' parable of the Prodigal Son is that the son was portrayed as 100% lacking in merit and a 100% failure. To counter shame, Jesus gave us the ultimate example. The Prodigal Son took his inheritance money, left his covenant land and position, squandered all his wealth on defilement, and ended up literally homeless and living with the pigs. To Jesus' listeners this represented the ultimate, unforgivable guilt and failure. Yet in the parable Jesus said that the father ran to him and restored him. In telling this parable, Jesus was sharing the nature of God the Father. If you are willing to return to Him, He will make everything new for you and manifest His Kingdom through you. Failure is not a bar to relationship with Jesus and Kingdom Finance!

That is why it is so important to conclude the past and move on. It doesn't matter that we have failed or that there are those that sit in judgement on our past actions. Our primary calling is to be in relationship with Jesus and to walk in love. He loves us, He has forgiven us, our relationship is with Him, He has borne our sins, He has paid the price for our redemption, and our rehabilitation. He has borne our shame, borne our lack, and become a curse for us. We do not have the right to wallow in self-pity – give yourself 53 days like

---

2. Luke 18:9-14 - The Pharisee is an example Jesus used of someone bound in religious pride - the religious spirit.

Peter, and then follow his example and proclaim Jesus as Lord over your vision and destiny and be victorious.

Your destiny is to run the race God has put before you. If you have fallen or been knocked down the metaphorical stairs, get up, dust yourself off and charge again into the race. In this race if we fall we must get up again running because that is our calling (Hebrews 12:1; 1 Corinthians 9:24). You cannot remain at the place of failure, either by not forgiving those who have done you wrong (including yourself) or by defining yourself by the judgement of others.

> If you have fallen down the stairs get up, dust yourself off and charge again into the battle. We are in a race and if we fall we must get up again running because that is our calling.

So what is critical in order to achieve our destiny? What releases Kingdom Finance to flow supernaturally? It is not a prophetic word, special university degree, money, or a blessing from someone anointed in this area, as much as these may be beneficial. The number one thing necessary for Kingdom financial release is the anointing that only comes through true intimacy with Jesus.

Freed from Shame

God wants us to enjoy liberty in our walk with Him. That means to walk in victory and to be radiant and free. From the time of the original sin of Adam and Eve, a characteristic of sin is to hide ourselves and to cover up in shame. Like the Prodigal Son, we have all come to Him broken and ashamed, but that is not the end of the story, is it? Imagine if the Prodigal Son continued with his life as if he were in the pigpen instead of in the restored position his father had provided. The Prodigal Son was not left in his condition, as the Father came running to him and restored him fully.

> **We are not just broken and fixed but remade in His image.**

In the same way, our Father God will restore us fully, not due to what we have earned or deserved, but because of His great love and His great purposes for our lives. Having dealt with our sins and concluded our pasts, we walk in an empowered lifestyle where each day is the outworking of our prophetic destiny. We are not just broken and fixed, but remade in His image. He has designed for us to be new creations and brand new people (II Corinthians 5:17). To be free from shame means we walk in liberty. We are empowered and transparent, we can choose our actions, and are not constrained by what people think or our pasts. We are also not chemically or psychologically driven to behaviours we do not want. A person who is walking in victory is a free, whole person with healthy relationships.

Some Tests for Shame

How do we know if we are affected by shame? There are a number of indicators, but here are some examples:[3]

1. If God really knew me, He would not love me.

2. It is hard to look people in the eye when they are speaking to me.

3. I am quiet, have trouble meeting with people, and crowds can be a struggle.

4. I suffer from rejection and it seems that people look down on me or are against me.

---

3. For a more detailed understanding see http://www.wholeperson-counseling.org/id/shame.html

5. I feel like love and acceptance is conditional and I have to work for it.

6. It is hard to accept a compliment or gift with thanks and positivity.

7. I struggle with depression, guilt, sin, hopelessness and anger.

8. Joy and light-heartedness seems foreign to me.

9. I lean to a negative expectation and sometimes feel like a failure.

10. I struggle to comprehend the goodness of God as my Father.

Each statement that you checked as being true for you may be an indicator of shame operating in your life.

Impact of Shame

Shame can affect us physically, mentally, relationally, and spiritually. Physically it can manifest itself by intense blushing and embarrassment, self-conscious posture, and poor eye contact. In extreme cases there can be nausea and panic attacks depending upon the situation. Mentally, shame can cause us to self-curse. Instead of saying what the Bible says about us (our positional truth) and confessing that we are blessed and the son or daughter that He loves, we self-curse and say that we are ugly, poor, broken, unloved, rejected, and the like. Shame means we don't declare His Kingdom over our lives on earth as it is in Heaven, and this allows the enemy to impact our lives and limit our victory.

Shame can also put us in a frame of mind in which we don't measure up to our perceived standards. We live our lives with reference to standards that enable our ongoing view of ourselves as failures and this perfectionism can cause a great deal of stress.

Shame can also hinder us in our relationships: "We feel ineligible for mutually respectful relationships if we believe that we are worth less than other people."[ii]

Shame and Hypocrisy

The truth is that Jesus bore all of our shame, and He was rejected so that we can be accepted.[iii] He showed us how the Father responds to us in the story of the Prodigal Son - He runs to us and restores us even though we do not deserve it. Shame is based on what we deserve and not the blessing. Shame focuses on what we have done or not done - it is linked to judgement and our punishment - getting our "just desserts". Shame is empowered by the law and not the free favour of what Jesus has done for us.

Shame aligns with fear, slavery, and sin- it is not our natural state if we are in the Kingdom, yet many in the church are enslaved by a false image, addiction, and shame.

> **Shame is based on what we deserve and not the blessing.**

Perhaps even more damaging in the life of the believer is that shame holds us back from making Jesus Lord of all our lives and, as a result, limits our capacity to walk in the anointing we desperately desire to walk in. This is because we can only make him Lord in our lives to the point where we are hiding from Him. When shame holds power over us, we often try to fix what is wrong ourselves and create a fabricated personality, one that resembles how we wish to be seen. Not a real personality, but a constructed one. Does this ring a bell with you? Dressing in a jacket and tie for church and putting on a "bless you" smile, while inside feeling pain and brokenness. Hypocrisy has its roots in shame and the lengths people will go to protect their image.

Jesus speaks of this in relation to the Pharisees who outwardly looked righteous but this was just an image. Shame makes us prey to the religious spirit and leads us to build a false life that cannot hold God's anointing.

> *"What sorrow awaits you teachers of religious law and you Pharisees. Hypocrites! For you are like whitewashed tombs—beautiful on the outside but filled on the inside with dead people's bones and all sorts of impurity. Outwardly you look like righteous people, but inwardly your hearts are filled with hypocrisy and lawlessness. (Matthew 23:27,28 NLT)*

Two people can act right and look right, but one person can be free and authentic and one can conform to an image empowered by shame and the religious spirit. One has authenticity and walks in anointing, and one rings false, like a cracked pot.

We want to move in blessing, to move powerfully in the Spirit, and to see God move in our lives in mighty signs and miracles, and then we wonder why it does not happen in our lives and churches. Could it be because we are not authentic and whole before Him? The anointing can not fully rest on us if we ask God to bless our religious constructs and fabrications.

> We make him Lord in our lives to point where we are hiding from Him. Where shame holds any power over us we can create a fabricated personality that is the image of what we would like to be and how we would like to be seen.

We can see this in ourselves or others in the church. A person can be pressing in and wanting to see the movement of the Spirit, but their actions seem "off". There is something that just does not witness with our spirit - it doesn't ring true. This lack of anointing can be compensated for by excellence and talent, but in the presence of someone who is authentic and connected to Jesus the difference is stark. Give me an anointed speaker or worshipper over a merely talented one every time!

> Give me an anointed speaker or worshipper over a merely talented one every time!

In this season, God wants us to walk in a new level of anointing, submitted fully to His Lordship. True empowerment is freedom, and freedom is not conformity with a religious image - He is calling us to a higher level of lordship and integrity in Him - to abide with Him in the vine without sinful connection to shame.

Remedy for Shame

So what can we do about shame? The remedy for shame is to be restored to our full godly identity. This restoration happens when we repent for walking with shame that is not surrendered to Jesus. We recognise that the shame of our sins belongs to Jesus as He paid the price for it on the Cross. He bore all of the punishment for our sin and bore our shame.

> The remedy for shame is to be restored to our godly identity.

He is also faithful and just to forgive us our sins and to cleanse us from all unrighteousness (1 John 1:9). Like Jesus' example of the Prodigal Son, we are not brought back to be servants cowering in the Father's house, but are restored to full sonship with a celebration, not shame. He will fully restore us as Jesus taught us and we also know that He will compensate us for the years that have been "eaten" and deal with shame:

> And I will **compensate you** *for the years*
> *That the swarming locust has eaten,*
> *The creeping locust, the stripping locust, and the gnawing locust—*
> *My great army which I sent among you.*

You will have plenty to eat and be satisfied
And praise the name of the Lord your God
Who has dealt wondrously with you;
*And **My people shall never be put to shame**...*
***My people will never be put to shame**. (Joel 2:25-26 AMP emphasis added)*

Isaiah 61 also sets out a divine exchange for shame:

Instead of your [former] shame you will have a [a]double portion;
And instead of humiliation your people will shout for joy over their portion.
Therefore in their land they will possess double [what they had forfeited];
Everlasting joy will be theirs. (Isaiah 61:7 AMPC)

So the steps to deal with shame are simple:

1. Recognise that shame may be at work holding you back.

2. Repent for any sins associated with shame.

3. Repent for shame. Here is an example prayer: *"Dear Jesus, I have walked in shame in relation to [name it if you can e.g. being divorced, business failure etc], and I was not entitled to do so as you bore my shame on the Cross. I cannot take it back. I give it back to you like a writ of shame that I place in your hand. I cannot use this as an excuse or reason not to move forward into my calling and destiny. Please restore me to my proper position and identity in You."*

4. Forgive anyone that has offended you or brought you into shame. This is an act of your will not based on how you may feel.

5. Deal with and repent for any fabricated personality. The Prodigal Son did not pretend to be righteous like the Pharisee. Here is a sample prayer: *"Dear Jesus, I have not been honest about who I am and tried like Adam and Eve to hide from you. I repent for all my sins [name them if there is something specific] and for building up a facade to hide who I am. I come to you like the Prodigal Son trusting you that you are a good Father. Please cleanse me from all unrighteousness and restore me to my position and destiny in you. Heal my emotions from the damage of sin and shame."*

6. When you are attacked, don't respond with how you feel, but with the truth of the Word. Reject shame and acknowledge to God that you are wrestling with shame and ask for His help. Example of dealing with shame:
• The enemy attacks with thoughts such as, "Who do you think you are?", or "You are just a [name the sin- failure, bankrupt, divorcee, victim, or similar]."
• Our Answer: "I am His beloved son/daughter and the righteousness of God in Christ, a new creation and a brand new person. All things are possible because I believe!"

7. When you fall into acting in shame or sin, repent for the sin and give Him the shame again and again. Keep doing this for the rest of your life as Jesus brings restoration and honour.

8. As you do this, take authority and command that all guilt, shame, fear, or any attack of the enemy be broken off you and command it to leave, in the name of Jesus.

9. If freedom is difficult or if there is a deep problem, then seek further Spirit-led counselling and inner healing. There are many excellent Church-led and Christian programmes that can support you in overcoming a stronghold of shame in your life.

Chapter 16

Giving

God is the Great Giver

As Christians we are called to be givers.

Give, and it will be given to you: good measure, pressed down, shaken together, and running over will be put into your bosom. For with the same measure that you use, it will be measured back to you (Luke 6:38 NKJV, emphasis added).

We are to capture the heart of God and to worship Him in spirit and in truth. God is the great giver. "... *For God so loved the world that he gave...*"(John 3:16 KJV). He gave His best for us - His only Son who left His throne in Glory and came to earth to be the sacrifice for our sins.

His gift was the only way that mankind's blood debt could be paid so that we could be reconciled to God. The first principle that we must learn is that God is all about giving and restoration.

> **It is clear that the people that are His and know Him are the givers.**

We are Called to be Givers

Our heart of giving and love is dramatically referred to by Jesus in the teaching on the separation of sheep and goats. It is clear that the people that are His and genuinely know Him are the givers - if you are not a giver then you do not know Him.

> *When the Son of Man comes in His glory (His majesty and splendor), and all the holy angels with Him, then He will sit on the throne of His glory. All nations will be gathered before Him, and He will separate them [the people] from one another as a shepherd separates his sheep from the goats; And He will cause the sheep to stand at His right hand, but the goats at His left. Then the King will say to those at His right hand, Come, you blessed of My Father [you favored of God and appointed to eternal salvation], inherit (receive as your own) the kingdom prepared for you from the foundation of the world. For I was hungry and you **gave** Me food, I was thirsty and you **gave** Me something to drink, I was a stranger and you **brought Me together with yourselves and welcomed and entertained and lodged Me**, I was naked and you **clothed** Me, I was sick and you **visited Me with help and ministering care**, I was in prison and you **came to see Me**. Then the just and upright will answer Him, Lord, when did we see You hungry and gave You food, or thirsty and gave You something to drink? And when did we see You a stranger and welcomed and entertained You, or naked and clothed You? And when did we see You sick or in prison and came to visit You? And the King will reply to them, Truly I tell you, in so far as you did it for one of the least [in the estimation of men] of these My brethren, you did it for Me.*

> *Then He will say to those at His left hand, Begone from Me, you cursed, into the eternal fire prepared for the devil and his angels! For I was hungry and you **gave Me no food**, I was thirsty and you **gave Me nothing** to drink, I was a stranger and you **did not** welcome Me and entertain Me, I was naked and you **did not** clothe Me, I was sick and in prison and you **did not** visit Me with help and ministering care. Then they also [in their turn] will answer, Lord, when did we see You hungry or thirsty or a*

> stranger or naked or sick or in prison, and did not minister to You? And He will reply to them, Solemnly I declare to you, in so far as you failed to do it for the least [in the estimation of men] of these, you failed to do it for Me. Then they will go away into eternal punishment, but those who are just and upright and in right standing with God into eternal life. (Matthew 25:31-46 AMPC, emphasis added and references removed)

If you look at this Scripture it does not say that they gave **when asked**. He could have said when I was thirsty and **asked you** for a drink you gave it. He did not! This Scripture shows us the heart of God that is active, that seeks out the need, that is looking for the need and that is walking prepared to meet it.

As we abide in Him and live from our Spirit connection to Him, we will act more and more like Him. Our lives and our walk as Christians are to be characterised by giving. God is the great giver, and when we walk in fellowship and communion with Him we are givers also - it is our nature, and God gives us the power to walk in this anointing.

> **Your closeness to God can be measured by your giving!**

> Let Christ himself be your example as to what your attitude should be... For it is God who is at work within you, **giving you the will and the power** to achieve his purpose. (Phil 2:5,13 Phillips emphasis added)

Your closeness to God can be measured by your giving! One of the first things that will show if your relationship with Jesus is cooling is how minded you are to give and to help others. If giving is a struggle or if you do not notice needs around you, then this is a sign that your relationship with Jesus is off track. Like a sore throat can precede a cold, so a reluctance to give indicates our relationship with Jesus is not right.

What is Biblical Giving?

A general biblical truth is that it is a good thing to give. This is particularly true where the giving is to meet the needs of the poor, disadvantaged, and oppressed. Moreover, we should be prepared, seeking out, and looking for opportunities to give. The requirement to be a giver can be found throughout the Bible, but here are a few key illustrations of this principle:

True religion - Caring for the widows and orphans in their affliction and need is what "true religion" is really about.

> *Pure religion and undefiled before God and the Father is this, To visit the fatherless and widows in their affliction, and to keep himself unspotted from the world. (James 1:27 KJV)*

I like how the King James Version starts this verse, and I like this phrasing as it implies there is a stark opposite also - false religion. If we do not have a focus on giving to others in our Christian lives, then could it be that our Christian walk is false, that it is not true religion but false religion?

Delivering the victim from the jaw of the oppressor - Job 29 is one of my favourite Scriptures as it describes how we should be living our lives in faith. It is ACTIVE not REACTIVE. Not responding to a request for funds, but living a life of active purpose - we exist to meet the needs of others and expect divine appointments to meet those of our neighbours.

> *Because I delivered the poor who cried, the fatherless and him who had none to help him. The blessing of him who was about to perish came upon me, and I caused the widow's heart to sing for joy. I put on [a]righteousness, and it clothed me or clothed itself with me; my justice was like a robe and a turban or a diadem or a crown! I was eyes to the blind, and feet was I to the lame. I was a father to the poor and needy;* **the cause of him I did not know I searched out. And I broke the jaws or the**

big teeth of the unrighteous and plucked the prey out of his teeth. (Job 29:13-17 AMPC, emphasis added and punctuation removed)

> **Love without action is not really love. Once you have seen you must act.**

Love your Neighbour - Central to Jesus' teaching was to love our neighbours as we do ourselves and and to do good unto others as we would have them do unto us. If our life of love to the Lord is first and our life of love to people is second, we have summed up really what God has been saying to us in the Bible. Love without action is not really love. Love requires expression, and the main expression is to give to the object of our affection.

A lawyer came to Jesus asking what is the greatest commandment: *"And He replied to him, You shall love the Lord your God with all your heart and with all your soul and with all your mind (intellect). 38 This is the great (most important, principal) and first commandment. 39 And a second is like it: You shall love your neighbor as [you do] yourself."* (Matthew 22: 37-39 AMPC) This should be our highest priority. Our next priority is to love our neighbour as ourselves. This involves action. Once we have seen, we must act.

> *If you know someone who doesn't have any clothes or food, you shouldn't just say, "I hope all goes well for you. I hope you will be warm and have plenty to eat." What good is it to say this, unless you do something to help? Faith that doesn't lead us to do good deeds is all alone and dead! (James 2:15-17 CEV)*

God's Chosen Fast Isaiah 58 - perhaps you have never fasted to seek the Lord, but I am sure that anyone pressing into God's heart for Kingdom Finance will fast. In part, like Hezekiah, we may fast because of the need for the Lord to move on our behalf to rescue us. More importantly fasting enables our hearts to be tuned to His heart. Isaiah 58 is a powerful declaration of God's heart. His heart is a heart of love evidenced by justice and giving. WE ARE TO BREAK EVERY ENSLAVING YOKE. His mission is to destroy the works of the devil and we do this, in part, through our giving - our love in action. Make no mistake, our love cannot have any action or reality without giving.

*Yet they seek, inquire for, and require Me daily and delight [externally] to know My ways, as [if they were in reality] a nation that did righteousness and forsook not the ordinance of their God. They ask of Me righteous judgments, they delight to draw near to God [in visible ways]. Why have we fasted, they say, and You do not see it? Why have we afflicted ourselves, and You take no knowledge [of it]? Behold [O Israel], on the day of your fast [when you should be grieving for your sins], you find profit in your business, and [instead of stopping all work, as the law implies you and your workmen should do] you extort from your hired servants a full amount of labor. [The facts are that] you fast only for strife and debate and to smite with the fist of wickedness. Fasting as you do today will not cause your voice to be heard on high. Is such a fast as yours what I have chosen, a day for a man to humble himself with sorrow in his soul? [Is true fasting merely mechanical?] Is it only to bow down his head like a bulrush and to spread sackcloth and ashes under him [to indicate a condition of heart that he does not have]? Will you call this a fast and an acceptable day to the Lord? [Rather] is not this the fast that I have chosen: to loose the bonds of wickedness, to undo the bands of the yoke, to let the oppressed go free, and that you break every [enslaving] yoke? Is it not to **divide your bread with the hungry and bring the homeless poor into your house—when you see the naked, that you cover him, and that you hide not yourself from [the needs of] your own flesh and blood?** Then shall your light break forth like the morning, and your healing (your restoration and the power of a new life) shall spring forth speedily; your righteousness (your rightness, your justice, and your right relationship with God) shall go before you [conducting you to peace and prosperity], and the glory of the Lord shall be your rear guard. Then you shall call, and the Lord will answer; you shall cry, and He will say, Here I am. If you take away from your midst yokes of oppression [wherever you find them], the finger pointed in scorn [toward the oppressed or the godly], and every form of* *false, harsh, unjust, and wicked speaking, **And if you pour out that with which you sustain your own life for the hungry and satisfy the need of the afflicted, then shall your light rise in darkness, and your obscurity and gloom become like the noonday. And the Lord shall guide you continually and satisfy you in drought and in dry places and make strong your bones. And you shall be like a watered garden and like a spring of water whose waters fail not. And your ancient ruins shall be rebuilt; you shall raise up the foundations of [buildings that have laid waste for] many generations; and you shall be called Repairer of the Breach, Restorer of Streets to Dwell In.** (Isaiah 58:2-12 AMPC, emphasis added and punctuation removed)*

We Give to God, Not Man

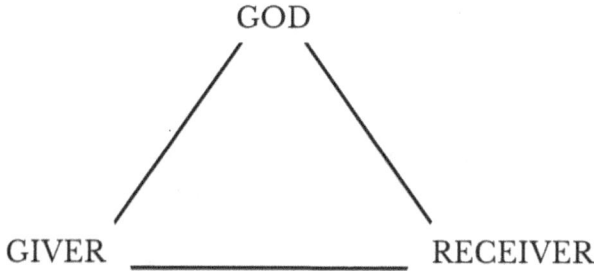

There is a central principle of giving that seems to be missed by much of the Church today with its emphasis on joining in the largely secular social welfare or social justice movement. We must adjust our thinking to align with true Kingdom purposes. It is a core Kingdom principle that our giving and service is to the Lord and not to man. Social justice dialogue is about man giving to man, usually in the context of concepts of equity - the rich giving to the poor or to those who are, according to some man made criteria, more deserving. Kingdom giving is about all giving to the Lord as He directs.

The greatest protection of this God-directed heart orientation is anonymity. Anonymity underlies all of our acts of service and giving.

> "Take heed that you do not do your charitable deeds before men, to be seen by them. Otherwise you have no reward from your Father in Heaven. Therefore, when you do a charitable deed, do not sound a trumpet before you as the hypocrites do in the synagogues and in the streets, that they may have glory from men. Assuredly, I say to you, **they have their reward**. But when you do a charitable deed, do not let your left hand know what your right hand is doing, that your **charitable deed may be in secret; and your Father who sees in secret will Himself reward you openly**. (Matthew 6:1-4 NKJV, emphasis added and some punctuation removed)

This point is critically important for a number of reasons, but all of these relate to the giving triangle.

The biblical orientation is that the giver gives to God and, on God's behalf, delivers the gift to the Receiver. This act should be done anonymously where possible as anonymity helps to ensure the integrity of our hearts and protects us from mixed motives. If you have given 100% anonymously, there is no chance you will be also trying to be recognised by man for your giving - only God can reward you because only He knows!

The receiver gets the gift and blessing from God and thanks for the gift goes to God. The delivery person giving the gift is acting like a courier. The recipient is thankful for the obedience and timeliness of the courier, but the orientation and thankfulness for the gift itself belongs to the Lord. Everyone can imagine their local post office or courier service. Imagine the distinctive UPS truck arriving. Now change that to a picture of GPS - God's Postal Service - and imagine yourself in a nifty gold uniform. You can take pleasure in a job well done making a delivery, but can you really take pride in relation to the actual gift in the box? When you thank the UPS delivery man for delivering a birthday present from your best friend, are you thanking him for the present or his role in getting it to you? Wouldn't he be surprised if you opened the parcel in front of him, started thanking him for such a nice gift, and tried to give him a hug! This is what not letting your right hand know what your left hand is doing means. The greater the degree of anonymity we can achieve, the greater we have preserved the honour for God in the process and the less we will be tempted to mis-appropriate His Glory.

Sadly, so much of our dialogue in the church in relation to giving has been transactional in nature: "You give to my ministry now and you will get an amazing return." This is usually connected to an event, need or with a sense of urgency that can in some cases be manipulative - if Kingdom love is not present and guiding our actions, then it is manipulative. Indeed, this mentality has led to ministers being recognised and called upon and rated for their ability to "pull" an offering. It may not be "bad" as we are helping someone, but it may not be what God intended for us to be doing.

Honour in Giving

However, asking for an offering is not always wrong. After all, Elijah asked the widow of Zarephath to give him food to eat from her last meal.

> *And the word of the Lord came to him: Arise, go to Zarephath, which belongs to Sidon, and dwell there. Behold, I have commanded a widow there to provide for you. So he arose and went to Zarephath. When he came to the gate of the city, behold, a widow was there gathering sticks. He called to her, Bring me a little water in a vessel, that I may drink. As she was going to get it, he called to her and said, Bring me a morsel of bread in your hand. And she said, As the Lord your God lives, I have not a loaf baked but only a handful of meal in the jar and a little oil in the bottle. See, I am gathering two sticks, that I may go in and bake it for me and my son, that we may eat it—and die. Elijah said to her, Fear not; go and do as you have said.* **But make me a little cake of [it] first and bring it to me, and afterward prepare some for yourself and your son.** *For thus says the*

Lord, the God of Israel: The jar of meal shall not waste away or the bottle of oil fail until the day that the Lord sends rain on the earth. She did as Elijah said. And she and he and her household ate for many days. (1 Kings 17:8-15 AMPC, emphasis added and some punctuation removed)

Elijah had a word from the Lord and could therefore act in faith, as we know that faith comes by hearing and hearing by the word of God (Ro. 10:17). Imagine if this happened today where an influential minister moving in high society appears to demand that a poor widow woman gives to him. Even worse, he says for her to meet his needs first! We must use our spiritual maps to understand this. It is not a scene that can be understood with the natural mindset, as the Kingdom is at work. Let me ask you a question that is central to understanding this dynamic: "In this story who was being blessed?" The answer is that it was the widow of Zarephath. Jesus made this clear when He was rejected in Nazareth:

*Then He said, Solemnly I say to you, no prophet is acceptable and welcome in his own town (country). But in truth I tell you, **there were many widows** in Israel in the days of Elijah, when the Heavens were closed up for three years and six months, so that there came a great famine over all the land; And **yet Elijah was not sent to a single one of them, but only to Zarephath in the country of Sidon, to a woman who was a widow**... When they heard these things, all the people in the synagogue were filled with rage.*

And rising up, they pushed and drove Him out of the town... that they might hurl Him headlong down over the cliff. But passing through their midst, He went on His way. (Luke 4:24-30 AMPC, emphasis added and brackets removed)

Jesus highlights that it was the widow who received the blessing. The crowd agreed and wanted to kill him. It may look like the widow is sharing her last meal, but the reality is that the prophet being "sent" to her was a great honour and blessing. The blessing in this context is on the one engaged in honour and giving, after which she had an amazing, miracle breakthrough.

In the same manner, when we come into connection with a genuine Kingdom person, we should be attuned to how to bless them and partner with them. We need to use our Kingdom map so that our perspective includes Kingdom realities. One of these realities is that giving to God in the context of blessing a Kingdom person means that we enter into a blessing. Honouring a prophet will result in receiving a prophet's reward (Matthew 10:41) and that is a blessing we would love to have. However, our orientation cannot change from being God-directed to being man-directed or we will stray into manipulation and mere human effort.

Giving Breaks Bondages

Unlike the social justice movement or other giving paradigms such as noblesse oblige[1], our giving does not come from a particular worldview, either left wing or right wing. It is not making a political statement, but the orientation of giving to God engages Him in our action, and there is an overlay of His dominion and bondage-breaking power that comes into play.

Giving is a physical act. It is something you do physically, but it is also a spiritual act when done with Kingdom purpose. When we give we must do it empowered by God's love and as Jesus showed us by His example. We would all agree that giving to the poor is good - we should do more and encourage others to do more - but there is a deeper principle at work here because the Bible warns us that even if we give all our goods to the poor and have not love it profits us nothing.

---

1. The idea that someone with power and influence should use their social position to help other people http://dictionary.cambridge.org/dictionary/english/noblesse-oblige

> *"Even if I **dole out all that I have to the poor** in providing food, and if I surrender my body to be burned or in order that I may glory, but have not love (God's love in me), I gain **nothing**. (1 Corinthians 13:3 AMPC, emphasis added and punctuation removed)*

NOTHING! Think about that truth. God wants us to give, and He has called us to operate in the Kingdom, but there is no Kingdom profit or blessing aside from Kingdom Love. This means that, from a Kingdom perspective, giving is not necessarily good - of course it is always better than stealing - but to get an eternal Kingdom reward it must not be separated from love. We must seek to operate in Kingdom giving so there is a reward but also so that there is a Kingdom impact!

> **We must seek to operate in Kingdom Giving so there is a reward but also so that there is a Kingdom impact!**

In order to operate with genuine Kingdom giving in love, we must operate as Jesus showed us: only doing what we see the Father do and only saying what we hear the Father say (John 5:19). As we walk in this Kingdom Love, our actions are Heaven-oriented and are totally different in nature from normal worldly giving. We are not social justice warriors righting wrongs or perceived wrongs; instead we carry the anointing of Heaven in love, and along with this, the power to break bondages.

This was brought home to me when I was walking out of a grocery store one day. There was an annoying drunk person begging there and really bothering people as they were leaving. I walked past him and felt a strong prompt to give him the largest note in my wallet. Immediately rejecting this, I kept walking. Again, I felt the prompt and said to myself that this was not God, as this person was drunk and would likely spend the money on drink. As I got to the corner, this prompt came very strongly: "Give him the note if you want your needs to be heard." I reluctantly headed over to the man and gave him the note and told him about the God that cared for him so much he prompted me to do this even though I had not wanted to. It was clear that even in his state the man was touched and held the note like it was precious. He then said that he would take it over to his friends in the park so they could see it and hear what I said. As I walked away I felt God say that I had been obedient to Him, and that they were all touching the note and there was a power dynamic released. The note was just a piece of paper, the money was not that relevant, but the release of God's power can break dominions of poverty, lack, and addiction. Someday, I will find out what God did in that moment.

Purposeful Giving

God is love and those that worship him must worship him in spirit and in truth (John 4:24). We must be in relationship with Jesus to have true release and reward. In short, our life must be anchored in Jesus. The Kingdom is all about the King and He must be the Lord of our lives, and we must have a genuine love relationship with Him (Matthew 22:37) and abide in Him (John 15:4-11).

I had a vision some time back of Christians operating businesses that were like large vending machines. Imagine two identical-looking drinks machines side-by-side. In the dream the machines seemed to do the same things, were selling the same product, and looked very similar. However, as I followed the power cord back further and further behind a covering, I could see where each machine was plugged into its power source. One machine was plugged into a normal socket and the other was plugged into a smoking and black socket.

It is clear from this vision that our source determines our output. The output may look the same, but one machine was not being energised and empowered by the Lord - it was plugged into the worldly system dominated by satan. I think God was showing me that our activities can look the same but be wrongly motivated and empowered. What is our source? What power are we tapping into? There is no fruit from our efforts where our supply is not Kingdom.

Two Christians doing similar things can have differing spiritual sources. Giving can be connected to the Kingdom or just be a social act connected to the world system dominated by satan.

We have two examples of giving set out in the Bible that look exactly the same at first glance. Two people giving all - one directed by Jesus (the Rich Young Ruler discussed prior) that would have led to an amazing blessed life, and one done without love:

> *If I give all my possessions to feed the poor, and if I surrender my body to be burned, but do not have love, it does me no good at all. (1 Corinthians 13:3 AMP)*

One is plugged into the white socket (or would have been had he obeyed Jesus) and one into the smoking black socket! Some may be thinking they are doing God's will, but if they trace the "power cords" in their life they will find they are not plugged into God's love. Their actions may be "good" in a worldly sense, but like the fasting of the Pharisees, they don't have the eternal value and connection to God's love.

> *"Not everyone who says to Me, 'Lord, Lord,' shall enter the kingdom of Heaven, but he who does the will of My Father in Heaven. Many will say to Me in that day, 'Lord, Lord, have we not prophesied in Your name, cast out demons in Your name, and done many wonders in Your name?' And then I will declare to them, **'I never knew you; depart from Me, you who practice lawlessness!'** (Matthew 7:21-23 NKJV emphasis added)*

I was pondering this scripture and felt drawn to the statement, "I never knew you". This is what we are talking about here. Knowing Jesus and being known by Him is what we do when we conclude our pasts. We are motivated by our relationship with Him, not by other influences. We begin to walk in His presence and in the anointing of

Holy Spirit in every act that we undertake. If we have this intimacy with Him then we will do the works of Jesus and represent Him to a suffering world.

I believe what God is saying is that there is a qualitative difference between giving, which even non-Christians do, and giving motivated and empowered by God's love. Giving which is motivated by the fleshly desire to be recognised or to reinforce our image or to get thanks and praise has more to do with rising above others in the Outhouse of Lack. Giving motivated by God's Love in us carries with it a powerful anointing that breaks the dominions and works of the devil in a person's life. It is this empowerment and connection to love that means we are plugged into the Heavenly source. We want to cooperate with Heaven in destroying the works of the devil.

> I believe what God is saying to us is that there is a qualitative difference between giving, which even non-Christians do, and giving motivated and empowered by God's love.

Actions and giving motivated and empowered by Love have dominion-breaking power over the enemy, and in order to break dominions and really set people free we need to have Jesus as our source and supply. God is love and what we do must be empowered, directed, and sustained by Him. We want to have profit from our lives and crowns to throw at His feet. Physical actions taken in obedience to God's Word allow us to partner with Heavenly power. When the Children of Israel shouted and blew the trumpets in obedience, it was not the force of the trumpet that took down the walls of Jericho - it was the dominion-breaking power of God. When Jesus broke the bread and fish it was not an amazing physical act: it was the miracle-working power of God. Our physical act of obedience to give according to His Word and empowered by love will break yokes of bondage and set captives free.

> **Kingdom Finance is different from just coming up with structures that increase giving to the poor as good as that may be. It is about carrying the anointing and aroma of heaven into a suffering world.**

For this reason, Kingdom Finance is different from just coming up with structures that increase giving to the poor, as good as that may be. Social Justice may be "a good", but to have eternal value, break bondages, and set captives free, it must be linked to Jesus and His love mission to destroy the works of satan! Money does not break the bondage of lack, but Kingdom giving does! Remember, poverty is not broken off by giving a person money because poverty is a curse - it is broken by the blessing that makes rich and adds no sorrow. It is about carrying the anointing and aroma of Heaven into a suffering world (2 Corinthians 2:15-17).

I emphasised the active character of giving in order to link it to the Scripture where Jesus says that not everyone who calls Him Lord will enter into the kingdom of Heaven (Matthew 7:21-23).

We cannot be in a position now that could give rise to a similar statement in relation to our actions! In our actions in life we must know Him, and more importantly, be known by Him. He must know our names. Put another way, we need God to say of us now that He knows us and knows our actions. The description used in Matthew 7 of *lawlessness* does not sit well with our worldly mindset - how can good works and wonders be equated with lawlessness? It is lawlessness when we are not motivated and inspired by Love. Our actions must flow from our relationship with Jesus who is Love. As He was in the world so must we be. We must do the will of our Father in Heaven - we must know Him and more importantly based on the Scripture above He must know us. This is particularly true when it comes to our giving. Following Jesus' example we must do what we see the Father do and say what we hear the Father say. This is the type of giving that accesses the miracle-working power of Heaven and will set captives free.

Let's break this down a bit with an example. We know that giving to the poor is a good thing to do. It is better than stealing from the poor which is condemned in Scripture. We would all agree with that, correct? However, on one occasion Jesus endorsed a higher form of giving where the ointment was poured as an offering over his feet, saying that the poor would always be with us.

> *In our actions in life we must know Him and more importantly be known by Him. He must know our names.*

> *For you always have the poor with you, and whenever you wish you can do good to them; but you will not always have Me. (Mark 14:7)*

> In 1 Corinthians 13:3 it says that even though "... *I bestow all my goods to feed the poor, ... but have not love, it profits me nothing (NKJV)*".

So in relation to the act of giving, we need to know Jesus is at the core of all of our actions and this is particularly true about giving. Giving is all about connecting with the heart of Jesus and entering into intimacy with Him.

The Trap of Earthly Honour - God will not share His Glory - and we should not be tempted to take it. The posture and orientation of the giver is between the giver and God. Our giving is not to the eventual recipient but to God, and as a result, our expectation of reward is from the Lord. The beauty of this is that our chance of disappointment is nil because Jesus never fails us! When we give the cup of water to the thirsty person we are giving it to Him (Matthew 25). If the recipient does not act appropriately that does not affect us as our service was to Him. This provides the context and framework for our giving.

Ideally, our giving should also be in secret as this allows this principle of honour to function more fully. The further we move away from secrecy the more we have to check our motivation and our heart attitude against the secrecy standard. Secrecy allows us to be confident of our motivation because man does not know what we have done - there is no possible mixing of motivation. In secrecy, no desire to be recognised, admired, honoured, or treated as a VIP can exist - we can be more confident that our motivation is pure. Indeed, we are not even looking to the person or organisation for our gratification, we are looking to God as the only possible reward is from Him. Also, for us to act in this manner we must be in relationship with Him in faith, hearing His word, and responding by giving. We abide in Him, believe what the Word says about the blessing of giving, and stand in faith that the Father will reward us openly (v4).

Let me illustrate the secrecy standard by a simple example: Imagine you are in a community of believers and a young couple are expecting a baby and praying for a crib and baby furniture that costs $500. As you hear about this, God drops into your heart to buy it for them either by a desire or by a direct rhema word. Here is the first decision point - you could give it to them directly or do it secretly. Doing this secretly, you could take $500 in $100 bills which are new and unused, put them in an envelope, and write something like this as God inspires you: *"God spoke to me to give you this money to buy your baby crib and furniture. He loves you greatly and is always looking for ways to bless you. This child is a gift from the Lord and you can always be confident that He will supply your every need."* It is then arranged to be given to them anonymously. What is the outcome of this? The receiving couple are thankful that someone was obedient to the prompting of the Lord and gave (the GPS Courier), but 100% of the praise and glory goes to God. "God met our need!", is the shout of praise and thanksgiving, and there is no one else in their mind's eye when they give praise to God. Likewise for the giver, there is the joy of obedience and the knowledge that God is being glorified and 100% of our expectation is towards God. There is no element of our basking in earthly praise or honour. By giving in secret we have protected our heart from the temptation of seeking man's praises.

> By giving in secret we have protected our heart from the temptation of seeking man's praises.

Anonymity is not always possible as certain projects require us to be involved in the giving process in order to find out the relevant details for telegraphic transfers or funding requirement dates. However, even if we are known, we should not slip into the trap of seeing ourselves as the giver but the instrument - every good gift comes from Him (James 1:17) and in giving we are His hand extended. We must see ourselves putting on our gold GPS delivery uniform and acting as His hand extended giving all glory to God.

Practical Points for Giving

At a practical level, are there any "best practices" in relation to giving? I think there are some common sense points to consider that are in line with our principles of obedience and the desire for anonymity.

The first is to do what God asks you to do. Learn to be sensitive to the leading of His Spirit. We are His sheep and the Bible says that we will hear his voice.

> *The sheep that are My own hear My voice and listen to Me; I know them, and they follow Me. (John 10:27 AMP)*

He may ask you to give in a way that seems odd or unusual to you. In this way it can become a prophetic act that means something to the person receiving.

For example, one time I felt led to give a specific high-value item to a ministry I was connected to, and put the item in an envelope and gave it to the leader who I knew. Anonymity was not possible but it was done without fanfare. He later said that the gift was something that he had been waiting for as it was the fulfilment of a prophetic word for his ministry and was part of his prophetic journey. Be ready to be obedient.

Earlier I mentioned the example of giving money for the baby crib and I mentioned giving crisp new $100 bills. Where there is time to be purposeful, I think this is best practice. New bills are clean and unsullied, they are not casual and mundane. By doing this we have brought a sense of occasion, a sense of honour and celebration. Our giving has become an offering which is holy to the Lord which is diametrically opposed to the spirit behind casually throwing some money at a problem. Are you giving to God or throwing money at an issue? I came across this when we were living in Singapore in a worldly context. At Chinese New Year, as was the custom, our friends came around and gave our daughter crisp unfolded red packets and inside were brand new bank notes. Every year this blessing of money was given, but a key part of it was the honour of the presentation. The value may not have been high, but there was a certain ceremony to this - care was taken. If we can capture this in a social giving context how much more in our giving to the Lord?

If you are giving to someone to meet a need, then cash also carries the most anonymity and it is the most useable for someone in need. When someone is in need, their need may be urgent and cash is immediate. You also do not know their circumstances and they may not have access to banking services. I know that if you are in need even a crumpled bill can be a blessing and buy some food, but we are talking about planned, purposeful giving. How can you be walking in this anointing and not planning? If you are planning to give to the Lord then we should do our best.

Another practical approach that has been my practice is to "pre-give". To take money out of my general use and availability and give it to the Lord. I do this by taking bills (new if possible) and tying them together in green thread to create a bundle. The bundle of cash is with me but not mine. I have it ready, waiting for God to give me a word for where this should go. I am prepared and having this with me assists in keeping my orientation to the Lord. Also, these funds are not cash in my wallet - if I need some cash I need to get it elsewhere. How can you seek out the needs of those you did not know and meet them as described in Job 29 without being ready? How could the Good Samaritan meet the needs of the injured man without having funds in hand?

I remember being in Harare, Zimbabwe advising on a project and meeting a Christian business person. We were having a meal and hearing about their story and I felt strongly impressed by God to give them some of this pre-given money which in this case was US$100 bills. As I did so, I was humbled to hear that this was a direct answer to prayer and met a critical need. Like the Kings of old we should come prepared with gold in a box to give to Jesus - I don't picture the box as being ugly and broken and gold is always shiny and beautiful. A gift from a king to the King of Heaven would be something to see. Preparation primes the pump for giving flow and keeps our hearts postured towards Jesus. We give Him our best! We are not the Christians that keep no cash in our wallet's to prevent us giving but we load them up! Now I am not suggesting we become the prey for every manipulative ministry pitch or sad story. Not at all: I am talking about purposeful, Spirit-led giving that releases the breaker anointing of Heaven.

For larger amounts, giving anonymously can be harder to achieve, but if you are serious there are a number of ways to keep anonymity to the maximum extent possible. This can be done through intermediaries or even special purpose companies or foundations for very large giving. Where there is an element of partnership with a ministry, anonymity is not practical as the relationship will need to be monitored and results verified for stewardship purposes. There is excellent support available for this type of giving but the posture of the heart is critical. We must not stray into taking His glory. We want our reward to be from Him not from the recipients or the public! We must seek Kingdom first and then all of these blessings will be added to us. He who sees in secret will reward us openly.

Also, as a general rule do not make promises to give, just give. Having been the recipient of unfulfilled promises this makes it difficult to maintain the giving triangle orientation. Your promise to give should be made to God and not to the recipient.

Giving Traps

Giving comes with a host of traps that can throw us off the Kingdom path and I have highlighted a few to avoid:

1. **The Trap of Mixed Waters** - this is where motivation gets blurred and we stray into the trap of seeing ourselves as meeting the needs of a person, not God. Like two rivers joining there is a "mixing of the waters" opening ourselves to a power dynamic which is very similar to the principle of the borrower being a servant to the lender. If we view ourselves as the giver, we trigger an expectation of gratitude owed to us. In doing so we have opted to receive the earthly reward by misappropriating the honour that should go to God. Indeed the Scripture says that God is removed from this type of giving and the FULL REWARD is the honour we can extract from others by our spectacle of giving. As a result, we have fallen into a trap where our giving may have **no Heavenly reward**. From a worldly perspective it may still be "good", as it is better than stealing, but it has no Kingdom reward. Think of the spectacle in the world of a VIP handing across a super-large cheque for all to see. This is the modern day equivalent of ringing a bell or blowing a trumpet to draw attention to our good works.

This line is crossed in many cases when we bring social justice into the church. From a Kingdom perspective it is not right to say that giving is good when it is divorced from the orientation of love and honour to God. In Kingdom giving, access to honour should be from the Lord's elevation of us in His time, not from self-promotion or self-aggrandisement around gift-giving. Of course, it is not wrong to be in a VIP room or meeting influential people, but if we are in this position of honour we should know that this is as a result of God's elevation which carries the anointing, not the dead hand of self-promotion. This is not the same as the reverse pride of "martyr-like" self-denial, but the recognition that this honour is from the Lord - it is His open reward of vindication and comes in His timing, accompanied by the deep seated knowledge that He has seen in secret and is openly rewarding.

At first this may seem to be an easy trap to avoid; however, this can be much more insidious, particularly where the relationship of giving is not one-off but ongoing in circumstances where our principle of secrecy is not practical. From what I have seen there is a widespread violation of this key principle as givers seek honour and recipients flatter and favour their key donors to manipulate them into giving. The more we enter into receiving honour from man and flattering the rich to get donations the more we evidence that we have no faith in the principle that God is the rewarder of those who give in the proper orientation - to God and in secret. As a result, our giving is not good, is not motivated and oriented in love, and has no eternal reward. Remember, if I give all, that means 100%, of my goods to the poor and sacrifice my body to be burned and it is not anchored in love it profits me nothing! (1 Corinthians 13:3)

Let's change our example slightly so that the young couple need a car for six months to a year and are praying about it. Imagine that God speaks to you to lend them your extra car and you offer this to them. In this case it is not practical to do this in secret as legal requirements and insurance need to be sorted out as well as other paperwork. When you go to them and let them know about the gift, then for both parties the motivation test against the above example must be used. How can I ensure that my giving is to the Lord? How can I ensure that my receiving is from the Lord? First, I must say it - speak it out and give God all the glory. For the giver: *"God spoke to me about providing this for you. God is your source and it is Him that is meeting your need. I am just being obedient."* I am sure that the couple will be grateful to you for your sacrifice and obedience, but as much as is possible direct that gratitude to the Lord. In the Bible when an angel appeared many people started to bow or worship there was an immediate correction given — this is our example of not allowing a situation to arise that means we share in God's glory. We must immediately correct the orientation for our sake and for the recipients by asserting that our role is as the GPS courier or messenger that is delivering God's gift - we are His hand extended. Let the couple be grateful for your obedience to the Lord in your role as courier, more than in your giving to them. In that manner you are giving the gift to the Lord and they are receiving the blessing of the gift from the Lord. For the receiver: *"Thank you for this gift and I honour your obedience to God. We are good ground to sow into and I declare that you will receive a full measure of blessing from the Lord."*

In this type of ongoing giving circumstance it is much easier for the enemy to slip in and for our God-directed orientation to slip. What do we do if something goes off track and our God-directed orientation slips? We may start dropping hints of our giving to others or slip into expecting more gratitude back from the couple. This is totally reasonable in worldly terms but not in Kingdom terms. Our friends and family can be unhelpful here as they may call for more honour for you saying: "After all you have done for them they should be more grateful!"

The best way to adjust our thinking is to repent of taking His glory and to reassert our orientation towards God. *"Father, forgive me if I have started in any way to take your glory and to seek honour from this act. I have given this to you and I know that you have me in the palm of your hand and will bless and reward according to your word. I give this to you as you have given so much to me that I did not reserve. I release any ungodly connection between myself and the recipient and ask that you would reinstate a righteous Kingdom relationship."*

2. The Trap of Judgement - We know that lending makes the borrower like a servant or slave as it is a biblical principle that the borrower is servant to the lender (Proverbs 22:7). An ungodly power dynamic can come into play where we have slid into taking the honour for the gift. If we have fallen away from the godly orientation, then there is no eternal reward and our heart orientation is to receive our reward from the lucky recipient and from those looking on and praising us for our actions. The less anonymity there is the more we have to be on guard against this trap.

Power seems always to come with its evil twin of judgement. Let loose, we can start to analyse or judge the receiver. This can seem very spiritual but the underlying spirit is not Kingdom but power and judgement. Instead of seeing the couple as being blessed by God, we can view them as being "bailed out" by us, after all, "what were they thinking" not to have planned better. Instead of their need being met by a loving God, we can drop hints that we are "helping them through a difficult time" or some other judgemental statement that makes us look powerful and important. God never gives a gift with shame, paternalism, condemnation, or diminution of honour attached.

The more "positive" side of power and paternalism can be that we may start to feel obligations to them which can result in false burden bearing. We may see ourselves as the giver of life to them and that can become a responsibility and weight that God never intended and this can result in resentment. Remember, our orientation has shifted - we are not giving to God now but to the couple - we have usurped God's role. If we are responsible for them, then they are seen to be subservient in some manner and we can start to judge how they got there and what they should be doing. Our sin of taking God's glory can also result in strife as we try to shake off this "dead weight". Instead of dealing in honour and calling forth God's destiny over the couple, it can lead to resentment and moaning. How silly - like the UPS delivery man becoming bitter that the recipients did not like the birthday gift they delivered! Should the couple do something wrong or if we find out that the reason for their need was some kind of mismanagement we can feel used. We are judging, full stop. We are no longer seeking a Kingdom perspective to seek God about what He wants to do. Remember, He is the God who deals justly and generously beyond our imagination. His view of Kingdom finance can pay the workers who work one hour the same as those who work all day (Matt 20)! We have become the elder brother of the Prodigal Son, resenting what the father had done in love. We are judging how they got there, how they are living, and what should be done. If our orientation is kept towards God, then our accountability is to God also. If God has given them a gift, then who are we to judge another man's servant? God can deal with the children He loves.

Welcome a man whose faith is weak, but not with the idea of arguing over his scruples. One man believes that he may eat anything, another man, without this strong conviction, is a vegetarian. The meat-eater should not despise the vegetarian, nor should the vegetarian condemn the meat-eater —they should reflect that God has accepted them both. ***After all, who are you to criticize the servant of somebody else, especially when that somebody else is God?*** *It is to his own master that he gives, or fails to give, satisfactory service. And don't doubt that satisfaction, for God is well able to transform men into servants who are satisfactory. (Romans 14:1-4 Phillips, emphasis added)*

The gratefulness of the receiver is owed to God and the reward of the giver is also from God even if the recipients somehow blow it in their walk with Him - it is not for us to judge. It is for God to deal with His servants and He can transform them in ways that we cannot. We cannot doubt that God is able to deal with the person effectively - he does not need our help!

3. The Trap of the One Eyed Goat - Closely linked to judgement and false burden bearing is a shortfall in our service. Put simply, if Jesus was getting water from you, would it be from the extra set of chipped "disposable" glasses headed for the charity shop or would it be from your best? Would it be a quarter full or overflowing? In Jesus' teaching was there anything left undone by the father of the Prodigal Son or by the Good Samaritan? No, all the needs were met in abundance. In Old Testament vernacular, are we giving Him a defective offering, a one-eyed goat?

> "A son honors his father, and a servant his master. If then I am a Father, where is My honor? And if I am a Master, where is the [reverent] fear due Me? says the Lord of hosts to you, O priests, who despise My name. You say, How and in what way have we despised Your name? By offering polluted food upon My altar. And you ask, How have we polluted it and profaned You? By thinking that the table of the Lord is contemptible and may be despised. When you [priests] offer **blind [animals] for sacrifice, is it not evil**? And when you offer the lame and the sick, is it not evil? Present such a thing [a blind or lame or sick animal] now to your governor [in payment of your taxes, and see what will happen]. Will he be pleased with you? Or will he receive you graciously? says the Lord of hosts. Now then, I [Malachi] beg [you priests], entreat God [earnestly] that He will be gracious to us. With such a gift from your hand [as a **defective** animal for sacrifice], will He accept it or show favor to any of you? says the Lord of hosts. Oh, that there were even one among you [whose duty it is to minister to Me] who would shut the doors, that you might not kindle fire on My altar to no purpose [an empty, futile, fruitless pretense]! I have no pleasure in you, says the Lord of hosts, nor will I accept an offering from your hand. For from the rising of the sun to its setting **My name shall be great among the nations, and in every place incense shall be offered to My name, and indeed a pure offering**; for My name shall be great among the nations, says the Lord of hosts. (Malachi 1:6-11 AMP, emphasis added)

We slip into this trap most easily when we view the giving we are doing as a gift to man and not to God. If we are giving to man then we can judge what is good enough. No natural man will pay workers a full day's wage for one hour but that is what God may ask us to do in His Kingdom.

What is a modern one-eyed goat? This was brought home to me when some ministry friends of ours heard they were being given a new van that they had been praying for. They were so excited - until the van arrived that is. I wont give all the problems with the van, but I would estimate that it would have taken $5,000 to $10,000 to make it roadworthy - bald tires, bad brakes, leaking fluids, broken windows, dirty, and more. It was not roadworthy. The net result was a substantial financial loss and burden on the recipient. When I saw this I immediately nick-named the van the "one-eyed goat". Now I am not saying that every gift must be new and shiny. If you have ever been without a car, even an older useable vehicle is a blessing, but in this case it was really unloading a problem and lacking in honour. It still may have had a small value but much better to have scrapped the van and given the cash to the couple to put towards a serviceable vehicle.

This was brought home to me personally when I bought a new appliance for our home and took the old one and had it refurbished and gave it to a young couple in the church. I think my spirit was right and I was pleased that we could give one that was fully serviced and fit for purpose. However, as I was driving away I drove past the Royal Mint and was thinking of the connection between Royalty and money and Royalty and God and the thought dropped into my spirit that if my giving was really to God maybe He should have gotten the new machine? I had kept the best. I did resolve to address this in my acts of service moving forward as God blessed. Let's rise up to be givers of new machines and new cars! Let's consider this as a call to radical giving! It is great to give a used machine (not a one-eyed goat mind you). It is even better to give a refurbished machine but let's challenge ourselves to move to and be blessed to a point where we can give a new machine! Let's keep our orientation on God and not on man and avoid any one-eyed goats!

4. The Trap of Shortfall - linked to the giving of a one eyed goat is what I would term a shortfall in service or pulling back. We may move forward with a vision in the Spirit but the flesh can take over and we can hold back. Imagine the Good Samaritan who dropped him off at the inn but refused to pay for treatment or accommodation. He has done a good deed and probably saved the man's life, but it was not the example of complete restoration that Jesus was illustrating. It would not be the Kingdom and certainly is not motivated by the principle of love which requires us to treat others as we would like to be treated. With God, cars have wheels, tires, and work; meals are full and include the extras; and service is complete.

I think in many cases our service of giving more closely resembles providing a T shirt to the wounded man, rather than being the Good Samaritan. We give a dinner mint to someone who needs a meal and couple it with some religious verbiage. I did hear a speaker's honorarium given with the statement that: "It is not much but I pray God will multiply it". It was clear God was speaking to the person that the gift should have been bigger. The Bible does speak of blessing the giver 40, 60, and 100 fold, but I have not found a principle of multiplying the deficient gift. As your giving is to God, He does not heal a "one-eyed goat".

God loves cheerfulness, abundance and extravagant giving.

> "... he who gives aid and superintends, with zeal and singleness of mind; he who does acts of mercy, with genuine cheerfulness and joyful eagerness...Contribute to the needs of God's people [sharing in the necessities of the saints]" (Romans 12:8,13 AMPC)

> "Let each one [give] as he has made up his own mind and purposed in his heart, not reluctantly or sorrowfully or under compulsion, for God loves (He takes pleasure in, prizes above other things, and is unwilling to abandon or to do without) a cheerful (joyous, "prompt to do it") giver [whose heart is in his giving]." (II Corinthians 9:7 AMPC)

We want to be radical givers and to be extravagant in our worship as we serve an extravagant God, but let's at least raise up to the challenge we see modelled in Scripture. We have the example of the Good Samaritan and the exhortation in James. Don't just wish someone a good day when we know there is a need or where God speaks to us to do something. In Jesus' example, the Good Samaritan left nothing lacking in his giving, which is the Shalom of the Lord - nothing missing and nothing broken.

If we are buying a meal for someone let it be a full meal. If you have a limited budget, then isn't it better to go to a more modest restaurant and bless someone with a full meal you can afford including dessert and coffee? If you are giving a car, why not make sure it is clean, insured and full of fuel? Wherever there is a tendency to pull back from generosity then push through with more giving, to keep moving in the Spirit. Seek the Lord for what He wants you to do in every circumstance.

We also need to avoid the trap of pulling back because God corrects our attitude. We can take a correction from the Lord as an excuse to pull back. Let's say we have strayed into taking God's glory. God may indeed impress on us that He is the source of supply not us. We must make sure that in repenting for taking God's glory, we do not use this to provide a spiritual cloak for the equally fleshly trap of pulling back. Using our Good Samaritan example, if we have strayed into taking God's glory and He corrects us, that does not mean we stop giving or helping? No, we repent, reorder our heart's alignment and continue to give to meet the need as God directs. In essence, there is a risk that we swing from moving in the flesh to do too much to moving in the flesh to do too little - finding an excuse to justify not doing what God has asked. We must not stop being the courier of what God wanted us to give. This is linked to the next trap.

5. The Trap of Pursing Lips - Closely, linked to the shortfall in service is the judgement that can accompany it.

> *But I am a worm, and no man; I am the scorn of men, and despised by the people. All who see me laugh at me and mock me;* ***they shoot out the lip, they shake the head, saying, He trusted and rolled himself on the Lord, that He would deliver him. Let Him deliver him, seeing that He delights in him!*** *(Psalm 22:6-8 AMPC emphasis added)*

Beware of the pursed lip that uses the truth that God is a person's supply as an excuse to shut off and not give or to back away - to cease to be the courier God intended. To say, in effect, let's see how that works out for them as it is up to God. This is a bit like saying to the man in the ditch that you cannot wait to hear how God rescues him! Like Pilate, we are washing our hands of our role in the outcome not seeking God for his heart and direction.

If God brings correction to you in this area, repent and adjust your heart to be the courier He intended.

6. The Trap of the Caveman - Perhaps drawing from all the other traps listed is not walking in the Spirit and not seeing in the Spirit. We can cease to act in honour and fail to honour the gifts and callings on people's lives. This underlies so much of Scripture, but I will give some key examples. Where we start to walk in the flesh there is a temptation to see in the flesh. David faced this as people were dealing with him in the worldly truth of his situation - in a cave, a wanted man, under threat of death. Was he an outlaw caveman, or was he really God's anointed King with a destiny that resounds through the ages? The spies that told the "truth" were the evil spies as they did not see with the eyes of faith (Numbers 13:32 and 14:37). Was Joseph an accused sex offender in prison, or God's redeemer with a great destiny? Was Jesus a carpenter's son from a place nothing good comes from or the Messiah? I can go on and on as this is a central theme of Scripture and fundamental to the faith walk of Kingdom Finance. Read Hebrews 11 for the annals of faith - those who walked by what the Word said not what the circumstance said. Honouring God means we are dealing with the King in a cave not a caveman.

Where our posture is as God's courier and giver, we are better able to pray for the real destiny over a person and to call forth what God is doing. When we have fallen from this orientation it can be a temptation to judgement, to cease giving, and to see a person as defined by their circumstances and failures not by their calling and anointing.

We can become like Job's friends who addressed him where he appeared to be, not where he was in the spirit - in the end it was only Job's prayers for his friends that restored them.

Traps from the Perspective of the Receiver

I have dealt with these giving traps from the perspective of the giver but the perspective of the receiver is also relevant. How do we deal with the requirement to see God as the provider and how do we deal with givers who may have fallen into one of the traps above?

Many of us are more comfortable being the giver. I think like our biblical examples, many of us with a Kingdom Finance calling have gone or are going through seasons of being receivers. Like David, I am sure that many of you reading this book right now feel like they are in some kind of cave. Will you be a caveman or a king?

The world around you, your family and many even in the church may be pursing their lips and giving a bad report. They may be seeing things as they are with the natural mind and justifying their approach with the use of terms such as "being realistic" or giving some "home truths". Like the bad report of the spies, they are calling out the facts on the ground not necessarily seeing with the eyes of the Spirit and calling forth words of anointing and destiny.

Having concluded the past and keeping short accounts, our Heavenly status as a king with a calling should be kept in the forefront of our minds and in our prayers and declarations. We must not come into agreement with those that may see us as cavemen because of our situation.

Another picture that may help is to think of yourself like a cork. We have the blessing and the specific words of destiny for our lives but sin, attack, or other factors may have pushed us underwater like a cork. But what is the reality? The reality is that as soon as these hindrances are broken and cut off the cork will shoot up! It works the same way with the word of God over your life when you are in a "cave". The word and the blessing in operation means that the cave cannot hold you. Your new spiritual nature is buoyant. You are going to rise up because the word of God over your life is the greater truth.

Like other heroes of faith in Hebrews 11 their faith was in the word of God over their life not the circumstances. When someone says, "what do you mean you are blessed you're short of funds and struggling", you can see yourself as a cork about to shoot up because God is dealing with the cords tying you down.

This is why we can be content in any state we find ourselves (Phillipians 4:11). We know that God's promises are sure and that the blessing is working for us. I can be content and not strive even if I am in a cave as I know that God will honour His word. I am a cork, my nature in the spirit is buoyant and the truth of His word and blessing will overcome the facts that I am facing.

Giving to Believers

> *But if anyone has this world's goods (resources for sustaining life) and sees his brother and fellow believer in need, yet closes his heart of compassion against him, how can the love of God live and remain in him? (1 John 3:17 AMPC, notation removed)*

I wanted to spend some time dealing with some of the areas where we need to greatly improve and grow in the Body of Christ. The general calling to give to the poor and oppressed is imperative and we should do more not less. However, some of our dialogue in this area has become tainted. We have created a category of "the Poor" which instead of being a trigger to action has become a block. What I mean is that when we think of the poor we should automatically think of giving, BUT we should not use this to limit our giving. We must not limit ourselves to giving to the poor. We must be ready to give and to be prepared to give to need or where God directs. The Bible speaks of being a father to the poor and needy but also speaks of **seeking out or searching out** the cause of those we do not know (Job 29:16).

How many people who may not meet our definition of "the poor" have been sitting in church with a great financial need wondering why this was not being met? Financial needs or a shortage of cash flow can affect people from time to time and we need to be alert to this as believers. Indeed, if we are on a journey of Kingdom Finance there may be times of battle and attack. Who is to be standing with you during these times of trial and attack? It is a call on the Body of Christ to stand with you in prayer but also practically.

How many are also praying for the release of funds for the destiny vision that God has placed on their heart? Jesus was born into His vision on the earth but it was the wise men who came bearing the provision needed for His survival in Egypt, including gifts of gold. Nehemiah's vision for the restoration of Jerusalem was met with the provision of a king. Where are the destiny helpers - - our "kings" and "wise men" -- who have seen the times and seasons and come bearing provision?

In some ways we have forgotten our calling to be searching out those with a need - to be using our spiritual gifts to be sensitive to the Spirit who wants to meet the needs of His people. The key Scripture for this is II Corinthians 8:14-15 which deals with sharing in the church.

> *But to have equality [share and share alike], your surplus over necessity at the present time going to meet their want and to equalize the difference created by it, so that [at some other time] their surplus in turn may be given to supply your want. Thus there may be equality, As it is written, He who gathered much had nothing over, and he who gathered little did not lack. (AMPC)*

Remember that our giving is to God and our blessing in relation to giving is from God. The principle at work is that a church that is mobilised in giving will be alive to the Spirit to see and to meet the needs of those who have a need. The principle at work is that believers who are givers will be alive to the Spirit to see the needs of those who have a need. The same mobilised group of givers will then be in a position to meet the needs of the givers who later have needs. Do you catch the vision of this call on the Body of Christ? Not just to meet the needs of the poor and disenfranchised, (as important as this is and let's do much more in this space), but also for there to be an anointing and resource where believers are caught short, are under attack, or have a destiny and calling that needs to be funded.

I remember a time where cash flow became very short for a number of reasons including outright attack of the enemy. I was not stripped to the point where people would classify me as "the poor", but I was facing some real issues and was in great distress and crying out to the Lord. I really went to the Lord about this Scripture as I had given and supported other people through various lean seasons they encountered. I sought God about where the equality was as now I was in my season where I needed another Christian in surplus to supply my needs! I did receive an answer but not in the manner I expected. I left an important business meeting and everyone jumped into their waiting cars or taxis and I made my excuses and began a long walk home in order to save money. To be honest, I was on the verge of bitterness about why I had met similar needs for others yet here I was walking. This triggered one of the most life changing visions I have ever had - it was real and vivid with great detail. First, I was taken in the spirit to Africa and I saw a young black boy gasping slowly looking at me and then dying. I knew in my spirit that as he died he could not believe that no one was there to love him and feed him. Perhaps I was shielded but it felt like I was experiencing his pain. Before I could wipe away my tears I was taken into a filthy brothel where a young girl was looking up in the middle of being defiled and I knew in the spirit, her despair and disbelief that she was there and that no one cared enough about her to rescue her. It was as if she was saying, "I cannot believe that no one has come to rescue me?" Immediately the voice of the Lord spoke to me and said that the child died and the girl is still in the brothel today because people I have spoken to to feed the boy and rescue the girl have not been obedient "AND YOU are walking today because people I have spoken to to meet your need have not been obedient". I was then shown as in a portrait gallery, the faces of several people He had spoken to about meeting my need so that I could forgive and bless them. I was truly shaken and humbled by this and also repentant for complaining about my needs when the gravity of the needs around me were so great. Even writing this now the memory of the heart of God and the pain of unmet needs is almost overwhelming. **Never** accept that God is holding out or holding back on you. We are called to be His hands and His feet in this world.

There are two great lessons from this vision. First, we are naive to think that there are no consequences for our sin. If we bless others and in turn are blessed this is a great result, but the principle works in reverse also. If we are not obedient in our life of giving others will suffer. If others are disobedient when we have a need, it is also true that we will suffer. Now God is working to make a way and He can do great things but we must not be deceived into putting onto God the responsibility that is ours. We must take personal responsibility to live the giving life that Jesus ordained for us to walk in.

> **Never accept that God is holding out or holding back on you. We are called to be His hands and His feet in this world.**

I think the second teaching from this vision is that God is very practical. If someone is on our heart and mind we must move in the Spirit to determine what our action should be. I believe that most times when you are thinking about someone or praying about someone, that God has brought this person before your mind for a reason. If this is true, then the question we must ask is what does God want and how can we bless them? I think our default position should be that God wants to give them a word or a practical blessing. After all God is the great giver and if we are in Him and abiding we cannot deal with people without giving. Instead, we process it in our mind and analyse the situation. Let's use an example of a friend in the church that is doing well as far as we know. God brings this person to your mind and we will track the two responses:

1. Fleshly response - we know that they probably have a bigger house than us and a fairly new car too - as a result, we have eliminated them as a giving recipient as they are not "the poor". We pray a blessing on them and perhaps next time we see them we tell them that they were on our mind the other day and we were praying for them.

2. Spirit-led response - we know that they probably have a bigger house than us and a fairly new car too - however, we know that God is practical and loves to bless. We quiet down our minds and tune into the Spirit and inquire of God what He would have us do? We approach this with the default position that God has brought them to mind to give to them in some manner. At this point we may feel to give them a word, pray for protection, or to give financially. Never be ashamed or afraid to give to a "rich" person - remember it is not you giving to them in any event as you are giving to God. I have had this happen on a few occasions and it was a real blessing. Indeed, it has also happened to me. When I was praying about writing this book I had someone give me 20 pounds. They were quite embarrassed and apologised but said that they really felt impressed to sow into the vision of the book. I was so encouraged as this was a real confirmation for me about the book. It is not up to us to judge the need or lack of need of the recipient. David gave extravagantly to Solomon which enabled the construction of the temple. We must break out of the worldly constraints and mindsets. Remember the vision of the faces God has spoken to to give to me? I am sure they had gone through the analysis much as above and their lack of obedience resulted in difficulty for me. Likewise I have had to repent for not responding to similar prompts on occasion also.

Let us be quick to adjust our default measure to that of giving. If you are thinking about someone, then ask: "How does God want to bless them?"

Later in the same teaching Paul says that:

> *And [God] Who provides seed for the sower and bread for eating will also provide and multiply your [resources for] sowing and increase the fruits of your righteousness [which manifests itself in active goodness, kindness, and charity]. Thus you will be enriched in all things and in every way, so that you can be generous, and [your generosity ... will bring forth thanksgiving to God.* (2 Corinthians 9:10-11 AMPC)

God has promised to provide seed to the sower as well as bread for eating. We need to activate this flow principle in our lives so that we are meeting other people's needs as God directs and by doing this with generosity we will activate two key giving flows:

1. **EQUALITY FLOW**- According to II Corinthians 8:14 if we give there will be a flow back to us should we have need of it in the future. This is the principle that should be operating in the Body of Christ. There is no equality or justice if we have met the needs of others in the Body of Christ and then our needs are not met in the same manner.

2. **FLOW OF INCREASE**- If I am a sower, then according to 2 Corinthians 9:10-11, I will also be given my bread for eating and my resources for sowing will be **increased** along with increasing the fruits of righteousness.

These principles also give us our key link to bearing godly fruit from our giving as He will definitely know us when we are being led by the Spirit in our giving. This is the model for abundant living and giving in love.

Radical Giving - The Special Anointing or Calling to Give

I think it already is a radical change to move our life's default from the fleshly setting of not giving to the Spirit default of giving. Put your own name in the blank:

For _____ so loved the world that (s)he gave.

Think about the needs of the world around us that God may be speaking to you about: bondages to be broken, captives rescued and released, families housed, the poor fed, good news proclaimed, etc. There are movies to be funded, rescue homes to be built, houses of prayer to be launched, Israel to be blessed, and the end times ministry of the church to be funded. I also know God is speaking to people to replace believers that were disobedient. Remembering my vision: Is God calling you to rescue the babies that are dying of starvation? Is he speaking to you to get the girl out of the brothel? I wonder if she is still there?

To do the things that need to be done to destroy the works of satan, our giving must rise past our own needs and the needs of our families. We must be established as prodigal sons and daughters restored, to the next level of being a Good Samaritan continually so that we can move to impacting our cities and cultures. Our giving must move from 10s and 100s, to the thousands and tens of thousands, hundreds of thousands, millions and beyond. Our giving must become radical.

The model should not be that those with money are being sought out and honoured by ministries, but radical giving by anointed men and women who have heard the voice of God and are connected to His giving heart.

I believe that God is raising up a generation of radical set apart called Nazarite givers. Nazarites of old were set apart like Samson for a specific purpose - they shifted cultures at pivotal times. John the Baptist prepared the way for Jesus. In like manner, people called to be Kingdom financiers and funders are those who are willing to challenge and change the existing status quo. They are willing to be conduits for His flow of funds and they understand that they cannot touch His glory in this process. It is not about us, radical giving is all about Him.

> **Nazarite Givers - I believe that God is raising up a generation of radical set apart called givers.**

When God first started speaking to me about Kingdom Finance and radical giving, I had a vision of conduits going to ministries and needs like pipes bringing water to plants. The needs or ministries we want to give to are like the plants and the conduits bringing the water are like the money flow. We are part of the mechanism for flow but in a sense we are just holding up the pipe and the size of the pipe is up to the Lord. Like the "delivery man" example, the attention is not on the support or the pipes but on the results.

I was praying about businesses and projects one day with the mindset that profits from these projects could go to various ministries. This was the business model I started out with - me owning businesses and then giving from the fruit to the needs. My mindset had been that when the businesses were profitable, then I could look for the various needs to give to. God really challenged me and I had to reorder my thinking. My focus was on the businesses and what roles I could have and not on the needs and ministries. God reminded me that He provides seed to the sower. God reminded me that I had not sown to these ministries so on what basis could I have faith that He would provide seed? Only a sower can truly have genuine faith for finances. I had to repent for rushing ahead, reorder my thinking and restructure my business approach.

First, I looked at what I was involved in and identified the projects that I did not feel were God ordained. Some I felt a strong leading to exit from fully. There were some surprised parties when shares were given back. Although there were some processes to walk through to exit from these ventures it was worth doing.

> **Only a sower can truly have genuine faith for finances.**

I then started praying about what He wanted me to give to - what ministries I should be connected to. Remember, this process happened before I had big money to give! The alignment had to be made first and when it did amazing things began to happen. There were divine encounters to various ministries and people that God began to connect me to. I had reoriented my approach so my face became ministry focussed not business focussed. I was looking at the plants that the conduits were going to feed even before the full flow of water (money) was put in the pipe! I then formally seeded the conduit for that ministry by giving usually a piece of silver or gold or a small amount of money. Like a first-fruits offering, this was done formally to bring into existence in the spiritual realm that I was now a sower in relation to that ministry. Think of the framed bills that you see sometimes in a business, usually the first note they received when they opened their doors. God had set up the connections and calling and I could now believe and pray in faith for God to release funds to me as a sower to bless them according to His word.

We are in a paradigm shift and realignment moving to new models of giving. We do not curse the old models, let them continue and increase, but God is establishing His purposes - He is calling Kingdom driven, anointed men and women who will do what He asks them to do and say what He asked them to say. Kingdom giving Nazarites that shift cultures, break dominions and destroy the works of satan.

Help, Lord! For principled and godly people are here no more; faithfulness and the faithful vanish from among the sons of men. To his neighbor each one speaks words without use or worth or truth; with flattering lips and double heart [deceitfully] they speak. May the Lord cut off all flattering lips and the tongues that speak proud boasting, Those who say, With our tongues we prevail; our lips are our own [to command at our will]—who is lord and master over us?

Now will I arise, says the Lord, because the poor are oppressed, because of the groans of the needy; I will set him in safety and in the salvation for which he pants. The words and promises of the Lord are pure words, like silver refined in an earthen furnace, purified seven times over. You will keep them and preserve them, O Lord; You will guard and keep us from this [evil] generation forever. The wicked walk or prowl about on every side, as vileness is exalted [and baseness is rated high] among the sons of men. (Psalm 12 AMPC emphasis added and notations removed)

Chapter 17

Offence

Perhaps more than any other area in our lives, offence can hold us back in our journey with the Lord. This is particularly relevant in the area of the release of finance for Kingdom purposes. Why is the area of offence so important for us as Christians and particularly for Kingdom Finance?

Before we can unpack the reasons we need to understand what offence means in this context. "Offence" has been defined as annoyance or resentment brought about by a perceived insult to or disregard for oneself.[i] This definition is only a starting point to understanding offence from a Kingdom perspective, as to be insulted or disregarded requires the *action of another person*. Offence requires a relationship. It implies that there is a third party "offender" acting in some "offensive" manner towards us that results in offence. The *offender* does the *offensive action* that may cause us an injury, but that injury results in us taking up an ungodly response we label *"offence"*, making it all a bit confusing. Further complicating matters, some actions taken against us are also labelled as offences under various laws or rules of conduct.

To bring some clarity it is helpful to break it down: we need an offender (the third party) who does something that is in some manner against our interests (the offending action or the offence) and results in us responding either in a godly manner or in a manner that results in us being offended (our reaction in either "taking offence" or not).

There are a range of actions that could come into play including:

- **Clear Offences** - these could be assaults or insults, the clearest examples of which may also be criminal offences.

- **Mixed Offences** - a clear slight or action taken against us, but where there may be some justification or fault on our part. An example of this could be someone who says that a person is "useless" or an "idiot" when a mistake is made.

- **Accidental Offences** - someone does or says something against us that is wrong but unintended. An example would be the inadvertent omission from a circulation list on an important email. This mistake could be easily remedied, but I have seen people take great umbrage and offence and come out with strongly worded attacks. A person taking offence in this scenario is in many cases described as prickly, difficult to deal with, and impossible to please.

- **Perceived Offences** - this category is very closely linked to accidental offences, however in this case, there is an offence taken when no action was intended, and perhaps when no action has been taken at all. An example may be a person who is suffering from deep wounds of rejection or other issues who takes offence at the slightest perceived insult. One example happened in a meeting I was attending. A colleague who was reportedly touchy and hard to please, stormed out of a meeting saying, "I'm no fool, I can see what is going on here!" There was an interesting discussion afterwards as it was clear that no one had any idea what the issue had been, and indeed someone was tasked with trying to find out! Clearly, he was acting in reaction to a perceived offence.

Offences are Wrong

First, let's deal with what is probably a bigger issue in the Body of Christ, as we tend to put the weight of dealing with the offence on the victim. Being an offender is always wrong as it is contrary to the law of love. If we commit an offence or sin against another person, we need to repent and ask for forgiveness. Let's get this basic truth firmly established - we should not sin against others, and when we do we should repent and ask for forgiveness to ensure there is no hindrance in our walk with the Lord. Forgive us for our trespasses (or sins) as we forgive those who trespass (or sin) against us is a key part of the Lord's Prayer.

Too often in the Church people put on the cloak of religion where they 100% believe that **you** should be walking in forgiveness towards **their** bad actions, without dealing with or being aware of their own bad actions. Expecting forgiveness almost becomes a licence to continue acting in an offending manner. I have seen this pattern in some Christian circles and organisations. Instead of operating in a manner that is an example to the world, they fall far below basic standards that are even expected in the secular world. I have seen people who have had their contracts varied with no regard for proper process and even a case where a person's employment was terminated by fax! In another case, a business owner who had lost large sums of investors' money through mismanagement, was acting as if he was a victim by complaining that the investors were obligated to forgive him.

I am convinced that there was a belief by these people that their Christian environment meant that they should have been forgiven, and that the challenge to their bad behaviour was somehow wrong and unexpected. They judge you for the splinter in your eye while being oblivious to the large beam of wood in their own!

> *Why do you stare from without at the very small particle that is in your brother's eye but do not become aware of and consider the beam of timber that is in your own eye? Or how can you say to your brother, Let me get the tiny particle out of your eye, when there is the beam of timber in your own eye? You hypocrite, first get the beam of timber out of your own eye, and then you will see clearly to take the tiny particle out of your brother's eye.* (Matthew 7:3-5 AMP, parenthesis and notations removed)

Our character as it relates to others is to be governed by love - love your neighbour as yourself (Matthew 22:39). If we are walking in love then we are not continually bullying, attacking, and judging others. We should be extra careful to protect and honour those we are dealing with. Our standard of operating should be a model for the world to study. We must press into Christ, letting the same mind be in us that was in Jesus:

> *If there be therefore any consolation in Christ, if any comfort of love, if any fellowship of the Spirit, if any bowels and mercies, Fulfill ye my joy, that ye be likeminded, having the same love, being of one accord, of one mind. Let nothing be done through strife or vainglory; but in lowliness of mind let each esteem other better than themselves.*
>
> *Look not every man on his own things, but every man also on the things of others.*
>
> **Let this mind be in you, which was also in Christ Jesus:** *(Philippians 2:1-5 KJV, emphasis added)*

When this Spirit of Love is not in operation we are open to the worst form of religious bullying. People can act in an aggressive or ungodly manner - their "beam in the eye" - and are quite shocked that someone would draw attention to their bad behaviour. They are blind to their own actions.

For example, when Jesus spoke to the Pharisees who complained about the actions of Jesus' disciples, they were shocked that He viewed their actions as being evil. They were blinded to the offensiveness of their own actions. I liken this to a bully who, every day for a week, steps on someone's foot. He is blind or has grown to ignore his own bullying behaviour. Finally, on the seventh day the person with the sore foot pushes back and says, "Stop standing on my foot!" The offender is surprised and taken aback, offended by the reaction. Because of his blindness, he does not see it as a reaction, but as a new action. He says, "Whoa, what's up with you pushing me?!" In essence, the Pharisees were saying that religion demands you cannot take offence, therefore you must put up with my offending! They are blind to their actions and view the response of the "victim" as being offensive!

We may have become used to our ungodly manner of dealing and need to press in to have the mind of Christ in how we live and deal with others. It is not acceptable to minimise our actions by common excuses such as, "It's just his way", or "It's my [name the nationality] temper". As noted earlier, we have all heard the curse that the "apple doesn't fall far from the tree", or "blood will tell", to explain how someone's bad behaviour is passed down in the family. These curses are broken and we can be free, because we are new plantings grafted into the tree of the Spirit. As we abide in the vine, we will be changed (John 15:4). However, we must be willing to address a manner of living and dealing with others that may be wrong and to which we may be unaware.

Dealing with Offenders

Dealing with the actions of an offender is not acting in offence. Abiding in Him and walking in love enables us to establish godly boundaries and those will enable us to stop people "standing on our feet". Avoiding offence does not mean that we act as if there has been no wrong done. It is a false peace to **pretend** that the wrong actions of someone did not occur. If someone is lashing out in a physical or verbal manner, forgiveness and not walking in offence does not mean we have to stay in such a dangerous place or ignore offensive behaviour. If someone has behaved wrongly, then dealing with it in love is not wrong.

This is best summed up in a quote from the movie *The Outlaw Josey Wales* where the character who is being manipulated and lied to says:

> "And there's another old saying, senator. Don't piss down my back and tell me it's raining."[ii]

People acting in this manner are really asking you not to respond to their bad actions and not to point them out - in worldly terms, this is blaming the victim. It is a perverse reaction, when an offender, blinded to their own offending actions, becomes offended by the reactions of the victims. This is double-offending and this is rife in our victim-defined society. The courtrooms are full of people who may be remorseful at being caught, but many are angry at the victims that turned them in or testified against them. This is not how we are to operate in Christ.

I remember a time that I met with a former client at a function who was unfriendly and curt with me. I was with a colleague who could not believe how rudely I was treated by this man, as he also knew that the man owed the firm I worked for a very large sum of money. I explained to him why I thought he was acting this way. Emotionally, he saw me as offending his constructed view of himself as a "successful mover and shaker". To him, I was an embarrassing reminder that he was not the person he portrayed himself to be. He was operating from an identity that was not secure but was constructed from what the world would consider to be success. In many cases the presence of the "victim" is disconcerting to offenders who have not dealt with the underlying issues in their lives.

This can even be enhanced where the offender is clothed with religion or self-righteousness. In these cases the presence of a person they have offended gives rise to a high level of discord and emotion. Look at the Pharisees as our example. Successful in their world-view as the movers and shakers of their day, but the presence of Jesus speaking the truth deeply offended and upset them. They came trying to trick him up and left offended and trying to kill him - yet He was perfect love, without sin, and did them no wrong.

Have we also acted in an ungodly manner and reacted badly when offences are brought to our attention? Let us determine to let the mind of Jesus be in us, to walk in love, not to offend people, and if we do, to be quick to repent and get on the right track.

> *So be subject to God. Resist the devil [stand firm against him], and he will flee from you. Come close to God and He will come close to you. [Recognize that you are] sinners, get your soiled hands clean; [realize that you have been disloyal] wavering individuals with divided interests, and purify your hearts [of your spiritual adultery]. [As you draw near to God] be deeply penitent and grieve, even weep [over your disloyalty]. Let your laughter be turned to grief and your mirth to dejection and heartfelt shame [for your sins]. Humble yourselves [feeling very insignificant] in the presence of the Lord, and He will exalt you [He will lift you up and make your lives significant]. (James 4:7-10 AMPC)*

The Field of Pain

Most of us know the famous prayer of Jabez:

> *And Jabez called on the God of Israel saying, "Oh, that You would bless me indeed, and enlarge my **territory**, that Your hand would be with me, and that You would keep me from evil, that I may not cause **pain**!" So God granted him what he requested. (1 Chron. 4:10 NKJV, emphasis added)*

There is a key truth hidden in this prayer that relates to our journey and relationships and how we must set boundaries with an offender. We each have a territory or field of influence in our lives that if we are godly, like Jabez, we are seeking to expand.

Jabez prayed that in his territory or field he would be kept from evil so that **he** would not cause pain. Applying this to ourselves, we are to have our field of influence and to live and operate in a manner that does not cause pain to others. Therefore, our first priority is not to offend.

Put another way, if we are not operating in a godly manner, we will cause pain. Given that more people seem to operate in an ungodly manner than in a godly manner, to the extent we are in their orbit or territory we are impacted, and this impact is what I refer to as the "field of pain".

> *The truly happy person*
> *doesn't follow wicked advice,*
> *doesn't stand on the road of sinners,*
> *and doesn't sit with the disrespectful. (Psalm 1:1 CEV)*

We don't stand in the road of the offender or sit with them. We need to stay out of their field of pain. If we are in their "orbit", we will have pain. This lesson has been costly to learn for those of us who have been let down by our Christian colleagues. We must separate ourselves from those who are offenders so that we are happy and not harmed. This is a godly boundary.

We have a saying in business that: "you cannot do good business with bad people". This is true, and we must limit the interaction with those who operate in sin, as the law of the Prayer of Jabez will hold true - we must avoid their field of pain.

Why is the field of pain relevant for us today? How many of us have had pain caused in their lives by parents, siblings, relationship partners, business colleagues, and friends? We are in their field of pain, and it can be a hard place to exist in, let alone flourish. Make no mistake, the prayer of Jabez makes clear that we cause pain to those in our territory if we are not living our lives in righteousness before God.

Pride Deceives

"The pride in your heart has deceived you..." (Obadiah 1:3 NKJV)

If we are not living in Christ and abiding in the vine, realising our true identity, then this verse is true. Our constructed identity of offence results in a strong deception caused by pride. Deception needs to be broken so that we can be changed by Jesus to become the people He intends us to be.

David is an example of this field of pain in operation as he had Uriah put to the battle-front to die to cover his sexual failure. He lived for a year in blindness, and it took a godly confrontation from the prophet Nathan (II Samuel 12) to shock him out of it so that he could deal with his sin issues and move on with his destiny. Uriah dies in David's field of pain.

In John 8:43, Jesus confronted the Pharisees and declared that they were blinded:

Why do you misunderstand what I say? It is because you are unable to hear what I am saying. [You cannot bear to listen to My message; your ears are shut to My teaching.] (AMPC)

Even dealing and interacting with Jesus directly did not break the blindness of their constructed religious personality. We must break open any element of this strong bondage in our lives so that we can be free to see what God wants us to see and to be who He wants us to be.

Prayer: "Father, search our hearts and see if there be any wicked way in us. Reveal this to us and break open any blindness in our eyes to see this. Help us to see and repent for our trespasses, and forgive us our trespasses as we forgive those who trespass against us. Help us to walk in love and have the mind of Jesus in our attitudes and actions. As we deal with offences in our lives, please forgive us for all our sins."

I would encourage you to pray this prayer and to allow the Holy Spirit to reveal to you areas and strongholds. For some this will not be a one-off prayer point but a process of concluding the past as we have discussed earlier.

Crooked Dealing

We must avoid offending by crooked dealings. "Crooked" is defined as:

Bent or twisted out of shape or out of place. Dishonest; illegal.[iii]

In common usage the standard seems to be "illegal", but in order to carry the fragrance of Heaven and be anointed, our dealings need to rise to a higher standard. Crooked or sharp dealings should not be named in the Kingdom.

Imagine a business-person looking to do a deal who sees a chance to move forward if they do not share the deal with their partner. Perhaps this person has not finalised their partnership agreement, but there is a clear moral expectation. The business-person keeps it quiet to avoid issues, but convinces themselves all is OK because they are not strictly legally bound as the contract has not yet been signed. One day, faced with an issue like this, I called some examples like this "crooked dealing" and people were shocked. The abundance of their heart has revealed their position. Our standards must be higher since our leader is Jesus and our advisor and counsellor is the Holy Spirit. God hates false measures, transactions, and deals that are not straight.

Taking Offence - Pierced but Not Wounded

Second to giving offence by a very long way is the problem of being offended or taking offence. When we take or hold onto offence, we reveal the facade of our flesh we have built. We show the lack of true, godly love in our lives. In Christ, we are seated with Him in Heavenly places (Ephesians 2) and are to call for His Kingdom to come daily. If we are with Him in this way, then the insults and offences thrown at us would have no impact at all.

In contrast, the worldly man without Christ walks in offence all the time, defending his constructed vulnerable identity, resulting in anger and violence. In this way, offence manifests in us to the extent that we have not surrendered our life to Christ. Offence becomes an instrument to measure how much we abide in Jesus - if offence rises up when we are attacked, it indicates we need to press in closer to Jesus.

> *"Yes, I am the vine; you are the branches. Those who remain in me, and I in them, will produce much fruit. For apart from me you can do nothing. ..I have loved you even as the Father has loved me. Remain in my love. 10 When you obey my commandments, you remain in my love, just as I obey my Father's commandments and remain in his love. 11 I have told you these things so that you will be filled with my joy. Yes, your joy will overflow! 12 This is my commandment: Love each other in the same way I have loved you. ...17 This is my command: Love each other.* **If the world hates you, remember that it hated me first.** *19 The world would love you as one of its own if you belonged to it, but you are no longer part of the world. I chose you to come out of the world, so it hates you. 20 Do you remember what I told you? 'A slave is not greater than the master.' Since they persecuted me, naturally they will persecute you. (John 15:5, 10-12, 17 -20 NLT, emphasis added)*

Have we built up ungodly walls to protect us, or even worse a fabricated worldly persona that we defend? Who are you? How do you want to be perceived? Why does it matter to you? Are you the suited and booted businessman adding this year's must-have accessory to your life and searing your conscience to issues of the day? Chasing "the dream" through destroyed relationships and pain but "looking good", while people you should care about suffer in your field of pain. Are you the rebel without a cause thumbing your nose at the system? Perhaps you are a teenager trying to find your identity through a constructed online image.

While the fruit of offence plays out in family feuds, tribal clashes, and wars, its root is deeply personal. It is a reaction to an attack or perceived attack against the identity of the person or group. To the extent we operate in offence, we are defending a vision of ourselves that may not be surrendered to and abiding in Christ. If our identity is founded on and abiding in Christ, then our mind is as the mind of Christ, operating in love. Actions of others against us cannot endanger our identity. "Like water off a duck's back", would describe how the actions of another against us should roll away. That does not imply a "rollover" or victim mentality. If you read the words and see the actions of Jesus, you will see that He had much to say to people about their actions and motivations, but he did not act out of offence but out of strength. It is not wrong to challenge the offender's actions or move to a safe distance outside their field of pain!

The key is that Jesus was not defending His identity as Messiah when He challenged wrongdoers, he was dealing with the person's issues. Likewise, we are spiritually seated in Heavenly places in Christ Jesus - that is who we are and the orientation from which we operate.

Just as a thermometer shows that we have a fever, so offence rising up in us when someone acts badly towards us shows us that we need to walk more closely with Jesus and abide in the vine (John 15:4).

I Have a Plane to Catch

Our reaction to any offence should flow from this positional truth of our identity and place with Jesus - seated with Him in Heavenly places (Ephesians 2:6). We are far above all the disputes and defilements that the world wants to drag us into. Avoid them and walk in love.

The Psalms are a great picture of the working out of attacks against David. David still was pierced and hurt by these attacks. He cried out to God: "How long", "Deliver me", and "Let not my enemies triumph over me". In the end of these Psalms he almost always spoke out his true identity, that God was his provider and deliverer, and that God would cause him to triumph. He may have been in a cave under attack by others, but his identity was confirmed as God's anointed. **He was not a caveman but a king in a cave.**

So I am not saying that there will not be painful, piercing attacks. What I am saying is that you can be pierced but not wounded, that you can live in your position in Christ and in your destiny and not be conformed to the attack.

> ...as much as I would love to stay and fling poo, I have a plane to catch to my destiny. Don't stop at the place of attack and take on wounding such that you miss the flight to your destiny.

I use our picture of an outhouse to help me with this. When someone attacks you, they do it from this place of ungodly defilement - they are figuratively down in the hole "flinging poo" like a monkey in a cage. My response is that as much as I would love to stay and fight, I have a plane to catch toward my destiny. **Don't stop at the place of attack and take on wounding such that you miss the flight to your destiny.** I do not want to climb into their mess and fight it out with them. If the enemy's plan is to delay and derail you in your destiny calling, what better way than for you to be locked in a defiling dispute? Forgive, repent for your own part even if small, and move on toward your calling.

Being Offended at God

I was praying one day and God spoke to me that one of the key things holding people back was that they were offended at God. They were offended at Him because of things that had happened or not happened. They were offended because they attributed to God the actions of the enemy, and the fruit of their own sin.

We must reassert and settle in our minds and hearts that God is good all the time. His nature is shown by Jesus when He described the Prodigal Son's father. It is God's will for us to dwell on earth "as it is in Heaven". The shortfall is due to the enemy and our actions, not His. He is blameless.

We were under the sentence of death and under the curse for our sins. Only through the blood of Jesus can this be dealt with and can we live in blessing. As we appropriate the Kingdom in our lives daily we must respond to attacks and to any element of the curse as being rooted in the enemy, not somehow an act of God. The enemy is the author of sin, sickness and death. If I step off the roof, God has a law that operates - gravity - that will strike me down. If I drive a nail through my foot, I will have pain and consequences. If there is a genetic fault that causes illness, it is the work of sickness in our generational line. For this, God is the healer not the cause and He wants us to be blessed. If there is lack and shortfall in our lives and family line, this is the work of the enemy who wants us enslaved and the curse in operation. At the same time God is working to bring us into the land of promise for our lives.

This truth is beautifully recorded in the prayer of Daniel for generational sin, discussed earlier.[iv] Daniel's reaffirmation of the goodness and righteousness of God is critical to his release. As you read it, Daniel is in a position of exile with his people and under ungodly domination. He has been harassed, sentenced to death, and put in a lion's den, but God delivered him. Can you detect any offence towards God in his prayer? There is none - Daniel continually asserts that God is righteous and blameless.

Remember that God put in place these spiritual laws of blessing and cursing. Like the law of gravity, if you violate these laws, the result is certain. However, God loved His people and made a way through for people; even in Daniel's time, there was abundant forgiveness for sin. How much more under our better covenant can we confess our sins and be cleansed totally by the blood of Jesus? The curse that should be poured out on us - that we rightly deserve - has been poured out on Jesus (Galatians 3:13).

If we are offended at God because of sickness, shortfall, or lack of funds we must acknowledge that this is a sin. He is not the author of any of these things and is continually seeking to bless us. We must repent for our false accusation and offence against God, come out of agreement with satan, who is offended at God, and ask for forgiveness. Like Daniel, we must assert that God is the God of blessing and that He is causing us to triumph.

Many Christians have simply adopted the religious mindset that exists in the world and in much of the church. This perception is that God is in Heaven relatively unmoved by our struggles and trials, but He looks over Heaven's parapet every once in a while to see a heroic act of faith and moves on that person's behalf. This idea seems to be modelled after the classical deities of old who meddled in the affairs of mankind. We have made Him to be like Zeus - capricious and unmoved by mere humans, toying with us and giving some a blessing and others a nasty outcome. In this manner, people reduce their conception of God to being an unreal force like karma, luck, or fate. This mindset sees healing is a lottery for the lucky or those who through their efforts have pressed in more. Indeed this kind of mercurial god can even inflict pain and hardship. The fact that healing seems to be less widespread can be used by people to support these views rather than seeing this belief system as part of the reason God's will and purposes in our lives may be hindered. It is almost completely opposed to the view of God as our father who loves us and goes running when he sees us coming home broken and ashamed. Blaming God also allows us to avoid looking critically at our lives, finding the problems, and pressing into His will for us to be victorious overcomers.

This attribution to God of the works of the enemy is also evidence that we do not really believe in Him. The reality is that He is the lover of our souls, our names are tattooed on his hands (Isaiah 49:16) and He sent His only son to die for us to save us (John 3:16). This salvation includes not just forgiveness from sin and eternal life but the power to live a life of victory now. There is a battle with spiritual forces and wickedness to stop this (Ephesians 6:12) being fully manifested in our lives. We do not want to give any credit to the enemy, but to the extent we do not give credence to the reality of this battle and the work of the enemy, we are living with offence towards God and do not believe in His true nature. He is not the source of this battle and the bad things that have happened. He is our deliverer and protector, our shield and fortress (Ps 91).

So let's get the picture straight. We have a God who loves us and has provided everything for us (John 3:16). We are seated with Him in Heavenly places in Christ Jesus (Ephesians 1-2) so our spirits are perfect in Him. Our mind, will, emotions, and body are still in this world, and we need to see them transformed (Romans 12:2), praying daily that His will be done and His Kingdom come (Matt 6:10). There is an enemy (1 Peter 5:8), and we are in a battle with his forces (Ephesians 6:12). This battle in the spiritual realm is real. Elisha's servant had his eyes opened to see the spiritual forces battling around the man of God (2 Kings 6:17). One of the biggest hindrances to the Church is our offence against God by attributing to Him the works of the enemy and thereby minimising the true nature of the spiritual battle.

Prayer: *Father, we have sinned against You by not believing in Your true nature and for blaming You for things that have happened or not* *happened to us. We recognise that in You there is no shadow of turning and that You are righteous and just all the time. We may not fully understand it, but these things were caused by our actions and the enemy's work in our life and generations. You did not cause this, but we did by not walking according to your plan of blessing. We are sorry and we repent and ask You to forgive us for blaming and being offended at You. Please cleanse us from this worldly twisted mindset that attributes evil to You and establish a right mind in us and a right alignment to you as our Father.*

Godly Confrontation

I am confident that we have all been offended against and we have all operated from a life that has not surrendered fully to Jesus. At time we have also offended others. Repenting and putting this behind us, how do we now live? Jesus must be our model, and Jesus was not shy to challenge and to place boundaries. He responded to Peter:

> *"But Jesus turned away from Peter and said to him, Get behind Me, Satan! You are in My way **an offense** and a hindrance and a snare to Me; for you are minding what partakes not of the nature and quality of God, but of men." (Matthew 16:23 AMP, emphasis added and parentheses removed)*

Strong words, yet Jesus walked in love and without sin and offence in his heart. However, He was able to identify and speak to the offence that Peter was bringing. He showed that confronting offence in love is possible.

Read again how He responded to the Pharisees and rulers:

> *"...They said to Him, We are not illegitimate children and born out of fornication; we have one Father, even God. Jesus said to them, If God were your Father, you would love Me and respect Me and welcome Me gladly, for I proceeded (came forth) from God [out of His very presence]. I did not even come on My own authority or of My own accord (as self-appointed);*

> but He sent Me. Why do you misunderstand what I say? It is because you are unable to hear what I am saying. *[You cannot bear to listen to My message; your ears are shut to My teaching.]* You are of your father, the devil, and it is your will to practice the lusts and gratify the desires *[which are characteristic]* of your father. He was a murderer from the beginning and does not stand in the truth, because there is no truth in him. When he speaks a falsehood, he speaks what is natural to him, for he is a liar *[himself]* and the father of lies and of all that is false.'" (John 8:41-44 AMPC, emphasis added)

Again, He was not operating out of offence, and his hard language to powerful people of the day was not designed to win over supporters or pander to some prideful, constructed persona. He was not trying to win votes; He didn't have a messiah complex- he was the Messiah! He was in our terms, the Man of God operating out of His calling and identity. Likewise, Jesus says that we are to operate in the same manner.

> Just as you have sent Me into the world, I also have sent them into the world...That they all may be one, just as You, Father, are in Me and I in You, that they also may be on in Us, so that the world may believe and be convinced that You have sent Me. I have given to them the glory and honor which You have given Me, that they may be one even as We are one. (John 17:18, 21-22 AMP, parenthesis removed)

Acting weak and subdued in some form of false piety is not what this is about. Acting in accordance to some formula for what we or a denomination thinks a Christian should be is not how we are to be. We are not to be Christian masochists taking offence after offence, but instead living as victorious overcomers. We are to operate as kings in godly anointing - our responses and actions should be rooted from who we are in Christ, not acting.

The Christian life is to be confrontational - truth against lies - provided we are operating and motivated by love and not offence. We are to raise a righteous standard in the world, directing people to Jesus. Remember that the mission of Kingdom Finance is to join with Jesus' mission to destroy the works of satan. Like Jesus we are to be truth bringers - Elijah confronted the priests of Baal with truth - he spoke the truth against the spiritual and economic wickedness of his day. Nehemiah confronted the ungodly financial practices that resulted in the trafficking of young girls (Neh 5:5). We have an example to break the jaw of the oppressor and release the victim (Job 29).

The Watchmen

Ezekiel needed to sound the alarm as a watchman:

> *Once again a message came to me from the Lord: 2 "Son of man, give your people this message: 'When I bring an army against a country, the people of that land choose one of their own to be a watchman. 3 When the watchman sees the enemy coming, he sounds the alarm to warn the people. 4 Then if those who hear the alarm refuse to take action, it is their own fault if they die. 5 They heard the alarm but ignored it, so the responsibility is theirs. If they had listened to the warning, they could have saved their lives. 6 But if the watchman sees the enemy coming and doesn't sound the alarm to warn the people, he is responsible for their captivity. They will die in their sins, but I will hold the watchman responsible for their deaths.'*
>
> *7 "Now, son of man, I am making you a watchman for the people of Israel. Therefore, listen to what I say and warn them for me. 8 If I announce that some wicked people are sure to die and you fail to tell them to change their ways, then they will die in their sins, and I will hold you responsible for their deaths. 9 But if you warn them to repent and they don't repent, they will die in their sins, but you will have saved yourself. (Ezekiel 33:1-9 NLT)*

If we walk in offence, we place ourselves in the proverbial outhouse toilet fighting it out with our offenders, but that is not our calling.

Instead, we are called to be Watchmen on the wall, challenging people with the shout of warning in relation to their lives. Our calling is to pursue our destiny as watchmen and not to miss the moment because of distraction and offence. Like Jesus, we challenge the distractions, deal with the issues, and press on.

Sometimes God's righteous standard is offensive to the sinful world. Yes, people may be offended at us when we speak the truth from our destiny calling and identity just as they were with Jesus. Can we expect less as, frequently, it is recorded that people sought to kill Jesus after He spoke. He did not pander to the powerful and was not a man-pleaser. Truth always confronts, and we speak the Kingdom truth of our destiny and the blessing we walk in. For example, the Word says that we are blessed, rich, and prospering. We are content as we know He is our champion, bringing this into reality in our lives. However, people may look at us and only see the natural - the lesser facts of attacks, losses, and setbacks. They can then curse you by saying you are destitute, poor, and deluded. They can be offended at your faith and calmness in a trial. They want you to "face the truth" or to "snap out of it". Just as they were offended at Jesus and did not see Him in His Messianic calling, people may not see you in your destiny calling in Jesus. They wanted Jesus to only live in His identity as the carpenter's son and tried to kill Him when He asserted His true calling (Luke 4:14-28).

It is the same for us as it was for Jesus - we must continue to speak the truth about our destiny calling. The truth is the Word. The truth is the Blessing. The truth is what God says about us and our destiny, not our feelings, circumstances, or how the world views us.

We may be like Joseph - a prisoner in the natural world, but really a dreamer with a destiny calling to lead. What about the jingling sound of the jailer's keys he heard everyday - were they the sound of continued "truth" of oppression or the sound of deliverance coming? One day the keys opened the door and Joseph was ushered into his high calling.

Likewise, was David a caveman cowering in the caves, or was he the anointed King? Have you been forced into difficult circumstances? Bankrupt, evicted, made homeless, businesses lost, marriage broken, etc? This state of affairs is not the truth of your life, just the facts on the day. His Kingdom is coming for you in your life today as it is in Heaven.

The Battle is the Lord's

Jesus was from another Kingdom and spoke from that Kingdom's perspective. He walked as a King in the land, and it offended people who wanted Him act as they saw Him - just a carpenter's son. Like Jesus, when we are attacked, there can be a hurt, but we must live from our true identity with Him. If we defend and try to deal with things in our own strength we are excluding God from working. We know that the fruit of sin is death and destruction, and that offending people put themselves in the enemy's hands. We must leave this to God. God has put in place the consequences of the curse, and we must allow God to deal with things. Indeed, because we have been forgiven so much, we must forgive and use the martyr Stephen as a guide (Acts 7). As he saw his home and place in Heaven, he was able to forgive.

Prayer: *Jesus I forgive {offender} for their {name their offences} and I release them to your mercy and righteous judgement. As I deal with this issue I pray that you will help me to walk in love, and I pray that my dealings with {offender} would be in love and aided by you.*

This Kingdom perspective changes how we see things and allows God to bring us into victory.

Chapter 18

Debt

What About Debt?

So far, we have dealt with things that have blocked victory in our lives such as concluding the past, dealing with shame, and offence, but where does that leave debt? What should we do about it and how do we get rid of it? How does God want us to live in relation to debt? What is His plan for us and how do we deal with debt in relation to Kingdom Finance?

So many people in the church are struggling under a heavy burden of debt. Our entire culture and economy is debt-driven and debt-oriented, and I don't think the church is materially different. In the UK personal debt was £1.853 trillion at the end of May 2024.[i] In the US household debt has climbed to $17.69 trillion in the first quarter of 2024.[ii] This does not even begin to address the unsustainable debt issues facing our nations.

Parents today train their children in the way they think they should go, namely how to get a good credit rating and loans (e.g. school loans and car loans) so that they can prosper in this debt-focussed society.

Students graduate from university with debt at levels that will require many years of working to eliminate. In the UK, it is estimated that three out of four graduates will be paying off student loans into their 50s.[iii] In the US, research has shown that the average bachelor's degree student will take 21 years to pay off student loans.[iv] These numbers can increase substantially for post-graduate and professional programmes.

Our ability to own a home and prosper is also seen to be directly connected to our ability to borrow and have a good mortgage. Indeed, given the increasing difficulty in qualifying for a mortgage, having a good mortgage is also viewed as an asset. I have heard people say that they cannot afford to move as they would never qualify again for their mortgage. It is not uncommon for people to make important life decisions based upon their debts and the ability to keep a good mortgage in place.

Debt impacts our freedom and our ability to do what we would like to do, as our ability to give is constrained by the need to service debts. Our ability to do something different is also limited as we can be locked into a monthly payment cycle that limits our freedom. Debt represents obligations that need to be met on a routine basis, usually monthly, over a long period of time. This type of obligation also has the effect of locking us into a lifestyle of work, earning, debt, and payments. The ideal borrower is a stable worker with a predictable cash flow and good job. This Mr or Miss Average is the creation of the lenders' financial models and will never take on the challenges of a Gideon or a David!

Many Christians I speak to are surprised that I tackle the issue of debt outside of how to get access to more! It is such a part of our culture and life that people cannot imagine a life without it. I have even heard ministers talk in admiring tones of their good credit rating and ability to borrow. Of course there is some truth, as an analysis of credit looks at character and good behaviour. However, before we begin to address what God has to say on this issue, we have to deal with this fundamental point - **God may have a better way.** So, how does debt fit into Kingdom Finance?

If our manner of thinking and model of living in relation to debt is influenced by the curse, we know that blindness will impact us. Here is a reminder:

> *And you shall grope at noonday as the blind grope in darkness. And you shall not prosper in your ways; and you shall be only oppressed and robbed continually, and there shall be no one to save you. (Deuteronomy 28:29 AMPC)*

Prayer: *Father, I pray that you would open my eyes to see your will in relation to debt and operating in a system that is debt-centred. Let me see what you want me to see and submit to your Lordship in my life in the area of money.*

What Does the Bible Say About Debt?

In looking at any issue, debt included, we must go to the starting point in God's plan for our lives. This point is set out in the Blessing, the benefit of which we inherit as believers:

> *He redeemed us in order that the blessing given to Abraham might come to the Gentiles through Christ Jesus, so that by faith we might receive the promise of the Spirit. (Gal. 3:14 NIV)*

Deuteronomy 28 sets out details of the blessing that we are to enjoy if we walk according to the Word. In relation to debt and the need to borrow the key passages include:

> *The Lord shall open to you His good treasury, the Heavens, to give the rain of your land in its season and to bless all the work of your hands;* ***and***

> *you shall lend to many nations, but you shall not borrow.* (Deuteronomy 28:12 AMPC emphasis added)

The curses set out in Deuteronomy 28 include the following:

> *The transient (stranger) among you shall mount up higher and higher above you, and you shall come down lower and lower.*
>
> **He shall lend to you, but you shall not lend to him; he shall be the head, and you shall be the tail.** *(Deuteronomy 28:43-44 AMPC, emphasis added)*

In Psalm 112, the description of the godly rich man it describes him as a lender and not a borrower:

> *...Blessed (happy, fortunate, to be envied) is the man who fears (reveres and worships) the Lord, who delights greatly in His commandments... Prosperity and welfare are in his house...It is well with the man who deals generously **and lends**, who conducts his affairs with justice...He has distributed freely [**he has given** to the poor and needy] (Psalm 112:1,3, 9 AMPC, emphasis added)*

We are also instructed to owe no one anything, which means not to borrow:

> **Owe no one anything**, *except to love each other, for the one who loves another has fulfilled the law. (Romans 13:8 ESV, emphasis added)*

Perhaps one of the critical verses in relation to debt is found in Proverbs 22:7 where the relationship between borrower and lender is set out. The borrower is described as being in slavery to the lender. There is an enslavement power dynamic that is at work in the borrower/lender relationship.

*The rich rules over the poor, and **the borrower is the slave of the lender**. (Proverbs 22:7 ESV, emphasis added)*

In the Lord's Prayer we are instructed to pray daily as follows:

Pray, therefore, like this: Our Father Who is in Heaven, hallowed (kept holy) be Your name. Your kingdom come, Your will be done on earth as it is in Heaven. (Matthew 6:9 AMPC)

When we take these Scriptures together, we have a picture of how God wants us to live. As we pray daily for His Kingdom to come and His will to be done on earth as it is in Heaven, we know that there is no slavery or debt in Heaven. We will not be paying off our car loan or credit card bill to a debt-collecting angel in Heaven. Jesus paid all of our debts and redeemed us from all vestiges of slavery. He whom the Son sets free is free indeed (John 8:36).

We can also see that God's plan throughout the Bible is for us to be blessed and to prosper; to have enough wealth to be a lender and not a borrower. We can also see that not having enough money and needing to borrow is listed in the curse section of Deuteronomy 28, and the Bible says that we have been redeemed from the curse as Jesus became a curse for us (Galatians 3:13).

> We will not be paying off our car loan or credit card bill to a debt collecting angel in heaven. Jesus paid all of our debts and redeemed us from all vestiges of slavery.

Am I Oppressed?

Are we open to look at this issue with fresh eyes? Are we open to seeing things in a different way and to having our minds renewed regarding debt? Our consumer culture and the economy we live in is so pervasive and compelling that we may not even be aware that we live in a manner that is less than God has planned and intended for us.

The Children of Israel in Egypt had been slaves for so long that they had forgotten what it was like to be free. In Exodus 6:9, Moses reiterated the vow of God to deliver the Israelites and to bless them and to establish them in the land he had sworn to them.

> *Moses told this to the Israelites, but they refused to listen to Moses because of their impatience and anguish of spirit and because of their cruel bondage. (Exodus 6:9 AMPC)*

It can be almost impossible to hear the word of God for our blessing and deliverance if we are steeped in a system that has us in bondage and slavery. Remember that the borrower is a servant and a slave to the lender.

The credit-based system we live in has tried to make debt more palatable and accessible by separating the slavery dynamic from the consumer experience, but it is still present. Prearranged lines of credit and credit cards make the slavery process relatively painless - like making a normal purchase. However, I have never had anyone describe the experience of applying for a loan as anything but disquieting. The experience makes people feel vulnerable and exposed. I believe this is the reaction in the spirit to an element of slavery entering into our lives. We have become good at ignoring this discomfort because it seems that basic living demands it, and in so many ways it makes sense. If our car is old and giving trouble with unpredictable bills, it is convenient to use it as a deposit and get a new car on credit that has a warranty and a predictable cash flow impact. This is particularly true where our cash flow is more squeezed due to the debts we carry to live.

This lifestyle seems to be okay but it is certainly a bondage. Should there be any glitch in our ability to pay, the situation with lenders and debt collectors can turn ugly very quickly. Remember that the same smiling face lending you the money has a busy full time legal department and debt collectors on retainer hounding defaulters who have fallen behind. Put another way, society has managed to hide the chains at the start of the process but they are clanging in another part of the building and come out very quickly if you cannot pay.

Like the Children of Israel, God is speaking to us that there is a better way, a promised land, and that He has made a way for us to live out of this bondage of slavery. However, it is critical to remind ourselves why He has done this. Moses is often misquoted as saying, "Let my people go", but that is not the entirety of what he said. His actual words repeated over and over to Pharaoh were:

> *...Let my people go,* ***that they may serve me...*** *(Exodus 7:16 AMPC)*

His goal for the Children of Israel was that they be free, living in His blessing, and serving Him. In the same way, His purpose in liberating us from the slavery of debt is that we may serve Him. His goal for us is the same.

> *For long ago in Egypt I broke your yoke and burst your bonds* ***not that you might be free, but that you might serve Me...*** *(Jeremiah 2:20 AMPC, emphasis added parenthesis removed)*

Let's personalise this for ourselves: In [your hometown] I broke your yoke of debt and burst your bondage to payments and interests, not so that you could just be free, but so that you could be free to serve Me! He wants us free to be able to execute our destiny and to worship Him. In the context of Kingdom Finance, that means to be free from the bondage of debt and this world's broken system so that we can join with Him in destroying the works of the devil.

Prayer: ***Father we have been under a slavery mindset that accepted the bondage of debt without really thinking about it or what God thought***

about it. Reveal to me your plan for me to be truly free and break off any blindness or mindset that would hinder me seeing what you have for me.

A New Mindset

So often we just go with the flow and do what seems right in our own eyes. Even in serving Him, we hear our calling and try to execute it using worldly thinking including debt. In relation to our finances and particularly debt, we need to have our minds renewed and be open to what God has to say to us. We cannot be so in sync with the world-system that we stop hearing or seeking God for His wisdom and revelation. We are to seek first the Kingdom or, as one translation put it, we are to set our hearts on the Kingdom. It must be our first priority, not chasing after our material needs and answering our own prayers through debt.

> *So don't worry and don't keep saying, 'What shall we eat, what shall we drink or what shall we wear?! That is what pagans are always looking for; your Heavenly Father knows that you need them all.* ***Set your heart on the kingdom and his goodness****, and all these things will come to you as a matter of course. (Matthew 6:31-33 Phillips emphasis added)*

King Asa should be our example as his story shows us how God wants us to behave towards Him. Asa was a good king and when faced with a battle, he cried out to the Lord. God spoke to him through a prophet affirming the King's approach saying:

> *... Hear me, Asa, and all Judah and Benjamin: the Lord is with you while you are with Him.* ***If you seek Him inquiring for and of Him, craving Him as your soul's first necessity****, He will be found by you; but if you become indifferent and forsake Him, He will forsake you. (2 Chron. 15:2 AMP, emphasis added and parentheses removed)*

We will find this admonition throughout Scripture. In describing those who would be cut off in the same era as Josiah, Zephaniah declared:

> *And those who have drawn back from following the Lord and those who have not sought the Lord nor inquired for, inquired of, and* **required the Lord [as their first necessity]**. *Seek the Lord inquire for Him, inquire of Him, and require Him as the* **foremost necessity** *of your life, all you humble of the land who have acted in compliance with His revealed will and have kept His commandments; seek righteousness, seek humility [inquire for them, require them as vital]. It may be you will be hidden in the day of the Lord's anger. She did not listen to and heed the voice of God; she accepted no correction or instruction; she trusted not in the Lord nor leaned on or was confident in Him, but was confident in her own wealth; she drew not near to her God but to the god of Baal or Molech. (Zephaniah 1:6; 2:3; and 3:2 AMPC, emphasis added parenthesis removed)*

We are to seek His will and purposes in our lives as our first necessity. This does not just apply to our relationships but applies to our money and our health, and again the story of Asa is relevant. Later on in the passage, he was faced with another armed conflict and made a sound decision likely based on good advice. He probably did what most wise kings would have done, and his plan worked well. He paid money to the King of Syria to back him up, which they did and he had a victory: a victory in the eyes of man. But this is what God had to say:

> *At that time Hanani the seer came to Asa king of Judah and said to him, Because you relied on the king of Syria and not on the Lord your God, the army of the king of Syria has escaped you. Were not the Ethiopians and Libyans a huge host with very many chariots and horsemen? Yet because you relied then on the Lord, He gave them into your hand.* **For the eyes of the Lord run to and fro throughout the whole earth to show Himself strong in behalf of those whose hearts are blameless toward Him. You have done foolishly** *in this; therefore, from now on you shall have wars."* *(2 Chron. 16:7-9 AMPC, emphasis added)*

Asa's victory was not what God would have intended. He had a greater victory in mind for Asa, but Asa did not seek the Lord's will as his urgent necessity. In relation to our finances, God wants us to seek Him as our urgent necessity - even if we think we can win in our own strength, we will miss the greater victory.

This also applies to our health - we are to seek Him first as our urgent necessity. Asa did not and the Word says:

> *In the thirty-ninth year of his reign Asa was diseased in his feet—until his disease became very severe; **yet in his disease he did not seek the Lord, but relied on the physicians.***
>
> *13 And Asa slept with his fathers, dying in the forty-first year of his reign.* (2 Chron. 16:12-13 AMPC, emphasis added)

In all things, we are to seek God as our urgent and first priority to determine what He wants us to do and not to rely on our own understanding.

> **In relation to our finances God wants us to seek Him as our urgent necessity - even if we can win in our own strength we will miss the greater victory.**

Another example is quite comforting for me, as it deals with times when we have really got things wrong! If we have got it wrong and wasted money what can God do? King Amaziah hired 100,000 men of war as mercenaries paying 100 talents of silver, which was a lot of money for the day. I am sure the military wisdom of the day would say that 100,000 extra soldiers would be a good thing. However here is what God said about it:

> *But a man of God came to him, saying, O king, do not let all this army of Ephraimites of Israel go with you [of Judah], for the Lord is not with you, For if you go [in spite of warning], no matter how strong you are for battle, God will cast you down before the enemy, for God has power to help and*

> *to cast down. And Amaziah said to the man of God, But what shall we do about the 100 talents which I have given to the army of Israel? The man of God answered,* **The Lord is able to give you much more than this.** *(2 Chron. 25:7-9 AMPC, emphasis added)*

Clearly, God had another view and plan that the king had not sought out. This is another example of not seeking God as our urgent necessity. The king had pressed ahead in his own wisdom and spent a fortune - good wisdom from a natural perspective, but not God's plan. Interestingly, this is an example of how we can waste time and money, yet when we repent and do things God's way, there is a simple answer regarding our financial losses. "The Lord is able to give you much more than this", which is an encouraging word for us when we have we have all got it wrong and done the wrong things by not seeking God. He is saying He can restore even the losses caused even by our own mistakes.

THE LESSON OF KING JOSIAH

Let me set the stage described in 2 Kings 22 and 23. Horses and chariots dedicated to the sun god lined the entrance to the temple. Everyone consulted mediums. Wizards and idols were everywhere. Inside the temple were vessels dedicated to the worship of Baal, Asherah, and the hosts of the Heavens. Asherah idols are in the temple along with altars for worship. Right beside the temple were the male cult prostitutes and people who served the Asherah. Nearby, the sacrifice of children to the god Molech was still in practice. This was the norm for the day, and everyone lived in this reality.

This is the picture of daily life (and worse) when a copy of God's lost law and covenant was found in the temple. It seemed like everyone had forgotten how to live and had been fully absorbed by the culture of their day. Defilement had not just crept in - it had become the norm.

> *Then Shaphan the scribe told the king, Hilkiah **the priest has given me a book**. And Shaphan read it before the king. And when the king heard the words of the Book of the Law, he rent his clothes. And the king commanded ...Go, inquire of the Lord for me and for the people and for all Judah concerning the words of this book that has been found. For great is the wrath of the Lord that is kindled against us because our fathers have not listened and obeyed the words of this book, to do according to all that is written concerning us. (2 Kings 22:10-13 AMPC, emphasis added)*

When he enquired of the Lord, he heard the grave news of pending judgement. Not knowing was no excuse, but here is how Josiah responded:

> *The king went up to the house of the Lord, and with him all the men of Judah, all the inhabitants of Jerusalem, the priests, the prophets, and all the people, both small and great. And he read in their ears all the words of the Book of the Covenant, which was found in the Lord's house. The king stood [on the platform] by the pillar **and made a covenant before the Lord**—to walk after the Lord and to keep His commandments, His testimonies, and His statutes with all his heart and soul, to confirm the words of this covenant that were written in this book. And all the people stood to join in the covenant.*
>
> *And the king commanded Hilkiah the high priest and the priests of the second rank and the keepers of the threshold to bring out of the temple of the Lord all the vessels made for Baal, for [the goddess] Asherah, and for all the hosts of the Heavens; and he burned them outside Jerusalem in the fields of the Kidron, and carried their ashes to Bethel [where Israel's idolatry began]. (2 Kings 23:2-4 AMPC, emphasis added)*

The king then went on to destroy the idols and framework for defilement that existed in the land.

His response is an example to us, illustrating what we are to do when the defilement of the world is found in our lives: repent, restore the covenant, and then destroy the works of the devil. Remember our definition of Kingdom Finance is to partner with Jesus in His mission to destroy the works of the devil (1 John 3:8).

Like the people in Josiah's time, we have forgotten the truths of the Kingdom. The culture of the world has so invaded the church that we are unaware of the altars of Baal in our midst. The curse is everywhere and we don't even know what is wrong. Yet when the word of our covenant is read, the truth brings realisation, revolution, and change. When we see things God's way, the temple prostitutes and pagan altars cannot remain. Like King Josiah, we see the defilement and bondage in contrast to the blessing of the covenant that God intended.

Our enslavement to debt is like this. We have a covenant from God to be blessed, yet a pervasive root of lack and debt has brought us into a form of slavery. It has crept into the church and is now viewed as the normal and essential way of living. Like slaves, we may not cry for freedom and may not see ourselves as ruling and being free. Instead, our lives can continue to be blighted by debt and despair which can give rise to jealousy and anger. These are not the emotions and attitudes of rulers and kings. We are to seek God's way as our urgent necessity.

Debt is not the answer, even if it allows us to purchase good things. God has a better, covenant way and wants us to seek him as our urgent necessity so that we can be truly free. And if we are truly free as individuals, then the church can be truly free. Then we will see the economic miracle of Kingdom Finance released.

I pray that we are now in a position to open our vision to what God may intend for us. Can we really live without debt in this world? Can we really believe God to move into a level of living where we can be the lender not the borrower? Does God really have a better way? Can we be debt free corporately when virtually 100% of the people in the churches have debts, and indeed the very church buildings are usually burdened by debts serviced by the congregation? Layers of debt upon more debt will need to be broken down just like the idolatry of Josiah's day.

So what do we know about God's will for us so far?

- We are inheritors of the blessing.

- The blessing says that we are destined to have abundance and to be lenders not borrowers.

- Debt is a form of slavery and evidence of the curse in operation in our lives.

- The borrower is a slave or servant to the lender.

- We are admonished to owe no one anything.

- There is no slavery, borrowing, or debt in Heaven, and we pray daily that His Kingdom will come and His will be done on earth as it is in Heaven - His will is for us to live a Heavenly debt-free life now.

Prayer: *Father, I realise that I may have accepted a way of living and dealing that puts my trust in things other than you. I repent for this and ask that Your covenant to me be reheard just like Josiah. I seek You as my urgent and first necessity and agree to do what You would have me do. Let me see debt as You see it and give me the plan and steps You would have me put in place.*

Is Debt Sin?

I am often asked: "Of course you don't believe that debt is sin do you?" Let's unpack this key question a little bit to understand and answer it. There are categories of sin that are "black letter" and very clear. Murder and theft would be clear examples of black letter sins.

Debt is not included as a sin in the Ten Commandments. Indeed, there are provisions for lending and borrowing in both the Old and New Testaments. For example, the Bible provided for the elimination of debts every 7 years (the Shmita year) and the restoration of property every 50 years (the Jubilee). This is where most people stop in their thinking.

Instead, we must approach the issue of debt from Scripture with an understanding of God's best plan for our blessing. Jesus said to pray daily that His will in Heaven is to be done on earth - His Kingdom is to come. In Heaven there is no debt, so the desired state of our blessing here on earth should be free from debt.

Remember that the borrower is a servant or slave to the lender. This is the slavery and bondage of debt. In 2 Kings 4:4, the widow's sons were about to be sold into slavery to pay for the family debts until God stepped in with a miracle. The Shmita and the Jubilee were put in place to deal with debt and to restore people who had fallen into debt. It was a season that the curse was reversed. This makes it clear that debt is not the state that God wants us to live in. He wants us to be free to serve Him.

In most modern Western societies the worst legal outcomes of debt have been moderated through legal protections and bankruptcy laws that provide a way of escape, albeit a difficult one. However, it is good to remember that in the past, remedies included debtor's prisons and slavery. Even today in certain countries, prison can be a real likelihood for unpaid debts and money problems.

We need to anchor in our minds the key truth that it is not God's will for us to be in debt- full stop. Using the slavery analogy, debt is a condition that God does not intend for us. Debt may not be a black-letter sin, but it is evidence of the curse in operation in our lives, which shows us that we

> **Debt is evidence of the curse in operation in our lives which shows us that we have strayed from following Him and obeying His commands.**

have strayed from following Him and obeying His commands. If we have generational debt and poverty we know that our generations have been walking in the curse due to sin in their lives. Deuteronomy 28:15 makes this abundantly clear:

> But if you will not obey the voice of the Lord your God or be careful to do all his commandments and his statutes that I command you today, then all these curses shall come upon you and overtake you... The sojourner who is among you shall rise higher and higher above you, and you shall come down lower and lower. **He shall lend to you, and you shall not lend to him.** He shall be the head, and you shall be the tail. (Deuteronomy 28:15,43-44 AMPC, emphasis added)

So we know that debt may not be a sin like theft, but it is evidence of sin. Debt is a consequence of sin and a manifestation of the curse in our lives. Therefore, if you have debts, God wants you to be free from them.

The Children of Israel were in captivity in Egypt and the oppression increased by having to make bricks with no straw and still keep to the same quota (Exodus 5:18). When we are in any form of bondage or slavery there are ways for our situation to be better or worse. Making bricks with straw is much better than making bricks with no straw. This is an example of "a blessing" but is not "the blessing that makes rich and adds no sorrow" (Prov. 10:22).

Think of it this way: A good interest rate or a consolidation loan to reduce borrowings and interest is like having a better slave owner. A lower interest rate is like being beaten less! Which is better, an owner who beats you ten times a day or five? In the same way, which is better, a loan with interest of ten percent or five percent? Five percent interest is the better master. Even in bondage God wants things to be better for us. In the captivity of the Jews in Babylon, God had instructions as to how to prosper in captivity:

> *And seek (inquire for, require, and request) the peace and welfare of the city to which I have caused you to be carried away captive; and pray to the Lord for it, for in the welfare of [the city in which you live] you will have welfare... For I know the plans and thoughts that I have for you,' says the Lord, **'plans for peace and well-being** and not for disaster, to give you a future and a hope. (Jeremiah 29:7; 11 AMPC, emphasis added)*

We can see that even under the curse, God has a plan for us to prosper. We must also remember that this is in the Old Testament, and we have a new and better covenant. We learned in Galatians 3 that through the sacrifice of Jesus, who was made a curse for us, we are redeemed from the curse and have a way of escape. Quoting this passage, Derek Prince described it this way:

> *"Christ has redeemed us from the curse of the law, having become a curse for us, for it is written: Cursed is every one who hangs on a tree."*
>
> *In other words, when Jesus hung on the cross, every Jew who knew his Old Testament recognized that Jesus was made a curse. Then we read the other side of the exchange in verse 14:*
>
> *"That the blessing of Abraham might come upon the Gentiles in Christ Jesus, that we might receive the promise of the Spirit through faith."*
>
> *Now, what are the two aspects of the exchange in that verse? What's the evil? Curse. What's the good? Blessing. It's very clear, isn't it? Jesus was made a curse that we might receive the blessing. Let's say it again.* ***"Jesus was made a curse that we might receive the blessing."*** *And you'll notice there's tremendous emphasis on curse in verse 13, the word occurs three times. Christ has redeemed us from the curse, having become a curse for us, for it is written: Cursed is every one who hangs on a tree.* [v] *(emphasis added)*

As a result, we know God's plan for us: to walk in blessing, like walking with Him in the cool of the day. His plan was the relationship He had with mankind in Eden and later what He planned in the

Promised Land. Through Jesus we are to live the Kingdom lifestyle now, daily calling down His Kingdom in our lives and moving from a debt-fuelled lifestyle into a debt-free, Blessing-fuelled, Kingdom Finance lifestyle.

So, the answer to our question is that going into debt is not a listed "black-letter" sin, but it is the fruit of sin and not a place or state that God wants us to live in. Our freedom from this slavery should be a key goal for us practically and in prayer. By all means get straw for your bricks and a lower interest rate, while at the same time repenting for not being in the place that God intended and believing and confessing that God is bringing about your deliverance, freedom, and Kingdom blessing.

Prayer: *Father, I recognise that You have redeemed me from the curse, and debt is a curse and bondage. I am sorry and repent on behalf of myself and my generations for not being in the place economically that you intended for me and for settling for less than Kingdom. Your plan is the blessing that makes rich and adds no sorrow and I ask that You show me Your plan and how to walk in it. I choose to believe You and not the world system we live in.*

Strategy for Victory over Debt

We must dare to believe. Dare to believe that God has a better way. Dare to bring every area of our lives under His Lordship. Like Josiah finding a lost scroll that shows us the truth of our current state, we must hear the word of the Covenant and God's plan and realise that our love affair with debt and this world's way of living must cease.

We know that debt is bondage and slavery, and it is not God's plan for us. We know that He wants us to walk in the blessing and to be a lender, not a borrower. We know that debt in our lives and families is evidence of the curse in operation, and this comes because we have not operated according to the Word - it is a fruit of sin. We also know that He has a better plan for us if we seek Him as our urgent necessity. As a result, we know that God has a plan to get us to the level of freedom and prosperity to be debt free and blessed so that, at a minimum, we can be the Good Samaritan continually as Jesus commanded.

What we tend to do is accept only the first step, that God wants to bless us, but then short-circuit His miracle provision by borrowing to get the blessing. We believe that God wants us to have the blessing of a new car, business, or a bigger church building, but then immediately go back to the world system to implement the vision. This pattern was exemplified recently by someone who came to me for prayer during a meeting because of a desperate financial situation. As he described it, God had clearly given him a calling to build an orphanage and school, and he had rushed into this heart and soul. I had a real witness that his calling was real. However, he had mortgaged his house to get money for this, spent all his money, racked up credit cards, and recklessly borrowed more. He was on the brink of losing everything and was struggling with the courts. It was a horrible and stressful situation. He had received the call from the Lord, but like the kings of old, had not sought God as his urgent necessity to get His vision and provision, which we know will NOT include debt because God is not going to put you into any form of slavery and bondage. God can untangle the mess and restore, but only if we repent for doing things our own way using the debt-fuelled world system.

A key verse for us shows us that this type of action is sin:

> ...*For whatever does not originate and proceed from faith is sin [whatever is done without a conviction of its approval by God is sinful].* (Romans 14:23 AMPC)

We cannot have faith in our debt and borrowing, as debt does not proceed from faith and is not God-approved. Now, like King Amaziah, if we listen to the word of the Lord and repent, God is able to restore us financially (2 Chron. 25:9).

Everything set out in this chapter is to lead us to this key point. Debt is part of the curse and we are to get out of its bondage. Like the kings in the Bible, if we seek Him as our urgent and first priority, He will turn things around for us and provide a way to be free. In our covenant this is called repentance.

> *If we refuse to admit that we are sinners, then we live in a world of illusion and truth becomes a stranger to us. But if we freely admit that we have sinned, we find God utterly reliable and straightforward—he forgives our sins and makes us **thoroughly clean from all that is evil**. For if we take up the attitude "we have not sinned", we flatly deny God's diagnosis of our condition and cut ourselves off from what he has to say to us. (I John 1:8-9 Phillips, emphasis added)*

I believe that one of the strongest bondages that Christians are under today is the belief that a good loan is a blessing, not just a benefit. Yes it is better than a bad loan in the same way a good slave owner is better than a bad slave owner. For this reason many of us do not take our debts to Jesus and seek the freedom He will provide.

Debt is not part of our inheritance and the blessing, debt is part of and evidence of the curse just as homelessness is not a sin but evidence that we are not where God wants us to be. Jesus has redeemed us from the curse - He paid the price for our debt and lack, but because of this mistaken belief, we do not bring our debts to Him in repentance and apply the remedy of His shed blood to this area of our lives. We may pray for a blessing, and we may pray to get out of debt, particularly if we are in financial difficulty, but have we recognised the cause and dealt with it?

We need to put debt fully in the NOT GOD'S BEST and SIN camp - part of the curse and part of the work of the enemy we are called to destroy. We need to repent for having it in our lives, entering into debt instead of seeking His way as our urgent necessity. We need to bring it to the cross and make debt part of what we ask Jesus to deal with in our lives. When we have done this, as with any sin, the guilt and punishment is His, not ours. He has paid it, He has redeemed us from the curse, and He can begin to undertake it for us. If we refuse to repent for it and keep full command and control of it, we are saying that in this area, we are managing our lives ourselves and do not need Him. The lie of the enemy has resulted in us hindering or resisting God from dealing with our debts and bringing us into blessing.

Prayer: *Jesus, we recognise that we have debt in our lives and families. We repent for not walking in the blessing but walking contrary to Your plans in the curse. Our families did not seek You in the area of money and debt and did not operate in the blessing the way You intended. On behalf of myself and my family line, we repent for debt and its causes. We repent for not looking to You for the solution, but going man's way. Just like in the Bible, You had a better way to bring about victory and a better way for us to walk in the blessing. Jesus, I bring each debt to You and nail it to the cross. I roll the burden over onto You, and I thank You that You are faithful and just to forgive us and to cleanse and restore us. I thank You that You are no man's debtor, and that each debt is paid and settled. I now seek You as my urgent necessity and declare Your Kingdom come and Your will be done in relation to my debts and the Blessing.*

What about Loans and Mortgages?

We have dealt with debt and had revelation of the fact that God's desire is to deal with our debts as they are not part of His plan for our lives. We can have faith in His finished work and plan for us. I am dealing with mortgages separately as most people have them and fully believe that a mortgage, like borrowing to invest, must be excluded as it relates to assets. Again, I am often told that: "Of course you mean credit card and consumer debt, not things like a mortgage."

Can we be so bold as to believe that God in all of His power can get us a home without a mortgage? Let's at least keep an open mind to the discussion.

Most of us have or have had mortgages since these borrowings allow us to have a home and shelter. Many would view a large, long-term loan or mortgage as the only way to make such a large purchase. As we have seen, getting a loan at a good interest rate or being approved for a mortgage can even be a benefit or a small "b" blessing. Given the state of finances that exists in the church, this is certainly the reality for all but a small minority of us. What has given rise to this state of affairs? Why is it we need loans and mortgages? Is it what God intended? Does God have a plan to take us out of our dependence upon loans and mortgages?

I would argue that the requirement for loans and mortgages is another illustration of the lack that exists in our family lines. As we have seen in Deuteronomy 28, borrowing is part of the curse.

> *Others said, "During the famine we even had to mortgage our fields, vineyards, and homes to them in order to buy grain."*
>
> *4 Then others said, "We had to borrow money from those in power to pay the government tax on our fields and vineyards. 5 We are Jews just as they are, and our children are as good as theirs. But we still have to sell our children as slaves, and some of our daughters have already been raped. We are completely helpless; our fields and vineyards have even been taken from us." (Nehemiah 5:3-5 CEV)*

Nehemiah had to deal with mortgages leading to human trafficking of girls. This is poverty and lack, and we have an epidemic of this in the world today. Like in Nehemiah's day, as sons and daughters we have been sold into the bondage of debt. There are no mortgages in Heaven, and the Word talks about receiving inheritances from our grandparents and our parents; that would be six inheritances! However, most of us have not seen this in a materially significant way. Why not? Surely, God's plan is for His chosen to walk in blessing, teaching their children to prosper and to be the heads and not the tails. Wouldn't six inheritances from Psalm 112 blessed people have resulted in sufficient blessing to have no mortgage? The Blessing of

Deuteronomy 28 should apply here as it is the word for our lives. There should be abundance in operation; instead our generations have needed borrowing, loans and mortgages.

Therefore, the reason we have mortgages is that we have had generational lack, generational sin, and the generational operation of the curse. We have been established in debt and how to access debt, not in blessing and how to access wealth. Abraham's children did not need mortgages, David's son Solomon did not need a mortgage, and God intended that we would inherit the blessing which covers housing.

As we repent for not living the way He planned in our generations and repent for being in a place where we have a mortgage, we bring our debts and mortgages to Him on the Cross. His blood paid the price for any element of the curse and lack in our lives. Once we have done this step, we have applied His remedy to cleanse us from sin and the curse and He can begin to move on our behalf.

Again, one the biggest lies of the enemy keeping us from blessing is to view our mortgage as a blessing. Yes it is *a* blessing to have a good mortgage and a home but it is NOT part of **the Blessing** as God intended. It is still a part of the curse - perhaps prospering under the curse, but still something He wants to take us out of. It is not the paradigm of Kingdom life in the Blessing. If you still struggle with this, answer this simple question. How many mortgages are there in Heaven? If we daily ask for His will to be done on earth as it is in Heaven, would this not include being blessed to the point where we can own our homes? Our daily prayer should include being debt free, mortgage free, capability to be the Good Samaritan, and to have sufficient to be a Kingdom transformer dealing with the ruins of our generations (Isaiah 61).

> **Solomon did not need a mortgage and God intended that we would be walking in the blessing WHICH COVERS HOUSING.**

I want to address the miracle loan stories that we have heard in testimonies where, against all odds, God broke through and made a way for people. I am not saying these testimonies are wrong. We believe in total healing, but still will take surgery or a drug that can benefit our illness. In the same way, until we break free in our generations into Kingdom Finance, God will work with us where we are. Like Joseph who continually prospered both in slavery and in jail. Be thankful for a great provision, but keep contending in prayer, actions, and belief for divine release. I don't want more straw for my bricks; I want to be free to worship Him as He directs!

In 2 Kings 7, the Captain could not see any way that the prophet Elisha's declaration could come true. In the midst of the siege, Elisha had declared a one-day turnaround whereby the next day the siege would be lifted and food would be cheap. The Captain could not raise his faith to believe or to see this, and asked how it could be even if the windows of Heaven opened. The story goes on to show how God brought about a great miracle economic transformation, but the

Captain did not enjoy it due to his unbelief. He was crushed to death in the rush for cheap food.

Likewise, it is not up to us to see how God can bring about the Blessing such that our debts are removed and our homes are owned. If we want to function in this level of blessing we must seek Him as our first priority, believe what He says, and then do what He would have us do.

Chapter 19

Victory

What About Victory?

So where are we on our journey towards Kingdom Finance victory? So far we have laid the foundations that God requires for victory in our lives and had our minds renewed to see what it means to be a godly rich man or woman. The requirement for intimacy with Jesus and hearing His voice underlines the need for us to really deal with anything that has been holding us back. We have concluded the past and specifically looked at offence against man and the disappointments that could give rise to offence against God. We then looked at our finances and brought them to the Lord, granting Him lordship. We have heard the word requiring us to abide in Him and to seek Him as our urgent and first necessity.

Normally, in the context of business we see the term *success* used, but Kingdom Finance is linked more closely to victory than to success. What does it mean to be a success in business and finance? The worldly view of success tends to focus on role, money, possessions, and power. Even in businesses which identify as Christian, that label can be a veneer or an add-on to the ungodly scale of measurements of wealth used in the world. It is the whitewash on the tomb (Matthew 23:27) or the washing of the outside of the cup. But God is now - at this time - holding a rule, a plumb line, over the actions of men and in particular those in business. His rule is the rule of righteousness and justice, not a thin veneer of religion and duty. He is not interested in the divided motives and the mixed waters characterising much of the current business discourse. We cannot impress him by being a better brothel-keeper - like the Pharisees, whitewash will not cover the stench of sin or a love affair with the world system.

> *Thus He showed me, and behold, the Lord stood upon a wall with a plumb line, with a plumb line in His hand. And the Lord said to me, Amos, what do you see? And I said, A plumb line. Then said the Lord, Behold, I am setting a plumb line as a standard in the midst of My people Israel. I will not pass by and spare them any more [the door of mercy is shut]. (Amos 7:7-8 AMPC)*

> *And I will stretch over Jerusalem the measuring line of Samaria and the plummet of the house of Ahab;* ***and I will wipe Jerusalem as one wipes a dish, wiping it and turning it upside down.*** *(2 Kings 21:13 AMPC, emphasis added)*

> *Therefore thus says the Lord: I have returned to Jerusalem with compassion (lovingkindness and mercy). My house shall be built in it, says the Lord of hosts, and a measuring line shall be stretched out over Jerusalem... (Zechariah 1:16 AMPC)*

His measure is the standard of Heaven's Throne Room purity. Justice is the measuring line and righteousness is the level. It is not about giving. It is not about helping the poor, as good as that is, and let's please do more! Generosity is good, but even that is not the point. Remember, if we give all our goods to feed the poor and are not motivated and activated by love then it profits us nothing (I Corinthians 13:3).

His plumb line has been stretched over the world of business and finance, and the time of forbearing is over. The time of sparing is over and the business "plates of defilement" will be wiped clean. I shared earlier the vision

> Take notice that success in this system can be failure in His.

I had of the table of celebration: glittery elegance and everyone dressed in party finery, excited about receiving the praise and approval of the King. However, on closer view the people were defiled and dirty and the tables were splashed with faeces and urine. This vision is totally disgusting but reminiscent of Jesus' statements to the Pharisees that they were like whitewashed open graves of defilement. Business men and leaders called to finance, take notice that the measuring rule of God has gone forth to establish his Kingdom purpose. He will not bless death and defilement and will not approve the works of man. Take notice that success in this worldly system can be failure in His.

> God is laying a new foundation.

I feel that we can learn from the parable of the talents as it relates to God's measure of victory in finances. Remember in the parable the man with one talent of silver buried it in fear, so God removed it from him and gave it to the man with ten (Matthew 25:14-30). This is the kind of justice God is enacting over our businesses and ministries. There was a season in the parable when the one talent was buried and there was no issue. In this "one-talent season" things appeared fine and the one talent-holder was not treated differently. However, there was a change of season when the Lord came back, measured or judged the actions, and removed the talent and reallocated it. I believe that we are in a time of measurement, assessment, and reallocation similar to that envisioned in the parable. Those that operate in the mixed table of manipulation, fear, and defilement will fail and have their influence and money distributed to those who operate in Kingdom Finance.

God is laying a new foundation. There is a requirement established for His Kingdom to be manifested.

> *Therefore thus says the Lord God, Behold, I am laying in Zion for a foundation a Stone, a tested Stone, a precious Cornerstone of sure foundation; he who believes (trusts in, relies on, and adheres to that Stone) will not [a]be ashamed or give way or hasten away [in sudden panic]. I* ***will make justice the measuring line and righteousness the plummet;*** *and hail will sweep away the refuge of lies, and waters will overwhelm the hiding place (the shelter). (Isaiah 28:16-17 AMPC, emphasis added)*

> *O you afflicted [city], storm-tossed and not comforted, behold, I will set your stones in fair colors [in antimony to enhance their brilliance] and lay your foundations with sapphires. And I will make your windows and pinnacles of [sparkling] agates or rubies, and your gates of [shining] carbuncles, and all your walls [of your enclosures] of precious stones. (Isaiah 54:11-12 AMPC)*

The Foundation that God is asking of us is founded in justice and righteousness and truth - sweeping away lies as the water overflows. It is also a foundation of Heavenly presence - foundations of sapphires, battlements of rubies, and gates of crystal. Can we really establish a foundation of genuine Kingdom Finance - Kingdom Presence here on earth? Can we bring the atmosphere of Heaven to earth in this arena? Can we be a righteous lampstand on the earth and blaze with fire and blessing? This is God's command and passion. It is not enough to have money and use it for good purposes. He wants us to bring the atmosphere of Heaven down, to break the yokes of bondage with the life and breath of Heaven. We are to be releasers of His power on earth. Breakers of bondage and builders of houses to dwell in. The

> It is not enough to have money and use it for good purposes. He wants us to bring the atmosphere of heaven down, to break the yolks of bondage with the life and breath of heaven. We are to be releasers of His power on earth. Breakers of bondage and builders of houses to dwell in.

anointing of the Lord is there for us to access and to declare daily, "thy Kingdom come and thy will be done on earth as it is in Heaven".

Victory requires that we are residents of Heaven as our primary identity, connected into Heaven's power sources, sweeping away the defilement of our love affair with the world system as characterised by Ahab and Jezebel - the archetypes of economic and political defilement.

> *But thanks be to God, Who in Christ always leads us in triumph [as trophies of Christ's victory] and **through us spreads and makes evident the fragrance of the knowledge of God everywhere, For we are the sweet fragrance of Christ** [which exhales] unto God, [discernible alike] among those who are being saved and among those who are perishing:*
>
> *To the latter it is an aroma [wafted] from death to death [a fatal odor, the smell of doom]; to the former it is an aroma from life to life [a vital fragrance, living and fresh]. And who is qualified (fit and sufficient) for these things? [Who is able for such a ministry? We?] For we are not, like so many, [like hucksters making a trade of] peddling God's Word [shortchanging and adulterating the divine message]; but like [men] of sincerity and the purest motive, as [commissioned and sent] by God, we speak [His message] in Christ (the Messiah), **in the [very] sight and presence of God**. (II Corinthians 2:14-17 AMPC, emphasis added)*

Principles of Victory

Victory gives us a direct link to our Kingdom Finance mandate to partner with Jesus in destroying the works of the devil. It speaks of battles that we face in which we overcome. David walked in victory over Goliath. Joshua walked in victory over Jericho. Moses walked in victory over Egypt. Victory is overcoming that which contends against our destiny and against the Word of God.

Victory is always the Lord's. We are His instruments, but the battle and the victory is His.

The horse is prepared for the day of battle, but deliverance and victory are of the Lord. (Proverbs 21:31 AMPC)

*Give us aid against the enemy, for human help is worthless. With God we will gain the **victory**, and he will trample down our enemies. (Psalm 60:11-12 NIV, emphasis added)*

Victory is found in the annals of faith in Hebrews 11 set out before us: faith in the Word of God empowering us.

*But thanks be to God, Who gives us the **victory** making us conquerors through our Lord Jesus Christ. Therefore, my beloved brethren, be firm (steadfast), immovable, always abounding in the work of the Lord always being superior, excelling, doing more than enough in the service of the Lord, knowing and being continually aware that your labor in the Lord is not futile it is never wasted or to no purpose. (1 Corinthians 15:57-58 AMPC, parenthesis removed and emphasis added)*

Obedience the key to victory

*At the time of the offering of the evening sacrifice, Elijah the prophet came near and said, O Lord, the God of Abraham, Isaac, and Israel, let it be known this day that You are God in Israel and that I am Your servant **and that I have done all these things at Your word**. Hear me, O Lord, hear me, that this people may know that You, the Lord, are God, and have turned their hearts back [to You]. Then the fire of the Lord fell and consumed the burnt sacrifice and the wood and the stones and the dust, and also licked up the water that was in the trench. When all the people saw it, they fell on their faces and they said, The Lord, He is God! The Lord, He is God! (1 Kings 18:36-39 AMPC, emphasis added)*

Elijah won a great victory over the defiled economic, political, and religious system of his day. This economic and political system was put in place, represented and led by Ahab and Jezebel, the King and

Queen, who suffered a major defeat when the great fire from Heaven fell.

The key for Elijah's victory was that his actions were done "at Your word" - he did as God asked, which meant that he heard the word of the Lord and acted on it in obedience and faith. He could act in faith because faith comes by hearing the word of God (Romans 10:17), and Elijah had heard the word of God for this situation. Clearly, the prophets of Baal and the evil acts had been going on for some time with no action such as this from Elijah - **both the timing and the action taken were in accordance with the word he had heard from God.**

> What was the secret of Jesus' miracle-working power? His secret was that He only did what He saw the Father do and only said what He heard the Father say.

What was the secret of Jesus' miracle-working power?

Like Elijah, His secret was that He only did what He saw the Father do and only said what He heard the Father say.

> *Jesus gave them this answer: "Very truly I tell you, the Son can do nothing by himself;* **he can do only what he sees his Father doing, because whatever the Father does the Son also does.** *For the Father loves the Son and shows him all he does. Yes, and he will show him even greater works than these, so that you will be amazed... I am able to do nothing from Myself [independently, of My own accord—but only as I am taught by God and as I get His orders]. Even as I hear, I judge [I decide as I am bidden to decide. As the voice comes to Me, so I give a decision], and My judgment is right (just, righteous), because I do not seek or consult My own will [I have no desire to do what is pleasing to Myself, My own aim, My own purpose] but only the will and pleasure of the Father Who sent Me. (John 5:19-20, NIV and 30 AMPC, emphasis added)*

> This is because *I have never spoken on My own authority* or of My own accord or as self-appointed, but the Father Who sent Me has Himself given Me orders [concerning] what to say and what to tell. (John 12:49 AMPC, emphasis added)

This indicates that when Jesus fed the 5,000 he was acting **as instructed by God**. He was not just testing the waters with God the way many of us do. He had been around crowds on many occasions, but on only two occasions do we have a record of a miraculous feeding of the crowds. Like Elijah, Jesus acted in faith to the word he had received, and He told us that the miracle-working power was the Father's - "the Son can do nothing by himself".

> **Could it really be that the answer to breaking through in the area of finances is as simple as hearing God's voice about our finances and doing it?**

In the same way, Jesus must have walked past the money changers in the Temple area many, many times. However, at one **appointed time** he made a whip and overturned the table and chased the money changers away (Matthew 21:12). Why that day? We know from the passage above that it was because the Father had instructed Him to do it that day, as He only did what He saw the Father do and only said what He heard the Father say.

Could it really be that the answer to breaking through in the area of finances is as simple as hearing God's voice about our finances and doing it? Let's take a look at one of Jesus' financial miracles and what can be learned from it. In Mark 6 we see that Jesus had a large crowd in an isolated place (v35-36), and the disciples asked Jesus to send the crowd away so that they could go to villages around and buy food to eat. Instead Jesus spoke to them and said:

> *...Give them something to eat yourselves. Shall we go and buy 200 denarii worth of bread and give it to them to eat? And He said to them, How many loaves do you have? Go and see. And when they [had looked and] knew,*

they said, Five [loaves] and two fish. Then He commanded the people all to recline on the green grass by companies. So they threw themselves down in ranks of hundreds and fifties [with the regularity of an arrangement of beds of herbs, looking like so many garden plots].

And taking the five loaves and two fish, He looked up to Heaven and, praising God, gave thanks and broke the loaves and kept on giving them to the disciples to set before the people; and He [also] divided the two fish among [them] all. And they all ate and were satisfied. And they took up twelve [small hand] baskets full of broken pieces [from the loaves] and of the fish. And those who ate the loaves were 5,000 men. (Mark 6:37-44 AMPC, emphasis added, notes removed)

What do we learn from this? It appears that they had a sizeable sum of money in their common purse held by Judas. A denarius was a small silver coin used by Rome, and the illustration pictured is of a denarius of Tiberius Caesar from the time of Christ. We can infer the common purse held about 200 denarii and at that time a denarii was approximately the wages for a soldier for one day.[i] Even though this money was approximately eight months' wages, it still would not have been enough to feed the crowd. A rough calculation is that it would have provided bread for 1,000 to 2,000 people. In short, they were carrying a fair amount of money, but not enough to supply the need in the natural realm, hence their practical response to Jesus.

Vision

The key requirement to have victory is vision. What mental picture comes to mind that we focus on as we respond to the issue we are facing or what God is asking of us? Let's consider this by comparing the disciples' reaction to that of Jesus in order to gain a perspective on how Jesus operated.

The disciples heard the command of Jesus to feed the crowd and IMMEDIATELY had in vision their own ability and resources. The disciples' perspective was:

Word————>Vision————>Wallet/Purse/Natural Capability

They were thinking about how they could obey Jesus' command in their own strength. I think in most cases we are the same. We have a word from the Lord and then immediately seek to deal with it in the natural sphere using our own resources and capabilities. A word from the Lord is supernatural and draws upon the supernatural resources of the Father, not the natural resources of man.

Jesus' perspective was:

Word————>Vision————>Father's Action/Miracle Provision

We know that Jesus was only moved to action by what He saw the Father do and only said what He heard the Father say. He had preached to many crowds on many occasions. Only on two occasions is it recorded that He miraculously fed the crowds so we know that He was being obedient to what He was instructed to do. Like Elijah, He was acting in faith on the word of God.

> *Have I been such a long time with you," returned Jesus, "without your really knowing me, Philip? The man who has seen me has seen the Father. How can you say, 'Show us the Father'? Do you not believe that I am in the Father and the Father is in me?* ***The very words I say to you***

*are not my own. It is the Father who lives in me who carries out his work through me. Do you believe me when I say that I am in the Father and the Father is in me? But if you cannot, then believe me because of what you see me do. I assure you that the man who believes in me will do the same things that I have done, yes, and he will do even greater things than these, for I am going away to the Father. Whatever you ask the Father in my name, I will do—that the Son may bring glory to the Father. And if you ask me anything in my name, I will grant it....**Indeed, what you are hearing from me now is not really my saying, but comes from the Father who sent me**. (John 14:9-14, 24 Phillips, emphasis added)*

So Jesus heard the voice of the Father and commanded the disciples to feed the people. The ACTION was God's - it was His work. He wanted this to happen and it was His will and therefore it was HIS RESPONSIBILITY.

This perspective brings us clarity on a passage of Scripture that I always found odd as it seemed disconnected. Immediately after the feeding of the 5,000, the disciples were on a boat and a storm arose.

And those who ate the loaves were 5,000 men. **And at once He insisted that the disciples get into the boat and go ahead of Him to the other side to Bethsaida,** *while He was sending the throng away. And after He had taken leave of them, He went off into the hills to pray. Now when evening had come, the boat was out in the middle of the lake, and He was by Himself on the land. And having seen that they were troubled and tormented in their rowing, for the wind was against them, about the fourth watch of the night [between 3:00-6:00 a.m.] He came to them, walking [directly] on the sea. And He acted as if He meant to pass by them, But when they saw Him walking on the sea they thought it was a ghost, and raised a deep, throaty shriek of terror. For they all saw Him and were agitated (troubled and filled with fear and dread). But immediately He talked with them and said, Take heart! I Am! Stop being alarmed and afraid.*

> *And He went up into the boat with them, and the wind ceased (sank to rest as if exhausted by its own beating). And they were astonished exceedingly [beyond measure],* ***For they failed to consider or understand the teaching and meaning of the miracle of the loaves;*** *in fact their hearts had grown callous [had become dull and had lost the power of understanding]. And when they had crossed over, they reached the land of Gennesaret and came to [anchor at] the shore. (Mark 6:44-53 AMPC, some punctuation removed)*

So the Bible says that the disciples' terror and astonishment in the storm were as a result of not understanding the teaching and meaning of the miracle of the loaves. I always found this passage to be confusing. How does feeding the 5,000 relate to the storm? The similarity and lesson Jesus is teaching must relate to the mechanics of the miracle. I have heard people discuss this correlation in terms of faith and knowing that Jesus would rescue them, but this argument is not convincing. There must be a deeper similarity between the feeding of the 5,000 and the storm. What is common to both? What were the disciples missing? Aside from both being miraculous, they do not seem the same.

Let's examine the similarities between the two miraculous events more closely and we will see they link to vision as set out above.

Comparison	Feeding of the 5000	Calming of the Sea
Step 1	Word - Jesus told disciples to feed the crowd	Word - Jesus told the disciples to go to the other side and He would meet them there
Step 2	Issue - Natural reality in their vision - 200 denarii and their capability to feed the crowd. Response rooted in lack	Issue - Natural reality in their vision - the storm and their inability to deal with it. Response rooted in lack and fear
Step 3	Action - disciples' vision was that they could not fulfil the word to feed the people	Action - disciples' vision was that they could not deal with the storm
Step 4	Jesus' Vision was accomplishing the word from the Father - held up bread and blessed it with faith in the capability of the Father to accomplish what the Father had commanded	Jesus' Vision was to fulfil the command of the Father to go to the other side of the lake with faith in the capability of the Father to accomplish what He had commanded
Step 5	Action - took steps in faith to accomplish the Word He had received - blessed the bread and broke it	Action - took steps in faith to accomplish the Word - stilled the storm

While there are always many things to learn from Jesus' teachings, the core message here seems to relate to the lack of faith of the disciples and their continued tendency to look to their own resources. Their map of reality did not include the supernatural world and God's ability to bring about what He intended. Indeed, in another storm, Jesus reproved the disciples for their lack of faith:

> And He said to them, [Why are you so fearful?] **Where is your faith (your trust, your confidence in Me—in My veracity** and My integrity)? And they were seized with alarm and profound and reverent dread, and they marveled, saying to one another, Who then is this, that He commands even wind and sea, and they obey Him? (Luke 8:25 AMPC, emphasis added)

So let's pull all of this together step-by-step.

The Word from the Lord

The disciples had a WORD from the Lord who created the Heavens and the earth. They were in the presence of Jesus and they had a direct WORD from Him to feed the 5,000 and to cross the lake. Both words were from Jesus who is one with the Father. We know that He only did what he saw the Father do and said what He heard the Father say. So these WORDS from the Lord were from the Father and were sure and fixed. We also know that the WORD does not return void.

> *So shall my word be that goeth forth **out of my mouth**: it shall not return unto me void, but it shall accomplish that which I please, and it shall prosper in the thing whereto I sent it. (Isaiah 55:11 KJV, emphasis added)*

The world was created by the WORD that became flesh:

> *In the beginning before all time was the Word (Christ), and the Word was with God, and the Word was God Himself. He was present originally with God. All things were made and came into existence through Him; and without Him was not even one thing made that has come into being. (AMP John 1:1-3, parenthesis and notations removed)*

So when the disciples heard the commanded word of Jesus, the VISION that should have come to mind was that of a sure command of God that cannot be thwarted and must come to pass. Their map of reality should have been heavily weighted with Kingdom reality and God's supernatural power. It was 100% certain if God had commanded it. Like the word of the Lord to bless Abraham, to release the Children of Israel from bondage in Egypt, and to bring victory to countless heroes of the faith: this was the power and quality of the word they received.

Obedience Through Faith

So we know that faith comes by hearing the word of the Lord (Romans 10:17). Vision is the key difference between Jesus and the disciples in the stories above. Jesus heard the word of the Father to feed the 5,000 and go to the other side of the Sea of Galilee and He responded by having the vision of the Father's ability to supply the need and do the work - He had a Kingdom map. He partnered with His Father in doing the works, and the miracle-working power was the Father's.

The disciples heard the Word of Jesus, which was also the word of the Father, and they responded with a willingness to do the work. However, their vision was not the supply of the Father but their own capability, or rather their lack of capability - they had a natural or worldly map. Their faith was in their ability, their money, or their knowledge as fishermen to handle the boat. This is why Jesus challenged them on their level of faith.

What then was the common lesson that they had failed to learn? **If they have the word of the Lord on a matter, then it is up to the Father to see them through and do the work.** There is no chance of failure where God has asked them to do something. Their vision should have been of the capability of God to perform His word. Jesus modelled this idea when he took their bread and fish and lifted them **up to the Father** and asked Him to bless them. It was the Father's blessing that He sought as He did the Father's will, and the miracle-working power was the Father's. He then gave the disciples back exactly what they had given him, loaves and fishes, and their actions guided by Him were to organise the people to be fed and to start distributing the food. The miracle happened in the hands of the disciples as they distributed the food.

In the same manner, the word of the Lord came to the disciples to go to the other side of the lake. This was the word of the living God. What are the chances they would sink en route? None! They could have faith that they would arrive in safety. More than that, they could have faith to rebuke the storm and see it calmed as Jesus did. Not just could have, they should have and so should we.

Lesson Learned - Faith, Hope and Love

It is clear that the disciples did learn this lesson. Herod, emboldened by the death of James, had Peter arrested, with his execution planned for after the Passover.

> *About that time Herod the king stretched forth his hands to afflict and oppress and torment some who belonged to the church (assembly). And he killed James the brother of John with a sword; And when he saw that it was pleasing to the Jews, he proceeded further and arrested Peter also. This was during the days of Unleavened Bread [the Passover week]. And when he had seized [Peter], he put him in prison and delivered him to four squads of soldiers of four each to guard him, purposing after the Passover to bring him forth to the people. So Peter was kept in prison, but fervent prayer for him was persistently made to God by the church (assembly).* **The very night before Herod was about to bring him forth, Peter was sleeping** *between two soldiers, fastened with two chains, and sentries before the door were guarding the prison. And suddenly an angel of the Lord appeared [standing beside him], and a light shone in the place where he was. And the angel gently smote Peter on the side and awakened him, saying, Get up quickly! And the chains fell off his hands. And the angel said to him, Tighten your belt and bind on your sandals. And he did so. And he said to him, Wrap your outer garment around you and follow me. And [Peter] went out [along] following him, and he was not conscious that what was apparently being done by the angel was real, but thought he was seeing a vision. When they had passed through the first guard and the second, they came to the iron gate which leads into the city. Of its own accord [the gate] swung open, and they went out and passed on through one street; and at once the angel left him. Then Peter came to himself and said, Now I really know and am sure that the Lord has sent His angel and delivered me from the hand of Herod and from all that the Jewish people were expecting [to do to me].* (Acts 12:1-11 AMPC, emphasis added)

In Acts 12, we learn that Peter was sleeping the very night prior to his planned execution. He was sleeping! In the storm he was not sleeping; he was panicked and afraid to die. He had learned the lesson of the feeding of the five thousand, the lesson to trust in the word of Jesus, who only said what He heard the Father say. What word was this? Clearly, it was the word from Jesus to Peter after He was crucified and resurrected:

> *I assure you, most solemnly I tell you, when you were young you girded yourself [put on your own belt or girdle] and you walked about wherever you pleased to go.* ***But when you grow old*** *you will stretch out your hands, and someone else will put a girdle around you and carry you where you do not wish to go.* ***He said this to indicate by what kind of death Peter would glorify God.*** *And after this, He said to him, Follow Me! (John 21:18-19 AMPC emphasis added)*

Unusually, Peter knew from Jesus the time and nature of his death. He had a prophetic word that he would be an old man, so in the storm of his imprisonment, he was able to sleep secure in the word that he would not die. He did not know what God was going to do about Herod's plans, but he had an expectation that God was going to move on his behalf. He had faith in the word of Jesus and had ordered his mind, will, and emotions in line with this. Like Abraham, it did not matter what the facts of the moment meant. It did not matter what Herod said. It did not matter that James had just been martyred - he knew this was not the end of his ministry.

Satan's If

Like Peter, many of us have words of destiny and words of release over our lives. We know that when these words are sown they are tested by the enemy (Matthew 13). We know that the Blessing includes the enemy challenging us one way but fleeing in seven (Deut. 28:9) and we also know that weapons will be formed against us, but that they will not prosper (Is 54:17). In short, every word we have received will be tested.

Jesus also was baptised and the Spirit descended as a dove and the voice of the Father said:

> ...*This is my Son, whom I love; I am well pleased with him.* (Matthew 3:17 CJB)

Immediately after this, Jesus was tempted in the wilderness and satan's attacks challenged this word of identity from the Father:

> *And the tempter came and said to Him,* ***If You are*** *God's Son...* (Matthew 4:3 AMPC, emphasis added)

> **We will all face the IF of the enemy in our lives and callings**

We will all face the IF of the enemy in our lives and callings. Circumstances will arise which contend against the word of God over our lives and our destiny. IF you are really called to be King over Israel, why are you in a cave? IF you are called to a financial position in the Kingdom, why has your business failed? IF, IF, IF, IF, IF - which one are you facing?

Circumstances will contend with the vision set out in the word.

Joseph had a vision of a large place with his brothers bowing but ended up bloodied in a hole. David was anointed King of Israel but was on the run in a cave. Joshua and the Children of Israel were given a land flowing with milk and honey, yet Joshua still had to pray about what to do about Jericho's impenetrable walls. The mighty warrior Gideon was hiding in a winepress. Jesus was announced as the saviour of the world and had to flee from the country of his destiny to Egypt. We are no different: our callings and visions will be challenged. We will have the opportunity to say, "Hey, I am in a small dark place - the cave". Or, we can agree with the word and thank God for the "large, bright place" and speak to the circumstances to conform to the truth of God's word over our lives. We speak to the darkness to be broken until the blockage of the enemy is removed and we can see and enter into our large light place. We persevere.

Do we need to repent for agreeing with satan's challenge to our true calling and destiny? We do not need to make sense of HOW God is going to work it all out, but we do need to agree with Him and to speak His word to the mountain of circumstances (Mark 11:23, 24). We are to call for them to be removed and use our faith to proclaim those things which are not as though they are. This is the trial of our faith that produces patience as we wait for the full manifestation of His word of Blessing over our lives. We need to continue to call for the full manifestation of the promises of God in the Word and over our lives in spite of the facts that may contend.

Eternal Victory

We need to conclude the past, focus on Jesus, abide in Him, be motivated by Love, and have the Spirit resting on us like He did. We need to focus on, remember and read out His illustrious acts. We needn't rehearse the enemy's actions and our disappointments and hurts that have come - that can lead to discouragement in a very short time. Instead, we rest secure in the goodness of our Father who is bringing our destiny to full fruition in our lives.

We have **hope** which is a positive expectancy of God acting on our behalf. Hope is an abiding truth:

> *Three things will last forever--faith, hope, and love--and the greatest of these is love. (I Corinthians 13:13 NLT)*

Our Hope is eternal. It is rooted in His word over our lives:

> *When God made his promise to Abraham he swore by himself, for there was no one greater by whom he could swear, and he said: 'Surely blessing I will bless you, and multiplying I will multiply you'.* ***And then Abraham, after patient endurance, found the promise true.***

*16-20 Among men it is customary to swear by something greater than themselves. And if a statement is confirmed by an oath, that is the end of all quibbling. So in this matter, God, wishing to show beyond doubt that his plan was unchangeable, confirmed it with an oath. So that by two utterly immutable things, the word of God and the oath of God, who cannot lie, **we who are refugees from this dying world might have a source of strength, and might grasp the hope that he holds out to us.** This hope we hold as the utterly reliable anchor for our souls, fixed in the very certainty of God himself in Heaven, where Jesus has already entered on our behalf, having become, as we have seen, "High Priest for ever after the order of Melchizedek". (Hebrews 6:13-20 Phillips)*

Like Abraham, we are inheritors of His promises (Galatians 3:6) and have the benefit of the other promises in the Bible as well as personal words over our lives. These are the WORDS that give us hope and positive expectancy. There can only be fleshly expectation anchored in works if we do not have the Word of God for our lives. The word of family or the word of a business plan can never result in faith unless it is rooted in the Word of God we have received.

> There can only be fleshly expectation if we do not have the word of God for our lives. The word of family or the word of a business plan can never result in faith unless it is rooted in the word of God we have received.

I call this "hopeium" a worldly hope masquerading as faith. Like its rhyming drug, hopeium leads us into fantasy, delusion, and fruitlessness. If we are motivated by our plans, desires or even religious teaching, instead of the word of God for us, then we will likely be offended at God and disappointed. This is the pattern we saw with Jesus. The Jews at the time were offended as they believed that the work of God and the Messiah was to oust the Romans and establish another global kingdom - they did not have faith in a true word from God, they had hopeium and they saw what the word of their religion told them to see. Hopeium, not faith, led them into sin.

> *Jesus answered, "This is the work of God: that you believe [adhere to, trust in, rely on, and have faith] in the One whom He has sent." (John 6:29 AMP)*

So how does this all work together? This is the model set out in the Bible.

1. Works to Walk In: We have works God has prepared for us to walk in. We have to do the works set before us as righteous servants.

> *For we are God's own handiwork (His workmanship), recreated in Christ Jesus, born anew that we **may do those good works which God predestined (planned beforehand)** for us [taking paths which He prepared ahead of time], that we should walk in them living the good life which He prearranged and made ready for us to live. (Ephesians 2:10 AMPC, emphasis added and parenthesis removed)*

2. Faith by Hearing: FAITH comes by hearing the WORD of God. If we are doing our own thing outside of these works then we cannot have real faith and this phoney faith - hopeium - will not bear fruit. Real faith draws on the Word including the works prepared for us to walk in and connects us to the miracle working power of God.

> *So then faith cometh by hearing, and hearing by the word of God. (Romans 10:17 KJV)*

3. Faith through Love: FAITH expresses itself through LOVE. If what we are doing is not empowered by love then can it really be faith?

> *For [if we are] in Christ Jesus, neither circumcision nor uncircumcision counts for anything, but only faith activated and energized and expressed and working through love. (Gal. 5:6 AMPC)*

4. God is LOVE: We must operate in Kingdom love.

> *God is love, and the man whose life is lived in love does, in fact, live in God, and God does, in fact, live in him. (I John 4:16 PHILLIPS, emphasis added)*

5. Hope to Endure: Our HOPE in Jesus inspires us to ENDURE and stand fast for the manifestation of the Word in our lives.

> *We remember before our God and Father your **work produced by faith, your labor prompted by love, and your endurance inspired by hope** in our Lord Jesus Christ. (I Thess. 1:3 NIV, emphasis added)*

6. Stand Fast: Like Abraham, we stand fast believing in the word of God even though circumstances may contradict.

> *[For Abraham, human reason for] hope being gone, hoped in faith that he should become the father of many nations, as he had been promised, So [numberless] shall your descendants be. He did not weaken in faith when he considered the [utter] impotence of his own body, which was as good as dead because he was about a hundred years old, or [when he considered] the barrenness of Sarah's [deadened] womb. No unbelief or distrust made him waver (doubtingly question) concerning the promise of God, but he grew strong and was empowered by faith as he gave praise and glory to God, **Fully satisfied and assured that God was able and mighty to keep His word and to do what He had promised.** (Romans 4:18-21 AMPC, emphasis added)*

Endurance and perseverance are only blessings if they are in line with the eternal values of the word, faith, hope and love. This connects us to the miracle working power of God that brings the breakthrough and overcoming victory. As we hear the word, move forward in faith, and persevere in hope we will hear from the Lord what to do and how to have victory.

The opposite is also true as greed, defilement, pride, ambition, covetousness, and any other ungodly motivations and influences have no eternal value. Also good works that are not the Word of God outlining the works prepared for us to walk in and done in love profit us nothing. There can be no faith in things that are not rooted in the Word of God for our lives. In financial terms, there can be no faith in a business plan that is motivated by greed, not the Word of God for our lives. There can be no faith in going into the slavery of debt, as this is contrary to His Word. Even if we have natural and material success, the reward will not extend to the eternal. Even if we give all our goods and our body to be burned but have not love, it profits nothing (I Corinthians 13.3). At the end of our labour we want to hear the words that He knows us, not that He never knew us (Matthew 7:21). If we are doing works, even good works, outside of His plans and word for us then we are lawless. He can only know us and the eternal value of our works if we operate empowered by His eternal values.

> He can only know us and our works can only have eternal value if we operate in His eternal values

Faith in Action - God's Strange Acts

As we stand in genuine faith contending for our destiny calling, we must seek Him for direction as our first and urgent necessity, not leaning on our own understanding. We know that in relation to the work God has for us to do, we can have faith in the word of God for us. We also know that faith without works is dead so we must take the actions that God shows us to take to move through to victory.

> *For as the body without the spirit is dead, so faith without works is dead also.* (James 2:26 AMPC)

As we do so, He will move on our behalf.

> *For the Lord will rise up as on Mount Perazim, He will be wrathful as in the Valley of Gibeon, that He may do His work, **His strange work**, and*

bring to pass His act, His strange act. (Isaiah 28:21 AMPC, emphasis added)

If we have a word from the Lord and we have faith in His ability to bring about His word in our lives, we need to know what to do. Our vision is to be of His ability to supply, not our capability to perform. We cannot lean on our own understanding and its inherent limitations. This is the Kingdom in operation. We are to call down His Kingdom in daily prayer over the situation, knowing that if we ask anything in His name, we will receive it.

And Jesus, replying, said to them, Have faith in God [constantly]. Truly I tell you, whoever says to this mountain, Be lifted up and thrown into the sea! and does not doubt at all in his heart but believes that what he says will take place, it will be done for him. For this reason I am telling you, whatever you ask for in prayer, believe (trust and be confident) that it is granted to you, and you will [get it]. (Mark 11:22-24 AMPC)

If you live in Me [abide vitally united to Me] and My words remain in you and continue to live in your hearts, ask whatever you will, and it shall be done for you. (John 15:7 AMPC)

... For truly I say to you, if you have faith [that is living] like a grain of mustard seed, you can say to this mountain, Move from here to yonder place, and it will move; and nothing will be impossible to you....And Jesus answered them, Truly I say to you, if you have faith (a [n]firm relying trust) and do not doubt, you will not only do what has been done to the fig tree, but even if you say to this mountain, Be taken up and cast into the sea, it will be done. And whatever you ask for in prayer, having faith and [really] believing, you will receive. (Matt 17:20; 21:21-22 AMPC)

This is where many of us have missed the mark. We may have clearly heard the word of the Lord about our situation or even a ministry issue, but we then rush ahead with our VISION - our reaction to that word which, like the disciples, may relate to our ability and our resources, not God's resources.

Remember the man who came forward for prayer about the situation he was facing as a result of borrowing for his ministry facility in Africa. He had clearly heard the call of the Lord but, like many of us have done, he had rushed ahead in his own strength and resources and ended up in trouble. He did not wait for God's "strange plan" for victory, but had leaned on his own understanding and plans. Using our understanding he had built a plan based on his ideas and moved forward in misguided hopeium or false faith. The lesson here is that we MUST seek the Lord for His further word as to what to do next. Where God has a Word and a calling, He also has the plan for supernatural execution. Thank the Lord that He is merciful if we repent, and He can even untangle the messes we make in rushing ahead to do the work. God is great at rescuing His people from their own folly - just look at the Prodigal Son!

Imagine if the disciples had heard the word of the Lord to feed the 5,000 and had borrowed from the moneylenders more denarii to supplement their 200, then ran about to try to get the bread delivered. Where God has given the word He also has a plan to give the victory.

> **Where God has given the word He has a plan to give the victory. Where God has a Word and a calling he also has the plan for supernatural execution.**

Indeed, if the plan is something that you can fully do in your own strength, then I would question whether you have actually heard from the Lord, for God chooses the foolish and weak things to confound the wise.

> *[This is] because the foolish thing [that has its source in] God is wiser than men, and the weak thing [that springs] from God is stronger than men. For [simply] consider your own call, brethren; not many [of you were considered to be] wise according to human estimates and standards, not many influential and powerful, not many of high and noble birth. No] for God selected (deliberately chose) what in the world is foolish to put the wise to shame, and what the world calls weak to put the strong to shame.*

*And God also selected (deliberately chose) what in the world is lowborn and insignificant and branded and treated with contempt, even the things that are nothing, that He might depose and bring to nothing the things that are, **So that no mortal man should [have pretense for glorying and] boast in the presence of God**. (I Cor 1:25 -29 AMPC, emphasis added)*

The story of Joshua is an excellent illustration for us. Joshua clearly had the call to take the land, but he still had to seek the Lord for each action. Indeed, where there was a setback, he had to have a fresh word from the Lord. Each step of his conquest of the land required him to seek the Lord for the plan as an urgent necessity (Joshua 7-8).

> **The lesson here is that we MUST seek the Lord for His further word as to what to do next. Where God has a Word and a calling he also has the plan for supernatural execution.**

Hearing a general directional word is great. According to Deuteronomy 28 we know that we should prosper. There is still the need to follow the pattern set out in the Bible and modelled by Joshua and Jesus. Jesus had a destiny as Messiah, but in specific actions He was praying and fasting and only did what He saw the Father do and only said what He heard the Father say.

In our modern, business-oriented world we have tended to relegate the moving of the Lord to our year end calculations - have we moved forward in sales or value? We give God a general acknowledgment that our skills and understanding are from Him, but the work is done primarily in our own strength. We use this trite acknowledgement to justify leaning on our own understanding. We attribute a generic trend such as better sales or performance as "blessing". I am sure there is some merit to this acknowledgment, and it can be true in a broad sense as even our breath is a gift from the Lord (Acts 17:25), but walking into Kingdom victory and genuine Kingdom Finance release is something more.

The God of the Kingdom is the God of the intimate supernatural lifestyle and He wants us to be intimate with Him and to abide in Him. This is more than an "In God We Trust" headline acknowledgement as we stumble along our own paths not seeking the Lord for our next steps. He is a God of dominion, and we are to establish and operate in His Kingdom under His Lordship and not in our own wisdom; certainly not in reliance on the wisdom and support of the defiled world system. While this type of business philosophy does not fit with our natural tendencies - it seems alien and foreign - we are to be submitted to His dominion in every area of our lives. Not only that, we must also seek first the Kingdom and hunger to know Him more because business is the Kingdom.

Our prayer must be in FAITH, and faith comes by hearing the Word of God for the specific situation or decision we are facing. God does give specific direction for specific situations - He has His strange acts! He does not share His glory, but over and over in Scripture and in life experience, He directs us in ways that seem strange to the natural mind. Here are some of many examples:

- Gideon's military plan for conquest was to send the majority of the soldiers back and attack with a vastly outnumbered army (Judges 7:2)

- Esther's plan to save her race was to host a dinner with her antagonist (Esther 5:4-5)

- Moses' plan for ultimate victory was to bring the Children of Israel to a dead end against the sea with Pharaoh's army attacking (Ex. 14:19-31)

- Joshua's plan for Jericho was to march around it with no sound and then shout on the final day (Joshua 6:2-5)

- Jesus paid his taxes with gold found in the mouth of a fish caught at His command (Matthew 17:23-27)

- Jesus had the disciples cast their nets in the deep water in the daytime for a great haul (Luke 5:4-11)

The list goes on and on. Indeed, the Scripture in Isaiah 28 referring to God's strange acts is based on II Samuel 5:19-25. In this scripture David sought God's instruction about attacking the Philistines and is told to go around behind them and attack when he hears the sound of marching in the tops of the mulberry trees. This is where God is described as the God of the breakthrough.

So, is there a pattern to breakthroughs? Yes, it relates to seeking and hearing the word of the Lord and acting in obedience, even if it is a strange act to the normal thinking of man. In a sense the pattern is that there is no pattern except submission to a God we know is there to love and bless us. Another translation for "strange" translates it as "alien". The process and approach that God uses is alien to us as it is from another Kingdom. It is not how we think and operate naturally so we have to develop this Kingdom mindset.

We have seen this in our personal walk with the Lord. When we started to seriously follow Him to establish His Lordship in the area of our business and finances I did what most people do: rushed ahead to make this exciting vision happen. I have described it as hearing the trumpet for Kingdom Finance and rushing from the tent in your underwear to attack the ranks of the enemy armed with a toothbrush. It is only the mercy of God that any of us are still here! The positive side is that by doing anything we are moving forward, and God can work with us if we are pressing into a deeper relationship with Him.

At one point we ended up in a very difficult financial situation and my wife really felt that we needed to seek the Lord for the "one thing" that He wanted us to do. What did God want us to do? We sought the Lord in prayer and fasting, and both of us felt that we should give a particular asset to a ministry person that God showed to us both. This was at that time the most valuable asset we had, and it made no sense to give it away as even the sale of it would have helped us a great deal. It was a strange and crazy act, however, we felt that God was directing it and that we had His word on what to do. As we began to move to get this gift to the person, the miracle unfolded. We were able to meet with someone that very night at the airport who was heading overseas to meet with this person. It was a miracle of logistics to get this gift to the Lord into that persons' hand, almost immediately, along with a word of what it meant for them. The next day a greater miracle occurred: we had a cash offer submitted for a property which had no offers for several years. The result was a quick, smooth sale. The strange act had brought forward the financial breakthrough.

Victory is to be an overcomer, hearing from God what to do in each battle and moving forward in the works God has prepared for you to walk in.

What about those of us who have gotten it all wrong, rushed ahead, and are in a total mess? Or, what if revelation has shown you that the success in your hands may not be as a result of victory through the power of God but through your own efforts? What if you are successful, but have missed truly knowing God in the process? Be assured that God is the great restorer, and that He is more than able to untangle the issues of your life and business no matter how severe. Repent and bring your mess to Him (review the section on Concluding the Past). In summary, He is faithful and just to forgive your sins and clean up all of your unrighteousness. Think about the Prodigal Son who came back from a total mess to his father who restored him fully, even though he felt he could maybe only be a servant. Maybe you have missed the mark and your calling and feel that all that is left for you is to maybe assist in some small way. Your failure is a failure only in relation to your aspirations and your plans!

God's way is still there for us, and He will restore and make all things new no matter how bad things are.

Prayer: *Father, I am sorry that I have run ahead of your plan and not sought your will or your direction for each step of its implementation. Forgive me for having a worldly view of success and not victory through your power. Forgive me and my family lines for doing business this way and not giving you lordship in this area. I stop now and listen to your voice and direction, and I make you Lord of my life and calling. Show me your way, your strange and perhaps alien way, and I covenant to walk in it as you direct. Untangle and untie the issues and problems that have arisen as I run to you like the Prodigal Son. I leave behind my plans and my solutions, my goals, and my success or failure, and accept the role and mantle that you have for me. Guide me each step of the way as I do your will.*

Greater Works and Financial Miracles

> *I assure you, most solemnly I tell you, if anyone steadfastly believes in Me, he will himself be able to do the things that I do; and he will do even greater things than these, because I go to the Father. (John 14:12 AMPC, emphasis added)*

How many of us have been challenged when we read about the acts of Jesus and his miraculous lifestyle? Even the apostles and early church seemed to walk in a level of the miraculous we have not seen in the church. It seems that there is a disconnect between the measure of the anointing we operate in and where we feel we should or want to be. Yet Jesus says that we will do even greater things than these! Our role is to walk in greater miracles and greater works than Jesus did. How can this be?

In the area of Kingdom Finance we also have callings that can only be brought to reality through His intervention, as it requires us to walk in anointing as we abide in Him. In the area of the release of

Kingdom Finance, it is not just about giving and doing good, but about breaking dominions and releasing the miracle-working power of Heaven in the area of finance. It is opening the doors for a flow of blessing not previously walked in by our families and communities. A new paradigm is revealed, not motivated by empty godless social justice or an "NGO mentality", but by a Nazarite-like commitment to see Jesus glorified and to join with Him in His mission to destroy the works of satan.

We need to be the people referred to in Isaiah 61 who stand in the ruins of the generations and rebuild. Kingdom Financiers who have been personally restored (Isaiah 61:1-3) as prodigal sons, have moved forward to be blessing people one-on-one as Good Samaritans, and now move beyond this to the great callings and works God has for them.

> *And they shall rebuild the ancient ruins; they shall raise up the former desolations and renew the ruined cities, the devastations of many generations. (Isaiah 61:4 AMPC)*

These are the Elijah-like cultural architects who transform culture and disciple nations.

Jesus emptied Himself of His godly power (Philippians 2:7) and was an example for us of a man operating under the anointing of the Spirit guided by the Father. As we saw above, He modelled for the disciples and us how to operate in the world. He was our example and we are to do the works He did and even greater works!!!!

Here are the key elements of this power transference:

1. We are commissioned to do Greater Works:

> *Do you not believe that I am in the Father, and that the Father is in Me? What I am telling you I do not say on My own authority and of My own accord; but the Father Who lives continually in Me does the (His) works (His own miracles, deeds of power). Believe Me that I am in the Father and*

*the Father in Me; or else believe Me for the sake of the [very] works themselves. [If you cannot trust Me, at least let these works that I do in My Father's name convince you.] I assure you, most solemnly I tell you, if anyone steadfastly believes in Me, **he will himself be able to do the things that I do; and he will do even greater things than these, because I go to the Father. And I will do [I Myself will grant] whatever you ask in My Name [as presenting all that I Am], so that the Father may be glorified and extolled in (through) the Son. [Yes] I will grant [I Myself will do for you] whatever you shall ask in My Name [as [presenting all that I Am].** (John 14:10-14 AMPC, punctuation removed and emphasis added)*

2. This applies to all believers:

Neither for these alone do I pray [it is not for their sake only that I make this request], but also for all those who will ever come to believe in (trust in, cling to, rely on) Me through their word and teaching, (John 17:20 AMPC)

3. The process is the same as modelled by Jesus:

*But the Comforter (Counselor, Helper, Intercessor, Advocate, Strengthener, Standby), the Holy Spirit, Whom the Father will send in My name [in My place, to represent Me and act on My behalf], **He will teach you all things.** And He will cause you to recall (will remind you of, bring to your remembrance) everything I have told you. (John 14:26 AMPC, emphasis added)*

*"I have much more to tell you but you cannot bear it now. Yet when that one I have spoken to you about comes—the Spirit of truth—he will guide you into everything that is true. For **he will not be speaking of his own accord but exactly as he hears, and he will inform you about what is to come. He will bring glory to me for he will draw on my truth and reveal it to you.** Whatever the Father possesses is also mine; that is why I tell you that he will draw on my truth and will show it to you. (John 16:12-15 AMPC, emphasis added)*

*And other sheep I have, which are not of this fold: them also I must bring, and they shall hear my voice; and there shall be one fold, and one shepherd...**My sheep hear my voice**, and I know them, and they follow me:* (John 10:16, 27 KJV, emphasis added)

So what is the secret to doing the greater works and walking in the financial miracles that God is calling many to walk in. How do we activate it in our lives? The pattern of breakthrough is:

- **WORD** - We have God's word for our situation and our destiny calling. We hear the word for our lives in Scripture and establish our walk in the blessing and not in the curse. We stand on the written word that applies for our life and on the destiny calling. God will also speak through dreams, visions and the prophetic.

- **HEARING** - We hear His voice. We are his sheep and hear His voice and not the voice of another. He is our advocate and we have the Holy Spirit working to speak to us what is the will and word of the Father.

- **VISION** - We operate with a vision of God's ability to perform not our limitations. As we abide in Him, our vision is of His ability to perform the word over our lives.

- **PRAYER AND DECLARATION** - With this vision, we have faith-filled prayer and call forth the vision. We declare daily His Kingdom come and speak, pray, and decree in line with what we are shown. Abiding in Him we, like Jesus modelled, only say what we hear the Father say and only do what we see the Father do.

- **ACTION** - We seek the Lord for direction as to what to do. We seek Him as our vital and urgent necessity, then we do the actions and strange acts that we are shown and we do not lean on our own understanding.

- **MIRACULOUS RESULTS** - we know that the act and responsibility is God's - He will perform and deliver and the victory is His.

Chapter 20

Kingdom Business as Usual

It is NEVER Just Business

I have heard the statement, "It's just business", often, usually when someone is justifying making the "hard decisions" that sometimes happen in the world and could be regarded as heartless except for the disclaimer. It separates a person's religious life from their personal or business life. In Nehemiah's day, it was "just business" to take children as slaves for debt. It is a statement that justifies our actions because it relates to business, therefore it is a sphere outside of our ability to comment or question. A sphere where other considerations are relevant and that the plans and operation of the business demands the action. It is a statement that can be used to deny the power of Jesus to transform situations and realities and to keep His plans from operating.

However, like everything else in our lives, business and our financial life is to be submitted to Jesus. "Just business" cannot be used to inoculate everyone involved from the Kingdom of God which is always supernatural and always the most relevant consideration. As radical as it may sound to us, our minds, plans, experience, money, connections, and understanding are of little value in pursuing Kingdom Finance. They are only valuable to the extent that they are fully surrendered and empowered by the Holy Spirit. We are commanded to offer these as a sacrifice to God and to have our minds transformed.

> *I appeal to you therefore, brethren, and beg of you in view of [all] the mercies of God, to make a decisive dedication of your bodies [presenting all your members and faculties] as a living sacrifice, holy (devoted, consecrated) and well pleasing to God, which is your reasonable (rational, intelligent) service and spiritual worship.*
>
> *Do not be conformed to this world (this age), [fashioned after and adapted to its external, superficial customs], but be transformed (changed) by the [entire] renewal of your mind [by its new ideals and its new attitude], so that you may prove [for yourselves] what is the good and acceptable and perfect will of God, even the thing which is good and acceptable and perfect [in His sight for you]. (Romans 12:1-2 AMPC)*

Nowhere in Scripture does it state that we should be guided by best-practice, training, and our own understanding. Rather, over and over again, we are commanded not to lean on our own understanding.

> *Lean on, trust in, and be confident in the Lord with all your heart and mind and **do not rely on your own insight or understanding**. In all your ways know, recognize, and acknowledge Him, and He will direct and make straight and plain your paths. (Proverbs 3:5-6 AMPC, emphasis added)*
>
> *Roll your works upon the Lord [commit and trust them wholly to Him; He will cause your thoughts to become agreeable to His will, and] so shall your plans be established and succeed. (Proverbs 16:3 AMPC)*

This idea is completely contrary to almost everything we have heard and all of our education and study. Our understanding and the rationalism of the age will not help us here. As we abide in Jesus, He will make our thoughts agreeable to His will. We will be guided by Him, He will place our feet on straight paths. It is the blessing that eliminates the striving (Proverbs 10:22).

Remember the disciples who had toiled all through the night fishing and caught nothing? In those days they had to gather in the nets by hand and skilfully throw them out and pull them through the water. Imagine this scene - over and over and over they threw the nets, and during the night they got more and more tired until they were exhausted and defeated. They slowly rowed back to shore. But Jesus, who was a carpenter, said to them to throw the nets again.

> *When He had stopped speaking, He said to Simon (Peter), Put out into the deep water, and lower your nets for a haul. And Simon (Peter) answered, Master, we toiled all night exhaustingly and caught nothing in our nets.* ***But on the ground of Your word, I will lower the nets again.*** *And when they had done this, they caught a great number of fish; and as their nets were at the point of breaking, They signaled to their partners in the other boat to come and take hold with them. And they came and filled both the boats, so that they began to sink. But when Simon Peter saw this, he fell down at Jesus' knees, saying, Depart from me, for I am a sinful man, O Lord. For he was gripped with bewildering amazement [allied to terror], and all who were with him, at the haul of fish which they had made;* (Luke 5:4-9 AMPC, emphasis added parenthesis removed)

They were the fishermen and they knew best what to do. Jesus was trained as a carpenter and His understanding was not in fishing; however, He was not leaning on His own understanding, and Peter recognised this. They were the experts, but they heard the word of Jesus and acted upon it. They did not lean on their own understanding that had taught them to fish at night. Instead, they were in tune with Jesus, obeyed His instructions, did this strange act, and had a great victory haul. How many of us would like a great haul and victory? This is an example of the godly use of mind, skills, and understanding. Jesus gave them the word, and in submission and faith to it they used their minds, plans, and skills to row to the site, assemble and use their equipment, and fish. They also had to be quick witted to avoid the loss of the catch and not sink. Their minds and understandings were used in submission to His will and revelation. IT IS NEVER JUST BUSINESS. The disciples understood this principle. It was supernatural and stunning.

In order for us to have victory and eternal reward we can only do what we see the Father do and only say what we hear the Father say. We must abide in Jesus, connected to Him and hearing His voice through the operation of the Holy Spirit

We, like the disciples, must press into intimacy with Jesus and give great weight to His words and little weight to our understanding. We must listen for his direction, which usually completely contradicts our understanding. After all, His ways are higher and all glory is to go to Him.

> *For My thoughts are not your thoughts, neither are your ways My ways, says the Lord. For as the Heavens are higher than the earth, so are My ways higher than your ways and My thoughts than your thoughts. (Isaiah 55:8-9 AMP)*

Get ready for your supernatural, stunning victory!

About the Author

William Abraham is the founder of The 7000 (www.the7000.com) an author, speaker, international lawyer and project financier with global experience working with governments, banks, utilities and major companies. William has closed over $20 billion in infrastructure project finance transactions. He was formerly the Head of International Projects and Finance for a leading global law firm based in London and is a leading expert on the commercialisation of emerging technologies. His work with governments in partnership with the University of Cambridge has led to international joint-venture initiatives in innovation and entrepreneurship. He is particularly interested in bringing transformation through business - how to bring genuine benefit to countries through business and projects. He is recognised as an Apostolic Voice in Kingdom Finance leading a movement to raise cultural architects who can bring about genuine Kingdom transformation. After studying business and taking a Doctor of Jurisprudence degree he completed a Masters Degree in International Law from the University of Cambridge.

Endnotes

3. Slavery

i. http://www.merriam-webster.com/dictionary/slavery
ii. https://themoneycharity.org.uk/money-statistics/#:~:text=UK%20Personal%20Debt,including%20mortgages%2C%20was%20%C2%A365%2C239. And see https://www.usdebtclock.org/
iii. The valuation of slave property in a sample of twenty-eight estate inventories indicated that older slaves usually had minimal or zero market value. John Badeau's twenty-four-year-old woman was worth 40, while his seventy-year-old woman was appraised at only 3... Abraham Depeyster's inventory of eight slaves reflected the decreased value of slaves over the age of forty-five compared to younger slaves. Three slaves between age forty-five and fifty were worth considerably less than slaves aged eighteen and thirty-four years.18 Old age for slaves began between age forty-five and sixty; this sector of the slave population became a progressive economic and social burden to be borne by both individual owners and the white community, with no prospect of future returns or gain on this depreciated human investment. This group included the 14.4 percent of all blacks and 21.5 percent of adult blacks who were over age forty-five. Only 6.1 percent of all blacks and 8.5 percent of adult blacks were over age fifty-five; in the mid-eighteenth century 6.8 percent of all male blacks and 11.2 percent of male black adults were over sixty years of age. (http://newyorkslavery.blogspot.co.uk/2007/08/chapter-nine.html)
iv. http://www.gutenberg.org/files/11485/11485-h/11485-h.htm

5. Breaking Free

i. https://www.federalreserve.gov/publications/2023-economic-well-being-of-us-households-in-2022-expenses.htm
ii. https://www.investopedia.com/most-americans-report-living-paycheck-to-paycheck-new-survey-finds-7970611

6. A Reality Check

i. "The coin would have been too valuable for everyday use. Common merchants in the Roman province probably would not have had change for such a high-value coin..." (http://edition.cnn.com/2016/03/14/middleeast/israel-gold-coin-found/index.html)

13. Generational Sin

i. http://www.bac-lac.gc.ca/eng/discover/immigration/immigration-records/home-children-1869-1930/Pages/home-children.aspx

14. Leaving the Past Behind

i. http://www.amblecotechristiancentre.org.uk/journey/lordship-prayer-3/

15. Shame

i. https://en.oxforddictionaries.com/definition/shame
ii. Shame, Sandra D. Wilson Ph.D., Intervarsity Press,1990
iii. http://www.derekprince.org/Articles/1000085725/DPM_USA/Archive_of_UK/Keys/The_Divine_Exchange/Jesus_Endured_our.aspx

17. Offence

i. Oxford Dictionary www.oxfordictionaries.com
ii. http://www.springfieldspringfield.co.uk/movie_script.php?movie=outlaw-josey-wales-the
iii. https://en.oxforddictionaries.com/definition/crooked
iv. See chapter 13, *Generational Sin*

18. Debt

i. http://themoneycharity.org.uk/money-statistics/
ii. https://www.newyorkfed.org/microeconomics/hhdc
iii. http://www.dailymail.co.uk/news/article-2601146/Three-four-graduates-paying-student-loans-50s-Most-face-having-debt-written-30-year-limit.html
iv. http://www.usnews.com/news/blogs/data-mine/2014/10/07/student-loan-expectations-myth-vs-reality
v. http://www.derekprince.org/Articles/1000085721/DPM_US/Archive_of_UK/Keys/The_Divine_Exchange/Jesus_was_made.aspx

19. Victory

i. A denarius was equal to 16 asses (an "as" being a smaller coin and a "dupondius" coin being worth 2 asses) A modius (two gallons) of wheat would provide 20 one pound loaves of bread which was food for 10 days. "During the early Empire a modius would sell for two denarii in Rome but could be had for half that price in the rural parts of Italy and only 8 asses (half a denarius) in the breadbasket of Egypt. Baked bread sold for a dupondius a loaf in the expensive cities like Rome and Pompeii and half that (one as) in more rural towns. By this time the legionary was earning nearly a denarius a day." (http://www.forumancientcoins.com/dougsmith/worth.html)

Scriptures taken from the Holy Bible, New International Version®, NIV®. Copyright © 1973, 1978, 1984, 2011 by Biblica, Inc.™ Used by permission of Zondervan. All rights reserved worldwide. www.zondervan.com The "NIV" and "New International Version" are trademarks registered in the United States Patent and Trademark Office by Biblica, Inc.™

Scripture taken from the New King James Version®. Copyright © 1982 by Thomas Nelson. Used by permission. All rights reserved.

The Holy Bible, English Standard Version® (ESV®) Copyright © 2001 by Crossway, a publishing ministry of Good News Publishers. All rights reserved. ESV Text Edition: 2016.

Scripture quotations marked (NLT) are taken from the Holy Bible, New Living Translation, copyright ©1996, 2004, 2015 by Tyndale House Foundation. Used by permission of Tyndale House Publishers, Carol Stream, Illinois 60188. All rights reserved.

Scripture quotations from The Authorized (King James) Version. Rights in the Authorized Version in the United Kingdom are vested in the Crown. Reproduced by permission of the Crown's patentee, Cambridge University Press.

Scripture quotations taken from the Amplified® Bible (AMP), Copyright © 2015 by The Lockman Foundation. Used by permission. www.lockman.org.

Scripture quotations marked (AMPC) taken from the Amplified® Bible (AMPC), Copyright © 1954, 1958, 1962, 1964, 1965, 1987 by The Lockman Foundation. Used by permission. lockman.org.

Scripture quotations marked (CEV) are from the Contemporary English Version Copyright © 1991, 1992, 1995 by American Bible Society. Used by Permission.

Scripture quotations marked ABT are from the *The Original Aramaic New Testament in Plain English* by Rev. David Bauscher, 2007.

www.ingramcontent.com/pod-product-compliance
Lightning Source LLC
LaVergne TN
LVHW041751060526
838201LV00046B/968